FROM WAR TO PEACE

FROM WAR TO PEACE
The Conversion of Naval Vessels after Two World Wars

Nick Robins

Seaforth PUBLISHING

Title pages: *Halladale*, the converted Townsend car ferry which ran on the Dover–Calais route, photographed in 1958 off the South Foreland. She had seen action in the Second World War as the 'River' class frigate HMS *Halladale*. (Julian Mannering)

Copyright © Nick Robins 2021
First published in Great Britain in 2021 by
Seaforth Publishing,
A division of Pen & Sword Books Ltd,
47 Church Street,
Barnsley S70 2AS

www.seaforthpublishing.com

British Library Cataloguing in Publication Data
A catalogue record for this book is available from the British Library

ISBN 978 1 3990 0958 4 (hardback)
ISBN 978 1 3990 0959 1 (epub)
ISBN 978 1 3990 0960 7 (kindle)

All rights reserved. No part of this publication may be reproduced or transmitted in any form or by any means, electronic or mechanical, including photocopying, recording, or any information storage and retrieval system, without prior permission in writing of both the copyright owner and the above publisher.

The right of Nick Robins to be identified as the author of this work has been asserted by him in accordance with the Copyright, Designs and Patents Act 1988.

Pen & Sword Books Limited incorporates the imprints of Atlas, Archaeology, Aviation, Discovery, Family History, Fiction, History, Maritime, Military, Military Classics, Politics, Select, Transport, True Crime, Air World, Frontline Publishing, Leo Cooper, Remember When, Seaforth Publishing, The Praetorian Press, Wharncliffe Local History, Wharncliffe Transport, Wharncliffe True Crime and White Owl

Typeset and designed by Stephen Dent

Printed and bound in India by Replika Press Pvt Ltd

CONTENTS

Preface 6

1	Beat their Swords into Ploughshares	7
2	Conversion from Minor Warship to Merchant Ship	17
3	Examples from the Nineteenth Century	23
4	The Great War – Cruiser to Liner and Minesweepers to Passenger Ships	33
5	Conversion of Smaller Ships after the Great War	45
6	German Naval Vessels – Some Conversions after the Great War	55
7	Second World War Convoy Escorts – Corvettes, Frigates and Patrol Craft	65
8	Other Escort Ships and Escort Carriers	78
9	Landing Craft, Tank and Derivatives from the Second World War	91
10	Landing Ships, Tank	102
11	United States Navy and Royal Canadian Navy Vessels after the Second World War	114
12	Admiralty Fishing Vessels and Tugs, Some Examples	125
13	The Fairmile Launches of the Second World War: Examples from the British Isles	136
14	Minesweepers and Other Small Vessels from the Second World War	150
15	A Valuable Role for Surplus Naval Vessels	165

Bibliography 172
Index 172

PREFACE

Large numbers of redundant minor warships were put up for sale after both world wars. Many were sold at scrap value while others attained a premium from buyers intending to convert them to merchant ships. Convoy escorts and minesweepers were popular targets for conversion into cargo and passenger vessels, as whale catchers and to fill a host of other roles. There were only a few conversions of vessels larger than frigates although some bigger ships were converted, notably German destroyers after the Great War.

Conversions from war to peace include a number of surprises and ingenious solutions to create cruise ships and emigrant ships, luxury yachts and houseboats. Other conversions are more obvious, with less structural modification, and include Landing Ships, Tank and Landing Craft, Tank, also fleet tugs, motor fishing vessels, motor launches and smaller vessels. Conversions took place all around the world and focussed on British, American, Canadian and German warships after the two world wars. At other times redundant naval ships were bought for conversion for a variety of purposes, one of the first being the sale of the entire navy of the German Confederation in the 1850s, of which most vessels were bought commercially, five by a single British owner to develop the near-Continental cargo and passenger trades.

A great deal of help in preparing this book has been received from a number of sources. Ian Ramsey has underpinned the chapter on the process of conversion and the constraints of naval architecture and Ian has also peer-reviewed the manuscript and provided valuable comments. Julian Mannering also provided valuable guidance on the contents and structure of the book. The author is also grateful to Richard Danielson for discussion regarding the fate of the numerous Fairmile launches in British waters and for providing photographs to accompany the text. David Whiteside is thanked for sourcing a number of images from the World Ship Society Photo Archive and Linda Gowans is also thanked for photographic material. All photographs are credited as appropriate, those without acknowledgement in the caption are either from the author's collection or the source is unknown.

Dr Nick Robins
Crowmarsh, Oxfordshire

1

BEAT THEIR SWORDS INTO PLOUGHSHARES

And many people shall go and say, Come ye, and let us go up to the mountain of the Lord, to the house of the God of Jacob; and He will teach us of His ways, and we will walk in His paths: for out of Zion shall go forth the law, and the word of the Lord from Jerusalem. And He shall judge among the nations, and shall rebuke many people: and they shall beat their swords into ploughshares, and their spears into pruning hooks: nation shall not lift up sword against nation, neither shall they learn war any more.
   Isaiah 2:3–4

In time of war it is normal for merchant vessels to be requisitioned and converted for active service. Roles have included armed merchant cruisers, Catapult Aircraft Merchant ships, anti-aircraft ships, minesweepers, guard and inspection ships, landing ships and many others. Some never saw commercial service under their owner's house flag. For example, the small excursion turbine steamer *St Seiriol* undertook builder's trials and was immediately requisitioned for use as a troop transport in March 1915 and as minesweeper *FY573* in December the same year. She was sunk by a mine in 1918. Others, such as the Belfast Steamship Company's *Ulster Queen*, which became a cruiser complete with 4in armour plating to protect her hull in the Second World War, were unrecognisable in their new naval roles. Stories of many of these conversions and the naval activities of the ships themselves have been well documented and, for the most part, are well known.

The North Wales passenger excursion steamer *St Seiriol* (1914) was requisitioned almost as soon as this photo was taken during her builder's trials, and was lost on minesweeping duties off Harwich in 1918. She never served her owners.
(Liverpool & North Wales Steamship Company Limited)

The conversion of redundant naval vessels for merchant service is less widely understood. This is partly because these were far less in number and partly because many of the conversions for civilian life were so comprehensive that few observers recognised their antecedents.

There was one occasion during the Second World War when five naval vessels were converted into merchant ships under the Red Ensign as part of a daring exploit to provide essential hardware for the war effort. In 1943 there was grave concern that Britain was running out of ball bearings. Neutral Sweden had supplied Britain in peacetime and was willing to supply them again, provided that Britain came to collect the goods. Germany, which now occupied neighbouring Norway and Denmark, would, of course, do its best to frustrate any such trade. Sweden made it clear that any naval ships or personnel entering a Swedish port would be interned, and the only possible option was to use merchant ships. As a consequence, Ellerman's Wilson Line, Hull, was approached to manage a fleet of five motor gunboats which would be specially adapted and would fly the Red Ensign.

Five boats of the so-called Camper & Nicholson type were selected for conversion. They were 117ft long by just over 20ft breadth, and their three Paxman engines provided a speed of up to 28 knots. As gunboats they were equipped with one 6-pounder Hotchkiss gun, one 2-pounder pom-pom, four machine guns and a pair of depth charges and they carried a crew of twenty-one men. They were named after famous whalers in their commercial guise: *Hopewell* ex-*MGB504*,

The former Motor Gun Boat *Gay Viking* (1943), flying the Red Ensign, was one of five similar boats that brought much needed ball bearings to Britain from neutral Sweden in the winter of 1943/44.

Nonsuch ex-*MGB505*, *Gay Viking* ex-*MGB506*, *Gay Corsair* ex *MGB507* and *Master Standfast* ex-*MGB508*. They retained the two pom-poms and the machine guns, and were provided with hold space to accommodate 45 tons of steel with a small derrick serving the hatch. They could make between 20 and 23 knots – slower than their naval counterparts because the propellers had to be modified to suit the draft and trim of the loaded boat. In the saloon of each hung a large picture of Winston Churchill, and in the captain's cabin was a picture of Sir Francis Drake, a master of derring-do.

Manned by volunteer crews from the Wilson line, the five boats attempted to make a trial run to the Swedish coast; this had to be abandoned off the Skagerrak due to bad weather and the boats returned home. The crew of each boat comprised twenty men; all were badly shaken by the ride, suffering strained arms and severe bruising; they could do little but hang on in the small deck house.

Two interned cargo ships were used as warehouses by the Swedish ball-bearing manufacturers. The ships lay alongside at Bröfjord, near the port of Lysekil, which is roughly midway between Oslo to the north and Gothenburg to the south. In due course, the Ellerman boats sailed singly to Lyeskil then went alongside the ball-bearing store ships and loaded their cargo, before returning to Lyeskil to await suitable weather for the dash home. German officials in the port reported on their every move. Given a dark night and poor weather the boats would make a run for open water.

James Taylor wrote in his book *Ellermans: a Wealth of Shipping*:

> This daring scheme, confined as it was by the requirements of weather and conducted in the most amazingly public fashion, succeeded far beyond expectation. Subject to weather conditions the sorties continued through the winter and spring of 1943-1944 and were responsible for bringing to Britain's war effort cargo after cargo of valuable war material …

The only major casualty resulting from enemy action involved *Master Standfast* commanded by Captain C W R Holdsworth. On 5th November 1943 the former MGB was lying in foggy water awaiting the pilot to take her into Lysekil. Suddenly they were surprised by a ship, apparently Swedish, but quickly revealed as German. Ordered to heave-to, Captain Holdsworth chose to attempt a getaway to the safety of Swedish waters. The German warship opened fire and raked the boat, wounding several. She was boarded and the crew taken prisoner. Sadly, the gallant Captain Holdsworth died from his wounds a few days later.

The only other loss resulted from a collision between *Hopewell* and *Gay Viking*. This took place on 5th February, off Chistiansand. *Hopewell* was badly holed below the water line, so seriously that her crew were compelled to blow her up with explosives kept for such an emergency. The two crews retuned to Lysekil in *Gay Viking* which was also seriously damaged. There repairs were carried out and she made a successful final dash to Britain.

During spring 1944 the three remaining vessels were converted back into MGBs and rearmed. *Gay Corsair* was renamed *MGB2007* and was lost to enemy action. *Nonsuch* became *MGB2005* and *Gay Viking MGB2006* – both survived the war.

The boom periods for the purchase of surplus naval hardware followed the end of major hostilities, for example from 1919 through the 1920s, and in the late 1940s. This was due to two reasons. The first was that many shipowners had lost vessels during the two wars and urgently needed to rebuild their fleets. The second was financial escalation; the price of a new ship was always significantly higher at the end of hostilities than it was at the start, simply due to competition for

The *Ascot* class paddle minesweeper HMS *Atherstone* (1916) became the passenger excursion steamer *Queen of Kent* in 1928. She is seen alongside at Calais waiting for the return of her passengers.

resources and the inevitable increase in prices for materials to build ships in a commodity-scarce post-war environment.

In most countries, Britain and the United States included, all naval assets are owned and administered by the state or nation. Advertisements in the press describing redundant naval ships for disposal ultimately require a successful bidder or fixed-price buyer to pay the state, although in many cases there was an agency prescribed to administer the deal and the subsequent financial transaction. After the Second World War, numerous British fleet tugs and Landing Craft, Tank were chartered to commercial operators, the 'agency' in this case being the Ministry of War Transport until April 1946, and thereafter the Ministry of Transport. The United States Maritime Commission or Foreign Liquidation Commission handled most sales of redundant vessels from the United States Navy, respectively lying in home waters or overseas, while in Canada it was the War Assets Corporation.

Of course, wartime standard merchant ships such as the 'War' merchant fleet of the First World War and the 'Empire', Liberty and 'Victory' ships of the Second, were also available and in great number. These, for the most part, satisfied the needs of the liner companies, the tanker owners and many coastal and towing roles but they did not satisfy niche roles. These could be filled by the purchase and conversion of surplus naval vessels, some such as fleet tugs, drifters, trawlers and whalers requiring little alteration for civilian duties. Others for use as passenger vessels required major reconfiguration and usually gave good service to their owners against modest financial outlay.

Sale of wartime-built standard merchant ships after both world wars moderated prices of second-hand tonnage, but only to a small extent. Conscious that putting vessels up for auction would attract declining offers as the market needs were increasingly met, the Ministry of Transport, post-war owners of these ships in the United Kingdom, and the United States Maritime Commission in America, sold them mostly at fixed prices. They were bought by British and American shipowners as well as counterparts from overseas to increase international merchant fleet tonnage such that normal trading could resume sooner than would otherwise have been possible. New ships were also ordered and built, but the lead time to completion was considerable.

Conversion of naval vessels was always a favourable option when the economy was growing and a merchant company needed new ships to keep up with demand for its services. Usually, such ships were a stopgap until purpose-built tonnage could be ordered and commissioned; such was the case with the trailer ferry *Duchess of Holland* when she was converted from a Landing Ship, Small that had been commissioned into the United States Navy in 1946, for use on the Great Yarmouth to Scheveningen service for Norfolk Line in 1970. Within two years she had served her purpose and was put up for sale, having been displaced by new purpose-built ships. An earlier example was the purchase in 1853 of six warships from the German Confederation (*Deutscher Bund*) by the General Steam Navigation Company of London, the purchase coinciding with a short-lived expansion in trade between the Thames and near-Continental ports.

Purchase of naval ships for conversion to merchant service was also attractive in those trades that had low financial margins. The passenger excursion trade was exactly that, with year-round expenditure which had to be balanced against seasonal income. There are numerous examples, including the two *Ascot* class paddle minesweepers from the Great War which became the popular *Queen of Thanet* and *Queen of Kent* in the fleet of the New Medway Steam Packet Company.

Naval vessels brought into commercial service include both small launches and much larger classes of fighting ship as well as everything in between. The largest were a pair of German cruisers, SMS *Gefion* and SMS *Victoria Louise*, which were converted into cargo ships after the Great War, although, for the most part, few ships larger than frigates were bought and converted for commercial use.

Key reasons against the conversion of warships to merchant vessels is the narrow beam of many of them and the sub-division of the hull into small watertight compartments. These factors limit the potential deadweight capacity of a merchant conversion. Bulkheads can be, and were, removed, but this often required some of the remaining bulkheads to be strengthened. Besides, warships are normally designed and built for speed and manoeuvrability with fuel-hungry boilers economically unsuitable for commercial operation.

Another issue was the reluctance of the Admiralty to allow inspection of its ships by potential buyers; purchase was something of a lottery, a bit like buying a house without a surveyor's report. The preference for many buyers was to wait until ships had been sold and delivered to a shipbreaker's yard where a comprehensive structural and engineering survey could take place and a fair price agreed for the ship. The price would always allow a profit for the shipbreaker who had bought the ship on a tonnage basis for recycling. Quite often ships were bought in pairs, or even larger bundles, from a single shipbreaker for conversion for civilian service.

There was a good number of conversions of warships to merchant service for passenger use; the Townsend Car Ferries *Forde*, after the Great War, and *Halladale*, after the Second World War, for example, are perhaps among the better-known. A number of conversions to passenger vessels were made successfully, the excursion ship *Rochester Queen*, later the Channel Islands ferry *Commodore Queen*, and later the roll-on roll-off passenger and car ferry *Jersey Queen*, for example, was one such following the Second World War. There were a number of conversions from Landing Ship, Tank to roll-on roll-off freight ferry; ships of the Atlantic Steam Navigation Company come to mind, many offering a number of passenger berths. Others were deployed by the Royal Army Service Corps under the Red Ensign. Perhaps the most bizarre conversion of this type of ship was that of the Type 1 Landing Ship, Tank HMS *Bruiser* into the twin-funnelled luxury Caribbean cruise ship *Silverstar*. Smaller landing craft were converted for use on estuarial services; Red Funnel's *Norris Castle* is a good example of this type.

A large number of seagoing Admiralty salvage tugs were converted for civilian duties, some with passenger certificates. These ships were sought after by salvage and towing companies around the world during the 1920s and from 1946 onwards. Ocean-going fleet tugs flew the White Ensign and crews were subject to naval discipline. Large numbers of these ships were built in both world wars but immediately became surplus to requirements at the end of hostilities. Sale of these ships to commercial operators was certainly a fillip to the salvage and towing industry worldwide although it slowed down the development of this class of ship in a market saturated with wartime-built vessels. Only one European company, Smit of Rotterdam, managed to break free from the ex-naval steamship mould and brought out innovative motor ships with state-of-the-art equipment in the late 1930s. After the Second World War, however, the motor salvage tugs built for the Admiralty in 1944 and 1945 were at a premium, while the American-built diesel-electric salvage tugs on Lend-Lease to Britain during the war were also in great demand by commercial operators when they came onto the market or were made available for charter.

One of the most visible class of conversions took place after the Second World War when many of the wooden-hulled Fairmile launches were bought commercially and set to many and varied uses. They were readily adapted for short ferry and excursion duties, as Geoffrey Hamer explained in *Sea Breezes*, July 1982:

> The Fairmile B Type launches were built in the war mainly for patrol work and, of the 340 built in this country, at least 20 [actually more like 30] were subsequently converted for excursion work. Originally driven by petrol engines producing a top speed of 20 knots, they were re-engined with diesels for economic and safety reasons, and most passenger versions could manage only about 12 knots. Most had Class V

The former *LCG(M)181* (1944) became the passenger excursion ship *Rochester Queen* in 1948, the German-owned *Hein Muck* in 1955 and *Commodore Queen* in 1961. She was converted into the roll-on roll-off car and passenger ferry *Jersey Queen* in 1971. (Author)

Golden Galleon (1942), built as Fairmile Type B Launch *RML162*, was used in the excursion trade at Great Yarmouth for over four decades. She is seen heading up the River Yare.

and VI certificates for between 200 and 250 passengers. With a promenade deck stretching 112ft from bow to stern, they were ideal for trips in fine weather but saloon space was poor – those below deck had no windows while stability requirements allowed only the tiniest of deck saloons. They were good sea boats but with a large complement of passengers on deck they tended to roll easily.

Over the years they appeared on excursion work from most South Coast resorts from Eastbourne to Falmouth and were also used from Great Yarmouth, Llandudno and Blackpool, on the Thames, the Firths of Clyde, Forth and Tay, and even on the Mersey Ferry service. Last summer [1981] only three were still operating with British passenger certificates – the *Golden Galleon* at Great Yarmouth, and the *Western Lady III* and *Western Lady IV* at Torbay.

At their age, maintenance costs are becoming prohibitive and they cannot be kept in service much longer.

A report in *Superyacht Times*, July 2019, described the immediate post-war situation and the attractive option of converting Fairmile launches into private yachts:

The large yacht market at this time had been decimated by the scrapping of older vessels and numerous war losses. The problem was that many shipyards had been badly affected during WWII and to build a new yacht of over 30 metres was simply a dream to aspire towards in the future. Admittedly there were several yachts of this size still in existence, but these were not available for purchase due to their owners being unwilling to sell them.

As many as 200 of these [Fairmile B Type launches] would be converted to private yachts and many others to passenger tour vessels. Some would be converted for private use with the minimum of alterations whilst others would undergo more sophisticated conversions to upgrade them to the luxury standards of the time … It was remarkable that so many of these converted yachts survived many years after their estimated life of around five years given their light construction. Of these 200 conversions, it is believed that less than 20 survive worldwide today [2019].

The various classes of fishing vessel and motor fishing vessel that provided valuable service in both world wars were of little value to the military in peacetime. Most of these small wooden-hulled vessels went to the fishing industry while others were used as survey and dive support vessels, one even becoming the David MacBrayne passenger ferry *Loch Toscaig*.

The breadth of the types of conversions of all kinds of naval ships is quite staggering and the roles adopted in merchant service have been numerous and richly diverse. The success of the conversions was not always guaranteed, and although many of the ships reaped profits for their new owners some failed at the first hurdle and were quietly sold at considerable loss.

There were a number of ships that came from overseas navies into British merchant service, notably from the United States Navy. Many surplus US vessels were also sold for merchant service under the American flag and the emerging flags of convenience such as Panama and Greece.

Some vessels came under the Red Ensign from unlikely sources. Two small ships were bought by Yacht Holidays Limited of London who operated cruises with British-registered boats along the Rhine from Rotterdam up to Mannheim before the Second World War. At the end of the war two of the three ships were returned to their owners, being found at Lübeck and Tromsø, but the third was never located. A third ship was added in 1947, *Master Standfast*, the fast ball-bearing runner boarded by the enemy off the Swedish coast. She was found at Keil and later bought from the Admiralty.

Two further small vessels were acquired in 1949 and given the names *Lady Adriana* and *Lady Constance*. These were former wooden-hulled German minesweepers (*R-booten*) built in 1944 by Abeking & Rasmussen at Vegesack, Bremen. Yacht Holidays Limited had them converted for passenger use in Holland with accommodation in single and twin-berth cabins for thirty-four passengers and a crew of fourteen. In 1957 *Lady Adriana* ran aground on the Seven Maiden Rocks near the Lorelei. She was refloated and brought back to Rotterdam but was condemned. *Lady Constance* was given a major refit in 1959 and continued as part of a four-ship fleet, some cruises going as far as Basle in Switzerland.

Permission was granted to the German authorities to convert some of their naval vessels into merchant vessels after both world wars. However, few of the proposed conversions that were agreed by the Allies actually came about, although there

Lady Adriana (1944) owned by Yacht Holidays Limited of London was one of two former German 'R' class inshore minesweepers bought and converted by the company for cruises on the River Rhine. (Yacht Holidays Limited)

were a number of passenger ferries, coastal cargo ships and a couple of oil tankers successfully built around naval hulls (see Chapter 6).

Not all ships were purchased, many also being chartered. Such was the case when Frank Bustard approached the Ministry of Transport to charter Landing Ships, Tank after the Second World War in order to start his pioneer roll-on roll-off freight service between the United Kingdom and the Continent and later also to Northern Ireland. It suited the Admiralty to make ships available for charter when they believed they might want them back at some point in the future. Indeed, the LSTs were brought back into government service during the Suez Crisis in 1956.

On one occasion in the Great War the Admiralty loaned a ship for adaptation to commercial work. The Bermudan Government had the damaged and laid-up cruiser HMS *Charybdis* converted to maintain a rudimentary ferry service between St George and New York; the passenger liner normally on the route was away on trooping duties and this left the island isolated and very exposed (see Chapter 4).

Another conversion to liner status was not so well received and indeed gained a degree of notoriety. In 1946 the one-time seaplane carrier HMS *Albatross* was bought by the South Western Steam Navigation Company Limited of Torquay and Bristol and registered as *Albatross*. She was intended for use as a luxury cruise liner and a start was made on the conversion until the funds ran out. She was resold in 1947 to a London-based Greek company, converted into an immigrant ship and renamed *Hellenic Prince*. She was certainly no luxury liner with dormitories for up to twenty people, as well as some eight- and four-bunk cabins with shared bathrooms. *Hellenic Prince* was chartered to the International Refugee Organisation. Nobody that travelled aboard the ship had a good word to say about the experience and stories of the way passengers were treated are quite alarming (see Chapter 8).

Not all swords beaten into ploughshares went to commercial operators. After the Second World War, two *Bangor* class minesweepers were transferred to the Royal Air Force as the long-range rescue ships HMAFV *Bridport* and HMAFV *Bridlington*, serving the needs of their aircraft and those of the burgeoning aviation industry. Commercial aviation required up-to-date weather information on the Atlantic routes and to this end, a series of 'Flower' class corvettes were put into service as weather ships, later succeeded by a second generation of ships which were built as the slightly larger 'Castle' class frigates. These ships were maintained by the Air Ministry.

Some warships were only beaten very gently for use as RN or RNR training and drill ships. Two naval ships based at the Victoria Embankment at London for many years were the RNR Drill Ships HMS *President* and HMS *Chrysanthemum*. HMS *President* was built as HMS *Saxifrage* in 1918 as a 'Flower' class Q ship, disguised as a merchant ship, and HMS *Chrysanthemum* was built in 1917 as one of the *Anchusa* class sloops. HMS *President* took up duty at London in 1922 and HMS

The 'Flower' class Q ship HMS *Saxifrage* (1918) became the drill ship HMS *President* in 1922. She was decommissioned and sold in 1988, and is currently laid up at Chatham

Chrysanthemum joined her to provide additional accommodation in 1938.

The pair last flew the White Ensign in 1988 when they were replaced by a shore establishment in St Katherine Docks. HMS *Chrysanthemum* was used under the name '*Tiber*' as a film set in *Indiana Jones and the Last Crusade* (1989), and then moved to the Medway where her hull deteriorated so badly that she had to be scrapped in 1995. *President* faired a lot better and was saved from the scrapyard when she was bought by the charity Inter-Action Social Enterprise Trust, keeping her berth on the Embankment. In 1987 ownership passed to HMS President London Limited. In 2001 the ship was sold to David Harper and Cary Thompson and resold again in 2006 to the MLS Group as a function centre. In 2016 *President* had to leave her berth at London where she had lain for 94 years, and was moved to Chatham where she now remains under the new ownership of Lisa-Marie Turner. In a bid to secure funding to restore the ship MP Dr Julian Lewis spoke in Parliament (*Hansard*, 15 December 2016):

HMS *Saxifrage*, as she was then called, was designed to protect the vital merchant shipping on which our country depended. Crewed by 93 men, she was a 'Flower' class anti-submarine Q-ship. These sloops were originally intended to be minesweepers, but with the growing threat from submarines they were transferred to convoy escort duties. What makes their tale, and that of HMS *President* in particular, so historically significant was that they were deliberately configured as bait for U-boats. They were fitted out to look like merchantmen in order to invite attack by submarines on the surface, sometimes when investigating why their first torpedo had failed to finish off a vessel which in reality was packed with hidden buoyancy aids and armed with hidden large-calibre guns.

At the start of a U-boat attack, 'panic parties' would frantically abandon ship while the gun crew stayed out of sight until the submarine came within range. Then, the Q-ship would run up the White Ensign, break out the concealed guns and open fire.

There are also many examples of decommissioned naval ships used as static training establishments or store ships.

2

CONVERSION FROM MINOR WARSHIP TO MERCHANT SHIP

Although the basic concepts of ship design apply equally to warships and merchant ships, the demands applied to their hulls are quite different. Most warships and merchant ships have vertical frames closely spaced along the hull length onto which the hull plating is fixed. Each deck is stiffened by transverse beams which are attached to the side frames forming, along with the double bottom structure, a strong transverse ring. In both types of ship the keel and bottom structure, along with the upper part of the hull at weather-deck level, are strengthened to provide longitudinal strength similar to that of a box girder. The upper part of a ship is made stronger by the sheer strake which is the topmost strake of hull side plating and the strake of deck plating that connects to the sheer strake. Both merchant and naval ships use watertight bulkheads to provide rigidity to the hull structure and protection from collision or grounding damage. In the event of the bow colliding with another vessel or a dock wall, the most important bulkhead is the one adjacent to the bow and aptly called the collision bulkhead. In both types of ship each bulkhead has to withstand a pre-determined water pressure which in merchant ships is specified by the flag state regulatory agency – in the case of the United Kingdom, the Board of Trade and its latest successor The Maritime and Coastguard Agency (MCA).

The distribution of bulkheads and the compartmentalisation of warships and merchant ships are fundamentally different. The large open hold spaces of a merchant ship are bounded by bulkheads at each end as are the machinery spaces and also the bunkers, usually situated at the sides and forward of the boiler room. The only other bulkheads are the collision bulkhead and an aft peak bulkhead that encloses the watertight stern tube within which the propeller shaft turns. Decks above the fore peak, aft peak deep ballast tanks and oil fuel bunkers are all watertight and have to withstand the same pressure as the bulkheads. In any passenger ship that was certified to carry more than twelve passengers, the number and spacing of the watertight bulkheads had to comply with the subdivision rules of the flag state regulatory agency.

In cargo ships the hold and machinery bulkheads had no watertight doors other than perhaps between an engine room and a generator room. These doors had to be open for operational requirements when the ship was at sea but were closed immediately in the event of an accident. In ocean and short-sea passenger liners several of the watertight bulkheads had sliding watertight doors in them, all of which could be automatically closed in the event of collision, grounding or fire by moving a lever on the bridge. Passenger ships are subdivided into a 'Two Compartment Standard' which means that a ship will remain afloat and stable in moderate sea conditions with any two adjacent compartments breached to the sea with free flooding of the compartments. The two most important compartments were the two immediately abaft the collision bulkhead and in preparing the subdivision calculation, the ship designer estimated the sinkage by the bow with these two compartments flooded and decided how high the collision bulkhead, and possibly the adjacent one, had to extend upwards to avoid progressive flooding.

Titanic was designed to a Two Compartment Standard. However, she sustained damage to the underwater part of the starboard hull over a length of some 300ft. Despite having fifteen transverse watertight bulkheads, it was inevitable that she would sink as she had too many compartments breached and open to the sea. She sank slowly due to progressive flooding both into breached compartments and over the top of some bulkheads into the next compartment. At a subsequent refit her surviving sister-ship *Olympic* had five of her bulkheads raised from E to D Deck level, ensuring that all subdivision bulkheads were terminated at D deck level. It is regularly ignored that *Titanic* was a very safe ship which remained stable, with little heeling and still with some electric lighting as she progressively sank over a period of 2 hours and 40 minutes. Cunard's *Lusitania*, on the other hand, which had longitudinal as well as transverse subdivision, capsized and sank in 18 minutes when torpedoed due to asymmetrical flooding caused by her longitudinal bulkheads.

Great care must be taken to ensure that openings or abrupt discontinuities cut into the hull and main deck 'box girder' during conversion, are amply compensated for by strengthening fitted around the opening. Ideally, all openings should be circular but if square or rectangular in shape they should have well-radiused corners. Merchant ships, therefore, need strengthening around hull doors designed for cargo handling and embarkation and disembarkation of passengers, and they also have built-in weaknesses around cargo hatches which have to be ameliorated by increased thickness of plating. Vertical support is provided by incorporated internal structure although it is occasionally provided by pillars. The last ships to have a row of pillars at the centreline between keelson and weather deck, however, were the steel sailing ships built in the last quarter of the nineteenth century.

The decks of merchant ships may have to be specially designed to withstand the weight of cargoes typical to that trade. The 'tween decks are only designed for lighter cargo and could not be used, for example, for heavy bulk cargoes such as coal and iron ore. Passenger and officer accommodation, lifesaving appliances and the navigation bridge are built over the machinery spaces to provide protection to those areas. Crew and further passenger accommodation were latterly often situated in the poop.

Warships on the other hand, were, and are, liberally subdivided by both transverse and longitudinal bulkheads. These create a grid of small watertight compartments that are designed to assist in keeping the ship afloat as a fighting unit in the event of flooding sustained by damage in action. Warships also have watertight decks and the only way into any compartment, including the engine and boiler rooms, is through a hatch in a watertight deck, there being no doors in the adjacent watertight boundary bulkheads. Naval discipline ensured that the watertight integrity of the ship was maintained at all times by the closure of the doors and hatches when the ship was at action stations. In the event of a compartment being breached to the sea by enemy action, there was no guarantee that the personnel assigned to that compartment would be saved.

Many warships were constructed from higher quality tensile steel than would normally be used for a merchant ship. This allowed the same longitudinal and local strength for a much lighter material weight. This greater tensile strength supported the concentrated weights built into the ship such as propulsive machinery and weaponry but, of equal importance, it allowed the ship to maintain high speeds in hostile sea conditions without the risk of structural failure.

The weaker points of a warship that require strengthening are quite different from those in a merchant ship. There are no cargo hatches or other large openings in the weather deck but there is the armament, often protected by armour plate, that requires local strengthening to incorporate that weight into the structure of the ship. Such strengthening needs also to withstand the stresses caused by the weapons firing.

As fighting ships are built for speed and manoeuvrability, they have a fine form, a higher length to breadth ratio compared to equivalent-sized merchant ships, and powerful machinery. In addition, they are strengthened forward to withstand panting, pounding and slamming of the structure whilst being driven at speed into a head sea.

Just as a merchant ship design could be anything between a full scantling hull design and a lighter open shelter deck vessel depending on the intended trade, so a warship could be of lighter or heavier design depending on its designated role. In both world wars, however, resort was made to adopt successful mercantile designs as the basis for mass-produced naval ships. The Second World War 'Flower' class corvette, for example, was built to merchant-ship standards based on that of a typical whale catcher of the 1930s and the motor fishing vessel was a continuation of a current commercial design in both world wars. The attraction of this was that shipyards unfamiliar with naval construction practice could be commissioned to build much-needed ships for naval use albeit to merchant ship construction standards.

Prefabrication was widely used in both world wars in order to produce volume quantities of the smaller types of warships. Typical were the various types of landing craft which were fabricated by numerous small yards, many with no previous experience of steel construction, from parts manufactured by structural and other fabricators often some distance from the coast. Many of these craft had short lives and became unserviceable after the wars had ended. That being so, the Z lighters of the Great War and Landing Craft, Tank of the Second World War were capable of surprising longevity, some surviving in commercial service for over five decades.

Quality of steel was also an issue for some shipyards, notably yards in the United States where impure steel plate with higher carbon content than its certificate stated was built into numerous naval ships as well as wartime standard ships such as the Liberty type (See Robins 2017, Chapter 15). This may have contributed to the early demise of a number of vessels including the commercially popular Landing Ship, Tank. Concern was also raised regarding the integrity of all-welded hulls but the method was vindicated after the war by its international acceptance.

Lack of maintenance during wartime meant that many vessels available for sale and adoption for commercial use after hostilities ended were in desperate need of repair and replacement parts. The Admiralty refused to allow inspection of ships on the sale list so a prospective buyer often waited until a breaker's yard had made the initial purchase so that the condition of the vessel could then be inspected as it lay at the yard. Less risky purchases were the many wooden-hulled ships, including the Fairmile B launches and many fast patrol boats which were sold without their original petrol engines; the engines were returned to the United States under the strictures of Lend-Lease.

Given the numerous structural differences between warships and merchant ships, it is perhaps surprising that so many minor warships ended up in commercial service. There were, however, three compelling reasons why warships were so attractive to commercial shipowners:

– Needs must was the first reason because post-war availability and the high cost of new or

second-hand tonnage as replacement for war losses was prohibitive for many shipowners. Besides, the lead time to order a new ship, when materials were in short supply, was extensive and shipbuilders were unable to commit to a delivery date.
- Secondly, some types of naval ship were attractive for conversion into specific commercial roles, the 'Hunt' class escorts built in the Great War, for example, were especially popular for conversion to fast coastal and cross-Channel passenger units, much as the 'River' class escorts were after the Second World War.
- Thirdly, there were numerous small ships which had an important role to play during hostilities but which were immediately redundant thereafter. Some of these types were readily adapted for commercial use, motor minesweepers, motor fishing vessels and numerous wooden motor launches and harbour craft are examples, while redundant Second World War Landing Ships, Tank were used to pioneer roll-on, roll-off cross-Channel freight services from the late 1940s into the mid-1960s.

So, just what was involved in converting a minesweeper into a commercial passenger and freight ferry, a survey vessel or any other craft that might be proposed? A prerequisite for disposal by the navy to shipbreaker or commercial shipowner required complete de-storing and removal or comprehensive disablement of armament; and the first task in converting a warship for merchant service was removal of all unwanted heavy installations such as any remaining armament, related machinery and, as far as possible, armour plating, reinforcements and mountings for guns. This had the immediate effect of reducing the displacement or floating weight of the vessel.

If the intended conversion was to produce a passenger ship then the flag state regulatory agency was required to calculate and assign the minimum freeboard in the fully loaded condition to the main or freeboard deck. The maximum load draft was made up of the weight of the completed hull when converted, plus fuel, stores, crew and effects, and finally the deadweight of cargo and passengers. Subtraction of the loaded draft from the moulded depth, or the vertical distance between the top of the keel and the main deck at the side of a ship, defined the freeboard, and this had to be greater than the minimum prescribed. If there remained a surplus of freeboard then, for example, a deck saloon or even a new sun deck might be considered for a conversion design for a passenger ship. Before a passenger certificate could be issued, a subdivision calculation had to be carried out in order to establish the required number and spacing of the transverse watertight bulkheads.

When removing the many watertight bulkheads in order to create clear spaces for holds and passenger accommodation, consideration needed to be given to the overall structural integrity of the vessel. Where previous structure had been removed, an investigation had to be carried out to see if structural compensation needed to be incorporated into the conversion. All aspects of a conversion from a warship to a merchant ship had to be to the satisfaction of the flag state regulatory agency whose requirements were extensive and included intact and damaged stability, safety of life at sea, master's and crew spaces, navigation arrangements, and even lights and sound signals. If the ship was over 150ft in overall length, a second mast might be required to carry the second masthead light as warships usually only displayed a single light.

Both warships and merchant ships are designed around Archimedes' Principle which states that a floating body will displace its own weight. All ships when floating at rest in still water obey two important conditions: that the force of buoyancy acting upwards equals the total weight of the ship and that the centres of buoyancy (B) and gravity (G) remain in the same vertical lines even when the ship is heeled over to one side. The centre of buoyancy can move up or down with respect to the waterline depending on the load being carried. The point at which a vertical line through the heeled centre of buoyancy crosses the line through the original vertical centre of buoyancy is called the metacentre (M); the metacentre always lies vertically above the centre of buoyancy (see illustration). There is increased buoyancy on the side that is heeled over, and decreased buoyancy on the other, and this promotes a righting lever that will brings the ship back to vertical.

Any ship is stable provided that the metacentre remains above the centre of gravity. If the centre of gravity is higher than the metacentre the stability is impaired and the ship can be in danger of ultimate capsize.

In preparing the design for a new ship the naval architect was faced with familiar but complex tasks when given a clean sheet of paper along with a technical brief on the trade, capacity and performance required of the new ship. It was a much more complex and challenging task fitting this same brief into an existing hull because a former warship hull was usually long and narrow for its length, and was not ideally suited for conversion to provide a viable cargo deadweight capacity compared with a conventional broader-beamed merchant ship. However, the warship hull was suitable for conversion to survey ships; oceanographical research ships; cruising pilot cutters, daylight excursion and cross-Channel passenger ships; and in one particular case a large steam yacht, *Cutty Sark*, based on a cancelled Great War 'V&W' class destroyer (see Chapter 4).

It was also likely that the machinery would need attention. For example, high-speed naval ships with four water tube boilers supplying steam to two turbine sets might only require two boilers to be in service to allow the ship to operate more economically at a reduced but still significant speed. In some cases, the flag state regulatory agency might insist on reduced superheat temperature or operational steam pressure in the interests of safety. In a few cases, where a highly volatile grade of pulverised coal was used to fire the boilers, adaptations might have to be made to allow for the use of readily available and cheaper coal or possibly oil fuel. Bunker spaces might also be reduced in volume where the proposed operational range of the vessel in her new role and frequency of bunkering allowed, so freeing up this redundant space for some other purpose.

Other specialised craft such as Landing Ships, Tank required less conversion, although for civilian use the troop quarters needed to be converted into money-earning cargo space and longitudinal bulkheads had to be removed between the engine rooms. Other measures were required to comply with a civilian role and included new crew accommodation and raising the wheelhouse by one deck to give satisfactory forward visibility, but the

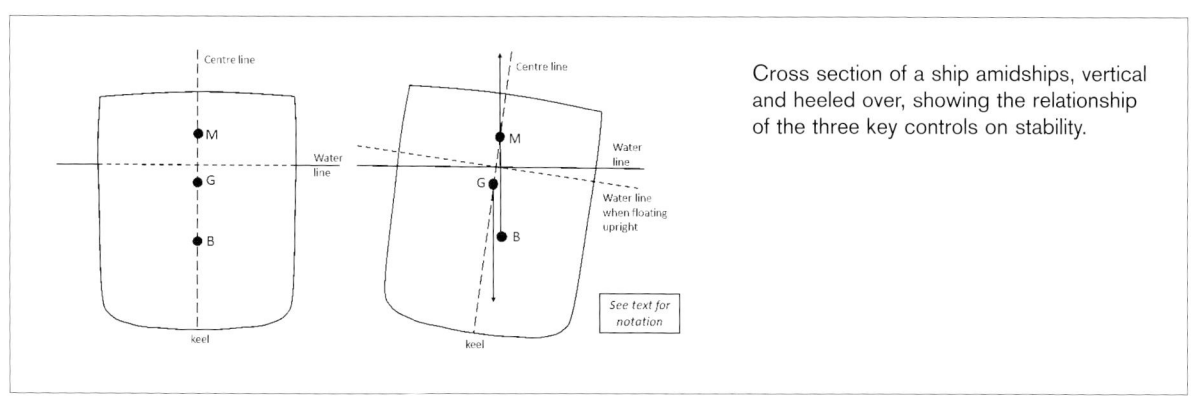

Cross section of a ship amidships, vertical and heeled over, showing the relationship of the three key controls on stability.

Some conversions led surprisingly long civilian careers. *Tucalif* (1943) was originally commissioned as Patrol Craft Escort HMS *Kilbirnie* and is seen in 1997 awaiting delivery to an Italian scrapyard after fifty years in commercial service.

Provided there was money available to commit to a contract for the conversion of a warship into a merchant ship, a yard could usually be found that was available to take on the business, while many, like Earle's at Hull, provided both naval architect services and rebuilding as a single package after the Great War. After both major conflicts there were a number of shipyards such as the Coaster Construction Company Limited at Montrose, and larger shipbuilders such as Harland & Wolff at its yards both at Belfast and on the Clyde, that specialised in the conversion of specific types of warship.

The bottom line of all conversions was simply availability, cost and suitability. If the cost of purchase of the redundant warship plus the cost of redesigning and rebuilding the ship as a merchant ship was less than the purchase price of a ready-made and available second-hand vessel then the deal was viable. This simple piece of economics assumes that the converted ship was in every way suitable for the trade it was to undertake and that it had an expected design life of sufficient length to repay the capital outlay. The second key factor was that purchase from the navy and conversion to merchant duties could be undertaken more quickly than trying to find and purchase suitable second-hand merchant tonnage.

overall costs of these changes were not great and the work took only a few weeks to complete.

Finally, there was the issue of putting the design into reality. There were severe material shortages following both the First and Second World Wars; there was competition for the attention of shipyards to overhaul and service war-weary ships; and there was a growing demand for new ships to be built to replace those lost to enemy action.

3

EXAMPLES FROM THE NINETEENTH CENTURY

The difference between merchantman and man-of-war was not obvious until the end of the Napoleonic Wars. Many of the commercial ships employed by the merchant traders, such as the East India Company, were armed. From the 1820s onwards, however, the need for merchant ships to carry guns declined and fewer ships were commissioned for private owners complete with an array of gunports. As the old wooden walls of the failing East India Company were taken out of service, many of those in suitable condition for further trading were sold for use in the emigrant trade to Australia – an early example of conversion of a fighting ship, albeit belonging to a privately-owned navy, to merchantman.

Opportunities for naval vessels to be sold for commercial use were otherwise few in the early part of the nineteenth century. The Admiralty was keen to get the best use out of its ships and tended to maintain them well until, with age and the weakening of their structures though use and decay, they lost seaworthiness. However, as the century progressed through the reign of Queen Victoria opportunities did arise and there are a number of examples of warships being put to commercial use under private ownership.

Bomb Vessels and Polar Explorers

Probably the first conversions from war to peace were seven of the eight *Hecla* class bomb vessels built between 1813 and 1826, one *Vesuvius* class bomb vessel and one gun-brig which were converted to Polar exploration ships. Bomb vessels, first used by the French, had been introduced to the Royal Navy in the late seventeenth century. They initially had a fixed high-trajectory mortar mounted forward of the mast that could fire explosive shells onto enemy positions on land. Later designs allowed for the mortar to be aimed without turning the ship. The vessels were strongly built with reinforced decks and strong thick-timbered frames and hulls in order to withstand the recoil of the mortars. As the ships became obsolescent, they were quickly identified as ideal vessels for use in polar exploration as their extra-strong construction would withstand the pressure of pack ice.

The *Hecla* class ships were 105ft length overall and had a beam of 28ft. They were full rigged and needed little conversion for use as exploration vessels although additional crew accommodation replaced the gun platform reinforcement timbers below the main deck. In due course, the accommodation aboard was insulated with cork and coal stoves were installed to provide some warmth and inhibit condensation. All the vessels were retained in the ownership of the Admiralty during their service as Polar exploration vessels.

HMS *Hecla* was the first ship to be adapted and she was put under the charge of William Edward Parry in 1819 to assist in his search for the legendary Northwest Passage. *Hecla* was accompanied by the smaller *Bold* class gun-brig HMS *Griper*. The ships were iced-in over winter and returned to England in November 1820. In 1821, HMS *Fury*, the second of the *Hecla* class ships to be completed, accompanied *Hecla* on two further trips to the Arctic. During the second voyage which began in 1824, HMS *Fury* was wrecked and abandoned in Prince Regent Inlet. HMS *Aetna* was converted in 1826, HMS *Meteor* in 1832 and renamed *Beacon*, HMS *Thunder* in 1833, HMS *Sulphur* in 1835, and the last of the *Hecla* class ships, HMS *Erebus*, in 1839. HMS *Erebus* and the *Vesuvius* class bomb ship HMS *Terror* were commanded by James Clark Ross for exploration around Antarctica. HMS *Terror* had been commissioned in 1813 and was converted for survey work in 1835. Both ships were then fitted with railway locomotive engines coupled to propeller shafts that provided a speed of 4 knots on trials and under Sir John Franklin they were later used in the search for the Northwest Passage – both ships and their entire complement of men were lost on this expedition. In 2014, a Canadian team located the wreck of *Erebus* in the eastern portion of Queen Maud Gulf, and two years later, the wreck of *Terror* was found south of King William Island.

HMS *Hecla* was used for survey work along the West African Coast in the late 1820s and put up for sale in 1831. She was sold to Sir Edward Banks and others and used on various trades until she was converted into a whaler in 1834. She was lost among ice floes in 1840. The last of the converted bomb ships were scrapped in the early 1850s after seeing service on harbour duties towards the end of their careers.

The German Confederation and the *Reichsflotte*

A unique opportunity arose in 1852 when an entire navy was disbanded, that of the German

The former bomb vessels **HMS** *Erebus* (1826) and **HMS** *Terror* (1813) in New Zealand, August 1841, from an oil painting by John Wilson Carmichael. (Wikimedia Commons)

Confederation. The *Deutscher Bund*, as the Confederation was known, was an association of thirty-nine states, mainly German-speaking, located in central Europe. It was created in 1815 to coordinate the economies of separate German-speaking countries. In due course the Confederation was weakened as divisions arose within it, and in 1848, revolutions established a unified German state.

A new provisional parliament first met in Frankfurt on 18 May 1848, and in June it decided to invest in a navy. The subsequent fleet took part in its only naval engagement at the battle of Heligoland against the Danes on 4 June 1849. The ships then became the property of the newly re-established German Confederation. This did not last long, and on 2 April 1852, the so-called *Reichsflotte* was dissolved. Most of the ships were put up for sale, although of the steam frigates were given to the Prussian Navy. At the time there were three steam frigates, including the former pioneer Cunard passenger steamer *Britannia*, six steam corvettes, two sailing frigates, one sailing corvette and twenty-nine gunboats. The ships were put on the market at extremely modest prices – it was a classic fire sale.

The early 1850s were the boom years of the mid-Victorian era and ships could not be built quickly enough to satisfy demand in some trades. The advertised sale of the *Reichsflotte* did not go unnoticed in London. The Directors of the General Steam Navigation Company (GSNC) were quick to assemble bids for the six steam corvettes as they came up for sale during 1853. The total price that was accepted was £35,700, a bargain at an average cost of just under £6,000 per ship; GSNC became proud owners of the corvettes *Großerzog von Oldenburg, Bremen, Frankfurt, Hamburg, Der Königliche Ernst August*, and *Lubec*. They were British built apart from the *Bremen* and *Hamburg* which were built at German yards, and they were relatively new. For example, the *Großerzog von Oldenburg* had been built at Bristol

The German Confederation corvette *Frankfurt* (1848), one of six ships sold for commercial service in 1853 and renamed *Holland*.

only in 1850. The corvettes each had a wooden hull apart from the *Lubec* which had an iron hull, and all were sail-assisted paddle steamers.

The ships were delivered in 1853 complete with guns, stores and well-stocked magazines. The six corvettes were brought across the North Sea to the GSNC yard at Deptford Creek, stripped of their naval hardware and in its place two holds were built, one forward and one aft of the machinery spaces, and accommodation was provided for a small number of passengers. The six corvettes were renamed respectively *Belgium, Hanover, Holland, Denmark, Edinburgh* and *Newcastle*, their new names reflecting the trade routes for which they were initially intended. In their new roles they were measured at between 383 tons gross in the case of *Holland* to the much larger 741 tons gross of *Edinburgh*.

The six former corvettes were kept in full employment until a mini-depression set in at the onset of the Crimean War in 1854. A buyer was found for *Newcastle* and she was sold. GSNC was able to charter out the largest of the ships, *Edinburgh*, to the French government for use as a transport. Robert Forrester explains in his PhD Thesis:

Der Königliche Ernst August (1850) was another corvette sold by the German Confederation after it decided it did not want the upkeep of a navy. She was renamed *Edinburgh*.

An exceptional income source from November 1854 was the charter of the *Edinburgh*, the largest of the six ships purchased from the Germanic Confederation in 1853, to the French Government for six to twelve months for service in the Crimea. She was sunk in fog in the Black Sea, likely in collision, during 1855. Though the company did not, as a rule, insure its ships when in service, they were insured when on charter.

Denmark was sold in 1859 and *Holland* followed her in 1860. *Hanover* remained in the GSNC fleet until 1868 having provided 15 years of profitable service to her owners while *Belgium* remained in service under the GSNC flag until 1877 when she was hulked.

Tugs and Gunboats

The Admiralty was next to demonstrate that warships could be adapted for more peaceful duties. By 1862 the Admiralty operated nineteen steam tugs mainly as harbour tugs to facilitate its own arrivals and departures. Seven of the tugs were purpose-built while others were former GPO dispatch boats. There were also five vessels used for towing that were originally commissioned as warships. Two of these were former paddle gunboats: HMS *Locust*, built in 1840, was a *Lizard* class gun vessel and HMS *Spitfire*, dating from 1845, was converted to a survey ship in 1851 then to a tug in 1862 – she was only broken up in 1888. Three were built as sloops, the paddle steamer HMS *African* in 1825, used largely as a survey ship and later a tug and demolished in 1862, the paddle steamer HMS *Echo* built in 1827 and converted into a tug in 1837 in which guise she served until 1888, and HMS *Confiance* also built in 1827, originally as a *Cherokee* class brig sloop but completed as a paddle steamer. Demoted to towing duties, *Locust* and *African* were stationed at Sheerness, *Comet* and *Echo* at Portsmouth, *Confiance* at Devonport and *Spitfire* was stationed at Bermuda. These tugs were all wooden-hulled vessels and none retained any armament.

Two of the *Philomel* class gunboats, both built at Pembroke, HMS *Pandoro* launched in 1861 (seven years after the keel was laid!) and HMS *Newport* completed in 1867, were both sold as yachts – both to the same owner, Allen Young. The ships were wooden hulled, rigged as barques and had a 2-cylinder horizontal steam engine and a speed of up to 10 knots. They were equipped with five guns. Young bought HMS *Pandoro* in 1875; she had been in reserve at Portsmouth for three years. He used her for two abortive attempts to find the Northwest Passage through the Arctic and then sold her to James Gordon Bennett who renamed her *Jeannette*. She was lost in pack ice in 1881 on another Arctic expedition. HMS *Newport* was commissioned as a survey ship and sold to Allen Young in 1881 and renamed *Pandoro II*. She was resold in 1890 to F W Leybourne-Popham and renamed *Blencathra*, and then sold again to Major Andrew Coats, both owners taking the ship to Arctic waters. In 1912 she was bought by Georgy Brusilov and given the name *Svyataya Anna* under the Russian flag. On yet another Arctic expedition she was lost in the pack ice – the ship never being found.

The former *Philomel* class gunboat HMS *Newport* (1867), in her final guise as *Svyataya Anna*, before leaving on her last trip to the Arctic where she was lost in the ice.

The wooden-hulled screw vessel HMS *Hyaena* was completed in 1856 by C J Mare & Company at Blackwall as one of the 98-strong *Albacore* class of steam gunboats. Although the main deck (gun deck) was 103ft long the ships had a shallow draught of just under 7ft. They were equipped with one 68-pounder and one 32-pounder muzzle-loading guns and two 24-pounder howitzers. In March 1870, HMS *Hyaena* was bought by Wm E Joliffe of Liverpool and converted for use as a salvage vessel. She served in this role until 1870 when she was sold to Robert N Dale of Liverpool and was eventually broken up in 1903. Another of the same class, HMS *Charger*, was sold in July 1887 to Canadian owners and renamed *Rescue* for use as an ocean-going rescue tug based at Halifax, Nova Scotia. She was only scrapped in 1921. Yet another of the class, HMS *Dove*, built at Northfleet in 1855 by W & H Pitcher, was bought by Peninsular & Oriental Steam Navigation Company in April 1873 for use at Shanghai as a tug and tender.

In 1870, Edward Bates & Sons of Liverpool bought three ships from the Admiralty: HMS *Recruit*, HMS *Sharpshooter* and HMS *Thais*. Bates typically bought redundant steam-powered ships and converted them into sailing ships to use on his long-haul cargo service between Liverpool and the Antipodes. Of his new acquisitions, *Sharpshooter* was the oldest of the three, having been completed in 1846 at Blackwall as an iron-hulled screw gunvessel. She was commissioned in April 1848 and served variously in the Channel Squadron, the Mediterranean, on the southeast coast of America and the West African coast. Bates sold her to owners in Singapore two years after acquiring her.

HMS *Recruit* was an iron paddle steamer of 389 tons displacement completed at London in 1850 by Robinson & Russell at Millwall for the Prussian Navy as *Salamander*. She was originally equipped with four 25-pounder mortars. In 1855 she became HMS *Recruit* as part of an exchange deal, but was laid up thereafter at Malta for much of the time. Bates kept this ship in commercial service for four years before reselling her to owners in Cape Town.

HMS *Thais* was a double-ended paddle tug and passenger tender built by Laird at Birkenhead in 1856. She had been ordered as a ferry by the Birkenhead Improvement Commissioners with the intended name of *Princess Eugenie*, but was completed to Admiralty specifications as a stores and personnel carrier. This was the third ship acquired by Edward Bates & Sons, and she was completely overhauled and lengthened by just 9ft in 1873. She was managed by T Readhead and based at Liverpool running occasional passenger excursions, but was sold in 1871. She was resold in 1877 to owners in Buenos Aires.

HMS *Mutine* was another mid-Victorian conversion to a merchant ship. She was completed at Deptford Royal Dockyard in 1859 as one of the two *Greyhound* class sloops (they were later redesignated corvettes). She was a wooden-hulled paddle steamer with a length of 172ft and breadth 33ft and was equipped with six 40-pounder breech-loading guns and twelve 32-pounder muzzle-loaders. She served on the Pacific Station throughout until she was decommissioned at Sheerness in 1869 and then sold in February 1870 to John Wade of London and renamed *Chieftain*. She ceased to be registered after 1873 (John Wade died in 1872). Wade had owned three fast clipper ships during his career, *Ziba*, *Ada* and *Eme*, which had all been employed in the China tea trade. *Chieftain*, however, was used as a tug and tender. Iron-hulled paddle tugs were introduced to the Admiralty from the mid-1870s. However, the Admiralty relied heavily on chartering tugs especially during hostilities such as the war in Egypt in 1882.

A series of twenty-six harbour defence vessels were built between 1862 and 1870. These had a 90-ton muzzle-loader which was fixed on deck and aimed by use of the helm and the twin screws; maximum speed was just 4 knots. Many of these ships were sold for use as platforms for pile driving, as floating cranes and other roles, some converted to barges. They mostly lasted a long time, the floating crane, formally HMS *Cuckoo* at Birkenhead, and the onetime HMS *Arrow* at Portsmouth survived into the 1950s, having enjoyed lengthy and fruitful civilian careers.

The composite screw sloop HMS *Elk* was built in 1868 by Portsmouth Dockyard. She was 155ft long by 25ft breadth and carried one 64-pounder gun and two 20-pounders. *Elk* was at Hong Kong in November 1874, departing in January 1875; and in Malta in April–May 1875. In 1890 she was converted for use as a tug at Portsmouth and in 1905 was sold to the Manchester Ship Canal Company and converted into the suction dredger *Elk*. She was not a success in her new role so the centrifugal pump was removed and a grab crane installed. She was then employed as a hopper dredger of 120 tons capacity. Her main role was to remove the 'hills' left by the larger dredgers in the Bromborough Channel approach to the entrance to the Ship Canal. She was also used to remove bulk cargo from barges sunk in the canal so that they could be lifted; lighters abandoned by their watchmen sank regularly once the bilge pump engine ran out of fuel, a common occurrence should there be a welcoming pub in the vicinity! *Elk* was retired from duty in 1930 and left to rot in the Lymm River above Latchford Lock. Had her owners known of the early history of the ship they might have looked for a home for her to go to. There were rumours, but only rumours, that the old dredger might have once been a gunboat as F D Roberts, Dredging Superintendent for the Manchester Ship Canal Company, wrote in a letter to *Sea Breezes*, April 1950:

Whenever she was drydocked for repairs, the

The composite screw sloop **HMS** *Elk* (1868) was converted into a dredger when she was bought by the Manchester Ship Canal Company in 1905. She is seen at Malta.

copper spikes with which she was fastened, so the story goes, were replaced by galvanised spikes, presumably for those concerned to sell the copper. These spikes were 18 inches long and 7/8 in diameter, and each one was marked with an arrowhead mark. These marks were used as evidence by the old boys to support their story that the vessel had been a gunboat.

For once the 'old boys' were absolutely right, and it is to be hoped that they received their share of the proceeds from the sale of the copper spikes!

The *Algerine* class composite screw gunboat HMS *Ranger* was built by J Elder & Company (later Fairfield Shipbuilding & Engineering) and first commissioned in 1881. She had a displacement of 370 tons, was schooner rigged and could maintain 9 knots under steam. She was assigned to the East Indies Station where she stayed until 1892. On return to Britain she was decommissioned and put up for sale. HMS *Ranger* was bought by the Liverpool and Glasgow Salvage Association and put to work in the commercial world as a salvage ship. She had a strong wooden hull up to 11in thick along the bilges and was well suited to the heavy and often arduous work she was engaged in. In 1901 she was taken in hand at Belfast where she was modified further for her salvage role and her original compound engine was replaced by a new triple-expansion unit.

A familiar sight at her berth in the Albert Dock in Liverpool, *Ranger* attended numerous casualties. These included the successful salvage of the cruiser HMS *Gladiator* which sank in collision with the passenger liner *St Paul* off the Isle of Wight in April 1908; the White Star liner *Suevic* aground on the Lizard; the submarine *K13* on her acceptance trials during the Great War; the submarine HMS *Thetis* which sank on trials in Liverpool Bay in 1939; and *Ulster Queen* ashore on Maughold Head, Isle of Man in February 1940. Desmond Young is quoted in *Sea Breezes*, June 1951, as writing of the old *Ranger*:

If you were on board of her and gazed up for any length of time at her stumpy masts, with derricks almost as massive as themselves, describing a leisurely arc across the sky, you might find her roll a little trying, for she rolls steadily, comfortably enough – but unceasingly … But she is not without a certain dignity, and, roll or no roll, she is an admirable sea-boat, shipping only an occasional dollop of spray over the forecastle head, even in bad weather.

Finally retired, the old salvage ship was broken up at Liverpool in 1954. Although *Ranger* is by far and away the best known of the Liverpool salvage boats, several other of these ships were also built as men-of-war. Two *Mariner* class composite sloops, HMS *Mariner* and HMS *Reindeer*, built in 1894, were loaned to the Liverpool and Glasgow Salvage Association between 1917 and 1922 and after a long period of idleness both were demolished in the late 1920s.

HMS *Melita*, another one of the *Mariner* class built in Malta in 1888, was sold to the Falmouth Dock's Board in 1920 and renamed *Ringdove's Aid* and resold to the Liverpool and Glasgow Salvage Association in 1927 and renamed *Restorer*. She was broken up in 1937. Finally, there was *Linnet*, later named *Linton*. Built as HMS *Linnet* by the Thames Ironworks and Shipbuilding Company, Blackwall in 1880 as a Gun Vessel Second Class, or composite double-screw gun vessel, she was sold to the Liverpool Association for Protection in 1904 and converted for use as a salvage vessel. She was sold for scrap in 1923.

A similar ship, HMS *Sparrow*, completed at Greenock in 1889, was sold to the New Zealand Government in 1905. She was converted for use as a nautical training ship and given the name *Amokura*, a role which lasted until seagoing training was abandoned in 1919 due to lack of funds.

HMS *Handy* was built on the Tyne in 1882 and acquired by the Admiralty two years later for use as a gun trials ship. She was successively renamed

Excellent in 1891, *Calcutta* in 1916 and *Snapper II* in 1917. In 1922 she was bought by Dover Harbour Board and converted into the floating crane *Demon*, lasting in this civilian role until 1971. She currently lies at Portsmouth and is a candidate for restoration and preservation.

Static Training Ships

Many fighting ships retired from active duty to adopt roles as static hulks loaded with fuel and stores, while others became static training ships. One of the longest tenures was that of the training ship *Worcester*, moored off Greenhithe for many years until retired in 1946. She was laid down at Portsmouth in 1833 as HMS *Royal Sovereign* but her name was changed in 1838 to *Royal Frederick*. In 1858, when she had engines and propellers installed, she was again renamed, this time as *Frederick William*. She was first commissioned in 1860, classed as a Third Rate, with 74 guns. In her later guise as a training ship from 1877 onwards, she was renamed *Worcester*.

HMS *Gannet* was an *Osprey/Doterel* class sloop ordered by the Admiralty in February 1876 and constructed at the Sheerness Royal Dockyard. She was launched on 31 August 1878, and commissioned on 17 April 1879. She served in the Pacific until 1883 and in the Mediterranean between 1885 and 1888 during which time she saw action in the defence of Suakin in the Sudan. HMS *Gannet* paid off at Malta in November 1888, and for the next seven years undertook survey work in the Mediterranean. Between 1900 and 1902 she was used as an accommodation ship for the South Eastern & Chatham Railway. Thereafter she became the drill ship HMS *President*, based in the West India Docks, but in 1911 she again fell into disuse. Her fortunes changed in 1913 when she reverted to the name *Gannet* and was sent to the River Hamble as an accommodation ship to the

The composite gunboat HMS *Ranger* (1880) was sold to the Liverpool and Glasgow Salvage Association in 1892.

HMS *Triton* (1882) was a paddle survey vessel which worked mostly in the Pacific. She retired to an anchorage off Gravesend as a training ship and ended up as an accommodation vessel until sold for demolition in 1961.

training ship HMS *Mercury*. This role ended with the closure of *Mercury* in 1968. HMS *Gannet* has since been restored to her original condition and is now preserved at Chatham Historic Dockyard.

Another, but less well-known, example from the Thames was the *Triton*. Built in 1882 on the Thames, this paddle steamer was completed as the survey ship HMS *Triton*. She undertook a number of commissions in the Pacific during the 1890s. As *Triton* she was later converted to a training ship minus engines, and anchored off Gravesend as part of the Gravesend Sea School. She ended her days in the West India Dock as an accommodation ship. She was broken up at Zeebrugge in 1961.

4

THE GREAT WAR – CRUISER TO LINER AND MINESWEEPERS TO PASSENGER SHIPS

After the Armistice in 1918 a large number of surplus naval ships were put on the market up to the mid-1920s. Vessels ranged from the smallest of naval pinnaces to many larger ships, including a number of minesweepers. Many redundant major fighting units were mothballed in reserve and slowly disposed of for scrap between the wars, while some survived in reserve to be reactivated prior to, and during, the Second World War.

HMS *Charybdis*

One of the more interesting disposals was not a minesweeper, but that of the cruiser HMS *Charybdis* (D56). Beating swords into ploughshares became a necessity when Bermuda lost its lifeline steamer, *Bermudian*, when she was requisitioned in September 1914. This left Bermuda quite exposed with no regular passenger and cargo service to and from the island. Fortunately, *Bermudian* was returned to her owners, Canada Steamship Lines of London, three months later ready to reinstate the connection between Hamilton and New York. She stayed in service until June 1917 when *Bermudian* was requisitioned again. The Bermudan Government tried in vain to charter a ship; Robert Aitken takes up the story in *Sea Breezes*, July 1965:

> Towards the end of 1917, a delegation from the Bermudan Government went to London with the hope of having the *Bermudian* released from the Admiralty … The outcome was that the Admiralty agreed to loan the cruiser *Charybdis* for conversion, with no strings attached and to be delivered back in 1921. The *Charybdis* at the time was laid up in Bermuda Dockyard, with all the fighting armament removed and with a teakwood dummy straight stem. The ram had been removed after a collision somewhere off the US coast.
>
> I think it was in the early part of 1918 that the *Charybdis* was taken to New York by the Royal Navy and deposited with the Morse Dry Dock Corporation to whom the Bermuda Government had given the contract for the conversion. She was 320 feet long, 49 feet beam and fitted with eight boilers; twin screw, triple expansion engines, forced draught and a maximum speed of 21 knots.
>
> The conversion was not easy and far from satisfactory. Accommodation for cargo and passengers had to be fitted and this meant cutting up bulkheads for handling cargo. After removing tons of steel plate, chill room space of 26,000 cubic feet was installed. When the work was completed, she was far from being an attractive ship to operate.

HMS *Charybdis* had been launched by the Sheerness Dockyard in June 1893 and commissioned in January 1896. She was a protected cruiser of the eight-ship *Astraea* class. The ships

The *Astraea* class protected cruiser HMS *Charybdis* (1893), ended her days on loan to the Bermudan government running the liner service between St George and New York.

were armed with two 6in guns, eight 4.7in guns, ten 6-pounders, one 3-pounder and four torpedo tubes, and they were protected by a 2in armoured deck. The *Astraea* class each carried a complement of 318 men. HMS *Charybdis* spent most of her career in British waters, with occasional voyages to the Indian Ocean and Far East stations. She became part of the 12th Cruiser Squadron at the outbreak of war, but was damaged in a collision in 1915 and it was then that she was laid up at Bermuda.

As a merchantman, two of her boilers had been removed in summer 1918 to provide more space for exporting vegetables from Bermuda. The remaining boilers were operated under natural draught to provide a speed of about 10 knots.

Charybdis maintained the New York to Bermuda service for 21 months and made thirty-seven voyages, which were essential to supply the 20,000 inhabitants of the island and to transport agricultural products to markets in New York. The ship had accommodation for just sixty-five passengers, but on many voyages, an additional complement of passengers had to sleep on mattresses on the dining saloon floor; the tourist trade was not resumed until much later. Robert Aitken again:

Up to December 1918, £55,000 was spent on the *Charybdis* and at the beginning it was estimated that she could be operated for £21,000 per voyage. This was afterwards found to be nearer £28,000. Some voyages ended with a small profit, but most of them were in the red. Last voyage of the *Charybdis* to Bermuda ended at Hamilton on 10 December 1919, and the vessel was handed back to the Admiralty on Thursday

1 January 1920. She was finally sold to a Danish firm for scrap and, later in the year, towed across the Atlantic.

Her replacement was *Fort Hamilton*, none other than the old *Bermudian* under a new name, now owned by Quebec Steamship Company Limited – Furness, Withy & Company Limited, Montreal. Once again, normal trading resumed between New York and Bermuda and once again the tourist trade was encouraged, although it developed slowly at first. *Charybdis* was never remembered with any affection by the islanders but she was recognised as an essential lifeline that protected their trade and wellbeing.

The name *Bermudian* was reinstated at Bermuda in 1923 when the former Admiralty steam whaler HMS *Arctic Whale* (Z15) was bought and converted into the passenger tender *Bermudian* for use at St George. She had been sold by the Admiralty in 1920 and used in the meantime as a commercial whale catcher, retaining the name *Arctic Whale*. She was a product of Smith's Dock Company at Middlesbrough, completed in 1915, and was 125ft long by 25ft breadth and capable of 13 knots.

Minesweepers

The small ships that were assigned to minesweeping duties were a popular target for commercial shipowners after the Great War. There was a considerable shortage of purpose-built commercial tonnage and prices on the second-hand market were greatly inflated compared with like-for-like values before the war. In particular, the 'Hunt' class minesweepers were ideally suited for commercial adaptation. These ships had twin screws and were equipped with forced-draught coal-burning boilers. They had a shallow draught of just 8ft. Typical armament was one 4in gun forward and a 12-pounder aft, plus two twin machine guns.

Four 'Hunts' of the *Aberdare* group were bought by the Bombay Steam Navigation Company Limited in October 1920. Bombay Steam Navigation, although an Indian company, was managed by a British firm of agents until the managers sold out to the Scindia Steam Navigation Company at the start of the Second World War. The minesweepers were converted into coastal passenger and parcel steamers with new oil-fired boilers; following conversion they were measured at between 765 and 781 tons gross. HMS *Salford* (N06, N.A5) became *Vegavati*, HMS *Bradfield* (T36, N8A) *Champavati*, HMS *Appledore* (N7A) *Kamlavati*, and HMS *Repton* (T65) *Rupavati*, 'vati' meaning goddess, *Rupavati* thus, 'Silver Goddess'. The first pair had only been completed in 1918, the second pair in 1919.

The four ships were set to work for the Bombay–Goa Line, departing Ferry Wharf, Bombay at 10 am for Ratnagiri, with six intermediate calls, finally arriving at Panjim in Goa at 7 am the next day. The total distance was some 220nm. One of the four 'Hunts' was used on the weekly round trip to Mangalore, departing at 10.30 am on Tuesday and returning to Bombay on Saturday at 6 am. The ships were also used for weekly relief on the other three coastal services, or lines, operated by Bombay Steam.

All went well for the Bombay-Goa Line operated by Bombay Steam until The Indian Co-operative Navigation and Trading Company acquired two ships named *Tilak* and *Boa Viagem*. These were also former 'Hunts'. HMS *Instow* (N.A4, N.A1), a product of J T Eltringham & Company, South Shields, and HMS *Monaghan* (N.A3) built by John Harkess & Sons, Middlesbrough, were both sold to A S Miller in November 1920 and renamed *Tilak* and *Boa Viagem* respectively. 'Boa viagem' is the Portuguese equivalent of 'bon voyage', and the name reflected Goa as part of the Portuguese Empire at that time. Tilak, of course, is the mark worn by Hindus generally on the forehead.

Tilak and *Boa Viagem* were converted for

passenger use on the Indian Coast in otherwise much the same style as the Bombay Steam Company ships. However, the pair did not have their boilers modified and still relied on expensive pulverised coal as boiler feed. With two other steamers they ran in direct competition to the Bombay company, with services at the same time to the same destinations.

In November 1924 *Rupavati* ran onto rocks off Venguria and had to be beached. All passengers and crew were safely taken off the ship, which was later repaired and returned to service. *Tilak* and *Boa Viagem* lasted in service until 1931 and were scrapped soon afterwards. *Vengavati* and *Kamlavati* were sold for demolition in 1936 following the delivery of purpose-built tonnage and the *Champavati* followed them to the breakers in 1937. *Rupavati* transferred to the Dabhol line, but she too was replaced in 1938 and scrapped. E C B Thornton wrote of the Bombay Company's former 'Hunt' class steamers, in *Sea Breezes*, December 1957:

> The 'Hunt' class steamers had four 2 berth cabins with a small saloon and 'mod-cons' immediately abaft the bridge on the boat deck where one travelled in reasonable comfort and complete seclusion from the 100 'upper class' and 600 or so 'lower class' deck passengers.

A number of other 'Hunts' were converted for passenger use. HMS *Wem* (T86, N.A6), built by William Simons & Company at Renfrew, was

The excursion steamer *Doomba* (1919) at Redcliffe Pier in the mid-1930s having just arrived from Brisbane which is 20 miles to the south. She was originally commissioned as HMS *Wexford*.

bought in 1921 by Kutch Steam Navigation Company, London and Bombay. She was converted for passenger service also for use at Bombay and renamed *Deshulper*. She was sold in 1924 to L H Meisheri, London and Bombay, and again in 1926 to Khimji Shamji, London and broken up in 1927.

HMS *Wexford* (N.A7) was sold in 1923 and converted for passenger use by Coaster Construction Company Limited at Montrose. She was sent to Brisbane under the ownership of the Doomba Shipping Company of Brisbane (Brisbane Tug & Steamship Company Limited) with the new name *Doomba*. She had a passenger certificate for 1,500 passengers and was used for day excursion work between Brisbane and Redcliffe. She was requisitioned in 1939 and in 1940 purchased by the Australian Navy as the auxiliary minesweeper HMAS *Doomba*. After the war she was sold and used as a linseed oil lighter under the name *Meggol*. The vessel was eventually scuttled off Dee Why, New South Wales, in December 1976.

Back in the UK, Captain Stuart Townsend was a partner in Townsend Brothers Shipping Limited, established in 1889 with the objective of ship delivery and management. He was a keen motorist who spent his summers exploring the Continent. This required putting his vehicle at the mercy of the stevedores at both Dover and Calais, and of rough-handling of the car by the ship's crew once on the cross-Channel steamer. The Southern Railway did not encourage motorists to ship their cars to France, preferring that passengers used their trains. Disillusioned by the Southern Railway service, Townsend chartered the steam coaster *Artificer* in summer 1928 to test the market and to get Southern Railway to reduce its prices; the railway company charged £5-15 shillings one way for a car and Townsend reckoned he could undercut this by 50 per cent and still make a small profit. He found that there was a growing number of like-minded people and repeated the experiment in subsequent years. Cars were carefully loaded aboard ship and their occupants put on the railway mail boat to receive their vehicles on the quayside at Calais. In 1928 Townsend put the coaster *Royal Firth* on the service and started looking for a more suitable vessel.

Stuart Townsend's search for a suitable second-hand ship to convert into a roll-on roll-off car carrier for cross-Channel service, took him no further than Dover where he spotted a vessel awaiting demolition. She was HMS *Ford* (T2, TN7), another of the *Aberdare* group of the 'Hunt' class. She had been built by Dunlop, Bremner & Company of Port Glasgow, and launched in October 1918 when her intended name had been HMS *Fleetwood*. She was equipped with triple expansion steam engines built by the Ailsa Shipbuilding Company Limited at Troon. Sold for scrap in 1929, she lay at Dover awaiting demolition. Townsend made an offer for the ship as reported by A D Townsend in *Sea Breezes*, December 1976:

> Now, a warship is usually unsuited to commercial purposes, but for our specialised requirements this one had several advantages – speed, subdivision sufficient to meet Board of Trade regulations, and a flush deck which made it possible to load and unload rapidly. We bought her – the *Ford* – for £5,000, and the conversion was carried out by Earle's Shipbuilding & Engineering Company Limited of Hull, to the design of Mr Norman M Dewar.
>
> She carried 30 cars and 200 passengers and was satisfactory except as to speed: on trial she had done 18 knots but the Board of Trade required the boiler pressure to be reduced to such an extent that in service her speed dropped to about 13 knots. The ship was coal-fired and for a time we had difficulty with smoke but at length discovered that coal from a certain pit in the Dover area was highly suitable to her.

Before: the 'Hunt' class minesweeper HMS *Ford* (1918) was destined to spend the majority of her career as the cross-Channel car and passenger ferry *Forde* after a subtle name change.

The conversion work cost Townsend Brothers (Ferries) Limited, of London £15,000. It included the fitting of two general saloons, a ladies' saloon and two staterooms to a standard between first and second class aboard the railway-owned mail ships. In addition, heavy belting or fendering was added to the hull to protect it. *Forde*, as she was rechristened, commenced service on 15 April 1930 with an 11.30 am sailing from Dover returning from Calais at 3 pm. The voyage time was about 2½ hours. Just two weeks after her maiden commercial voyage she collided head on with the Quai Paul Devot at Calais, due to an engine telegraph error. Stuart Townsend was dining with the Mayor of Calais at the time, and when told his ship was sinking, he sat stoically at the table until the meal was over and paid for; his ship had not sunk, but was badly damaged and was out of service for the next month.

Forde had a Steam 2 passenger certificate and this allowed for far more passengers than accompanied just thirty cars. Cargo ships were chartered in the height of the season to carry more cars and their drivers and passengers were accommodated aboard *Forde*. The advertised fare was set as before at £2 per car one way and £3-15 shillings return for car and driver, plus 2 shillings per passenger. Unfortunately, the Southern Railway decided to take up competition with Townsend Brothers Ferries and put their modified cargo ship *Autocarrier* on the Dover to Calais route at which a rate war ensured. *Autocarrier* was originally ordered as the cargo ship *Camberley* from D & W Henderson of Glasgow, but reconfigured as a passenger and crane-loading car ferry on the stocks. She commenced service on 31 March 1931 in direct competition with *Forde*. Commercial rates were only estab-

After: Townsend Brothers Ferries' cross-Channel vehicle ferry *Forde* (1918) seen at Dover towards the end of her career on the English Channel.

Right: The 1929 sailing pamphlet for Townsend Brothers' *Forde*. (Linda Gowans collection)

lished in 1937 when Townsend was admitted to the Dover Pool of companies operating to Calais. Takings were distributed: 53 per cent going to the Southern Railway, 28.5 per cent to Townsend and the remaining 18.5 per cent split between two French companies.

Forde was also obliged to crane load and unload cars despite being equipped with a stern gate. In June 1936 a three-week-long general strike in France allowed *Forde* to back onto the quay and discharge her cars over the stern. This was only possible at the right stage of the tide, but it kept the service going while there were no crane drivers available. The stern ramp was also used on a couple of occasions at the request of car owners about to be confronted by British Customs officers at Dover; cars could be ejected over the stern into the sea as the cheaper option! In August 1932 *Forde* carried the three Talbot cars and their drivers to Calais on their way to win the coveted Coup des Alpes prize in the gruelling International Alpine Trial.

Forde was requisitioned in the Second World War as a salvage vessel and returned to her owners in 1947. The Southern Railway introduced the converted car ferry *Dinard* on the service mid-summer and it was obvious that something bigger and more modern than *Forde* was now required. After further service at Dover, she was sold in 1949 for £20,000 to M H Bland & Company Limited of Gibraltar and again employed as a car ferry, with the new name *Gibel Tarik*. She served between Gibraltar and Tangier until sold for demolition at Malaga in 1954 following the failure of her boilers the previous year; she had remained a coal-burner throughout her career. Her replacement was a larger ship, the Second World War frigate HMS *Halladale* which was purchased in 1949 for £15,000 (see Chapter 7).

Lady Cecilia (1918), one of two similar passenger excursion ships based at Vancouver, was originally the 'Hunt' class minesweeper HMS *Swindon*.

The 'Hunt' class minesweepers HMS *Swindon*, (N91, N.5A) renamed HMS *Bantry* in 1918, and HMS *Barnstaple* were bought from shipbreakers at Dover in 1925 by the Union Steamship Company of British Columbia Limited. They were both products of the Ardrossan Dry Dock & Shipbuilding Company Limited. They were converted for use on coastal day passenger and excursion services based on Vancouver and given the names *Lady Cecilia* and *Lady Cynthia* respectively.

The ships were converted for passenger use by Coaster Construction Company at Montrose during 1925. An upper deck was added, and to maintain stability, flotation sponsons were added on either side of the hull with a large blister just forward of the cargo doors at the forward end of the ship and just above the water. The sponsons had a slight inhibiting effect on speed. On one boiler the ships operated at 15 knots, the second boiler rarely being used. The rebuilt ships had two funnels but the aft one was a dummy. *Lady Cecilia* was 944 tons gross and *Lady Cynthia* 976 tons gross, the difference being in the below-deck tonnage spaces available on each ship. As day passenger ships they could accommodate 900 persons in summer and 500 in winter. The ships arrived at Vancouver in 1925 and *Lady Cynthia* was placed on the Vancouver and Powell River service while *Lady Cecilia* was put on the Bowen Island service, where Union Steamship Company owned and operated a popular resort. *Lady Cynthia* joined this service the following year when ownership passed to Union Steamships Limited. On 27 December 1925, *Lady Cynthia* collided with and sank another Union company steamship, the *Cowichan*, in thick fog. On 28 October 1953, *Lady Cynthia* collided with and sank a tug, although there were no injuries. *Lady Cecilia* was sold to Coast Ferries Limited of Vancouver in 1951 and scrapped shortly afterwards, and *Lady Cynthia* was withdrawn in 1956 and scrapped the following year.

One other 'Hunt' class minesweeper was sold for passenger service. HMS *Fairfield* was bought in March 1920 by South American Tours Limited, Buenos Aires and renamed *Flechas*. She was altered considerably and like the Canadian 'Ladies' had a new upper deck added, which extended almost to the stern of the ship, and which was protected by an awning. The forward part of the upper deck abaft the bridge was extended the full width of the ship. She carried permanent ballast to compensate for the additional top weight and sat slightly lower in the water than she had as a warship. Her appearance was that of a mini-liner with all-white paintwork and a buff funnel. She was provided with passenger cabins, most with a porthole and private bathroom, and there were a number of attractive public rooms. In 1936 her registered owners became J G Fernandes & Dr M de Freitas Valle e Silva, Porto Alegre but the following year she was on the Brazilian Navy List as the survey ship *Jaceguai*. In 1942 she was rearmed and commissioned as a corvette, but was scrapped in 1945.

Ascot Class Paddle Minesweepers

There were two *Ascot* class paddle minesweepers that joined the merchant service. This class of vessel had been based on the design of P & A Campbell's Bristol Channel excursion steamer *Glen Usk*. She had been designed and built by Ailsa Shipbuilding Company at Troon and was found ideally suited to the work of minesweeping; *Glen Usk* was equipped with compound diagonal engines. The only problem with the design was that in heavy seas paddle steamers lost speed when the paddle wheels and paddle boxes became choked with water and the preference was to stay in harbour during the worst weather.

The *Ascot* class, built in the Great War, were all named after racecourses. They had two boiler rooms, one forward and one aft of the engine room, and as a consequence the two vertical funnels were widely spaced apart. HMS *Ascot* was the first of the paddle-steamer minesweepers in a class of thirty-two ships. Each was fitted to carry two seaplanes. Five of the class were lost at sea, taking with them nine officers and seventy-two men. HMS *Ascot* was commissioned in April 1916, and was employed in the Firth of Forth till August 1917, then at Grimsby till May 1918, and Portsmouth until October 1918. She left Portsmouth on 7 November 1918, bound for Granton but was torpedoed three days later, and sank off the Farne Islands with the loss of her full complement of fifty-three men, the very last ship to be lost in the war. This loss occurred despite orders given on 20 October for all U-boats to return to Kiel; the motivation of the U-boat commander can only be guessed at.

All but five of the steamers had been sold for scrap by 1922, and those remaining were retained in reserve. Two of these, HMS *Atherstone* (T09) and HMS *Melton* (T94), came into the coastal passenger excursion trade while they were being sold off for demolition during 1927 and 1928. They were stripped of look-out turrets, mine wire derricks and the boom that once hung over the stern. Only the silhouette remained the same, with still widely spaced but now well-raked funnels and prominent navigation bridge behind the foremast, as well as the distinctive cruiser stern characteristic of the *Ascot* class. Charles Dance reported in *Sea Breezes*, September 1978, in an article recount-

The paddle minesweeper HMS *Melton* (1916) was one of a class of thirty-two ships based on the design of P & A Campbell's steamer *Glen Usk*.

ing the history of the New Medway Steam Packet Company of Rochester:

Probably one of the company's best loved steamers was the *Queen of Kent*, which joined the fleet in 1928. She was bought from the Admiralty, and, under the name HMS *Atherstone*, was one of a class of 32 paddle minesweepers. After an extensive refit she became the company's first ship to operate cross-Channel sailings, running from Chatham to Southend, Margate, Calais and Boulogne.

During 1930 she sailed from Dover and in 1933 made Wednesday sailings from Clacton to Calais, while in the 1937-38 seasons the pattern was Southend to Margate, Calais, Boulogne and Dunkirk. Laid up at the end of that season she went on war work in 1939.

After refitting, the *Queen of Kent* was put on the London-Southend service, with some cruises from Ramsgate in 1947 but at the end of the 1948 season she was sold …

Late in 1928 her sister-ship HMS *Melton* was bought from the Blyth shipbreakers Hughes Bolckow. Renamed *Queen of Thanet* (792 gross tons) she was also fitted out at the company's own Acorn yard and entered service in 1929. Her career ran along similar lines to the *Queen of Kent*, with which ship she was ultimately sold in 1948.

Captain Tommy Aldis was put in charge of first *Queen of Kent*, moving to *Queen of Thanet* when she started in service. It was largely down to Captain Aldis and his congenial attitude that both ships were dubbed 'The Happy Ship' while under his management. The two ships were converted to oil-burning and given new sets of paddle wheels in time for the 1932 season. With new motor excursion ships arriving in the joint

The *Ascot* class paddle minesweeper HMS *Atherstone* (1916) became the Thames excursion steamer *Queen of Kent* when she was bought from the scrapyard in 1927.

New Medway Steam Packet Company and General Steam Navigation Company fleets, both *Queen of Thanet* and *Queen of Kent* were laid up at the end of the 1938 season to await decisions on their future. They were requisitioned for naval duties the following year as minesweepers once again, initially based at Dover and later in the Forth. They returned to commercial use in time for the 1947 season but were put up for sale in autumn 1948, being now surplus to requirements. *Queen of Thanet* and *Queen of Kent* had together provided their owners with 23 years of summer excursion income in addition to serving the nation for a further seven years, surely a sound investment once they were rescued from the scrapyard and converted for commercial use in the late 1920s.

Red Funnel purchased the two ships from the New Medway Steam Packet Company for just under £15,000 each in time for the 1949 season. *Queen of Kent* was renamed *Lorna Doone* and *Queen of Thanet* became *Solent Queen*. They were refitted and ready to start work for their new owners just in time for the 1949 season. Red Funnel's full title was the Southampton, Isle of Wight and South of England Royal Mail Steam Packet Company Limited. *Lorna Doone* was stationed at Bournemouth, operating trips previously run by the paddle steamer *Bournemouth Queen*, which then went onto the Swanage ferry service, while *Solent Queen* was stationed at Southampton, taking over the excursions from the motor passenger ferry *Vecta*, including the day trip round the Isle of Wight. *Solent Queen* was

HMS *Melton* (1916) was given the name *Queen of Thanet* when she was converted into an excursion steamer by the New Medway Steam Packet Company in 1928.

extensively damaged by fire in June 1951 while refitting and was sold for demolition in October 1951. She was replaced at Southampton by *Lorna Doone* for the 1951 season, and although work was put in hand in the autumn to prepare her for the 1952 season it was decided to sell her and she too went for scrap in March 1952.

Minelayers HMS *Anglesey* and HMS *Sheppey*

In November 1914 the London & North Western Railway ordered from William Denny & Brothers at Dumbarton a fast quartet of cross-Channel ferries for their Holyhead to Kingstown passenger service. The keels of the first two were laid in February 1915 but the work was abandoned shortly afterwards. In July 1918 the Admiralty requisitioned the incomplete hulls with the objective of completing the ships as fast minelayers with the names HMS *Anglesey* and HMS *Sheppey*. The work was never finished and stopped altogether towards the end of the war. Later, much of the work ordered by the Admiralty was stripped out so that they could be completed as originally ordered. They were delivered to the railway company as *Anglia* and *Hibernia* respectively.

Anglia was found to be inferior to her three near-sisters, *Hibernia*, *Cambria* and *Scotia*, and she was withdrawn after only 18 months service running from Holyhead and then kept in reserve. Structural faults were found during collision repairs after the ship hit the breakwater at Holyhead, and work was never put in hand to ameliorate these deficiencies. It was presumed that the faults were the result of the work carried out on behalf of the Admiralty, although this was never proven. The only remnant of the Admiralty work in the two ships was that the 'tween deck height on the main deck was an extraordinary 9ft, a design feature that allowed for stowage of mines on that deck. The last two ships of the quartet, the *Cambria* and *Scotia*, also incorporated this design feature, as all four ships were built to the same drawings.

Steam Yacht *Cutty Sark*

At the end of the Great War Yarrow at Scotstoun had completed seven 'S' class destroyers (part of the 'V&W' class) for the Admiralty and had already started to cut the plates for an additional vessel for which the keel had been laid. Thereafter, building continued to the order of Major Henry Keswick of Jardine Matheson & Company. The ship was launched on 18 March 1920 as the steam yacht *Cutty Sark*. She had the same dimensions as the destroyers with a length of 263ft and a breadth of 25ft and a shallow draught of 16ft. Her gross tonnage was 883. She had four Yarrow turbines of 5,000bhp which provided a cruising speed of 24 knots.

In 1926 *Cutty Sark* was bought by the Duke of Westminster. For the next thirteen year she was host to the rich and famous until requisitioned as HMS *Cutty Sark* in 1939 and converted for anti-submarine duties, later becoming a submarine tender. After the war she was briefly used as a training ship minus her engines and boilers, moored first at King's Lynn, later moved to Grays, and eventually broken up in 1948.

The steam yacht *Cutty Sark* (1920) was laid down as a 'V&W' class destroyer but completed to the order of Major Henry Keswick as his private yacht.

5

CONVERSION OF SMALLER SHIPS AFTER THE GREAT WAR

Fleet Tugs

There was an increased need for ocean-going salvage tugs during the war for rescue work. These tugs were of two basic designs, and, as they were built by specialist shipyards, incorporated mercantile rather than naval features. However, they were armed with a single 12-pounder gun, equipped with radio and flew the White Ensign. The majority were of the 'Saint' class; sixty-four were ordered and forty-six were completed and commissioned before the end of hostilities. The second class was the *Resolve* or *Rollicker* class, comprising six more large ocean-going tugs, but these were only completed after the Armistice. There were also three tugs of the *Frisky* class.

Many of these large tugs were sold to commercial operators after the Great War and applied to a variety of duties based across the world. The 'Saint' class tugs (not all of which had pennant numbers) were popular with commercial owners after the Great War, some even sold after serving between the wars and through the Second World War:

– HMS *St Anne* (W36) was sold in October 1922 to R MacGregor, without change of name.
– HMS *St Aristell* went to J & A Brown at Newcastle, New South Wales, in April 1926 without change of name.
– HMS *St Arvans* (W05) went to the Canadian Coast Guard Service in 1923 and was later renamed *Ocean Eagle* in 1923 and *Aigle d'Ocean* in 1946. She sank in the Hudson Strait in 1975.
– HMS *St Athan* (W40) joined the British Petroleum Tanker Company fleet in November 1924 without change of name.
– HMS *St Aubin* (W18) was sold to the Shanghai Tug & Lighter Company.
– HMS *St Bees* (W23) was acquired by Moller Towage Limited in 1922 and renamed *Henry Burton*.
– HMS *St Boniface* (formerly *St Fergus*) (W20) went to the New Zealand Government and was renamed *Toia*.
– HMS *St Catherine* (W44) was sold to A H Raid, Vancouver in 1922 and renamed *Canadian National No 2*. Later named *Polaris* and then *Gulf Freda*.
– HMS *St Claude* (formerly HMS *St Mary*) was sold in 1925 to J Fenwick, Sydney, New South Wales and renamed *Lindfield*.
– HMS *St Clears* (W06) was sold to Risdon Beazley in 1948.
– HMS *St Day* (W55) went to the Polish Government in 1948 and was renamed *Ursus*.
– HMS *St Dominic* was sold in 1919 to Gibb-Livingstone, Hong Kong.
– HMS *St Enoder* (formerly *St Osyth*) was sold in 1925 to Danish owners and renamed *Garm*.
– HMS *St Erth* (W130) was sold to J Fenwick, Sydney New South Wales in 1925 and renamed *Heros*. Served as HMAS *Heros* in the Second World War.

- HMS *St Ewe* was sold in 1926 to the Iraqi Government as a pilot tender at Basra and renamed *Alarm*. Served in the Second World War as HMS *Alarm* and from 1942 as HMS *Alarm II*. Returned to owners 1946 and renamed *Shu'Alah* in 1966.
- HMS *St Finbarr* (W22) went to the Canadian Government in 1923 and was renamed *Franklin*.
- HMS *St Florence* was sold in 1924 to the Canadian Pacific Railway and renamed *Kyuqot*.
- HMS *St Giles* (W96) was sold to J & A Brown, Newcastle, New South Wales and renamed *Khalifa*.
- HMS *St Helier* (W08) was sold in 1920 to Chrichton Thompson.
- HMS *St Hilary* was sold in 1926 to Waratah Tug & Salvage Company.
- HMS *St Keyne* was sold in 1926 to Brazilian owners and renamed *Times*.
- HMS *St Kitts* was sold to the Adelaide Steamship Company and renamed *Uco*.
- HMS *St Mabyn* (W09) was sold in 1926 to J & A Brown, Newcastle, New South Wales. Later renamed *Caroline Moller*. Served as HMS *Caroline Moller* (W09) in the Second World War.
- HMS *St Minver* was sold in 1925 to Cie de Remorquage et de Sauvetage Les Abeilles, Le Havre and renamed *Abeille XXII*.
- HMS *St Olaves* (W40) was sold in 1922 to J & A Brown, Newcastle, New South Wales.
- HMS *St Teath* was sold in 1922 to Brazilian owners and renamed *Parana*.
- HMS *St Tudy* was sold in 1926 to F P Barney and later renamed *St Eileen*.

In 1922 the twin-screw *Resolve* class tug HMS *Rollcall* (W81) was bought by Alexandra Towing Company Limited of Liverpool. She had been built in 1918 by Ferguson Brothers at Port Glasgow as a twin-funnelled fleet tug. She was completely rebuilt, and given two triple-expansion engines and oil-fired boilers to provide a service speed of 14 knots. She was renamed *Romsey*, and remeasured at 889 tons gross.

Romsey was stationed at Southampton as a passenger tender with luxurious first class accommodation to convey passengers and the mails to and from passenger liners calling at Southampton Roads, before they continued to and from northern European ports mainly on the transatlantic routes. She was replaced by a new *Romsey* early in

Before: The *Resolve* class fleet tug HMS *Rollcall* (1918) was sold to Alexandra Towing Company Limited in 1922.

Rollcall (1918) in full Alexandra Towing livery at Liverpool prior to conversion and renaming for use at Southampton. (Max Cooper)

1930 and was sold to Compagnie Générale Transatlantique as *Minotaure* for use as a tender at Le Havre. Although she was scuttled by the retreating German army in 1944, she was raised and partially rebuilt for further use by Compagnie Générale Transatlantique, and only sold in 1958 to Belgian owners, and shortly afterwards resold for demolition.

Lead of the class, *Rollicker* (W95), was chartered to J & A Brown, Newcastle in New South Wales, in 1922, and passed to the Government of Nigeria in 1926 before reverting to the Admiralty seven years later. In both cases the ship was registered locally – at Newcastle, Australia and in Lagos, Nigeria. On return to the Admiralty in 1934 she was based at Gibraltar. She served throughout the Second World War and was broken up in 1952.

HMS *Frisky* commissioned in 1919, was sold to Atlantic Ocean Towing Company of Hamburg as *Gustavo Ipland* in 1924 and then resold in 1930 to Foundation Maritime of Halifax and renamed *Foundation Franklin*. She was scrapped in 1950 following damage caused during a salvage operation at sea. Of her sisters, HMS *Saucy* was bought by the Shanghai Tug and Lighterage Company and retained the name *Saucy*, and HMS *Jaunty* was sold to Beira Works Limited, Portuguese East Africa, in 1930 and renamed *Rio Tejo*.

After: The tug and passenger tender *Romsey* now fully converted and bearing little resemblance to her former self as a Royal Navy fleet tug.

Admiralty Trawlers

The Admiralty ordered about 580 trawlers in three classes during the Great War: 'Mersey', 'Castle' and 'Strath' class, but some 82 were subsequently cancelled after the Armistice. They carried a crew of up to twenty men and were equipped with a single 6-pounder gun. In all over 120 'Mersey' class, the largest ships of the three classes, nearly 300 'Castle' class and 160 'Strath' class ships were ordered and they were given names taken from the muster rolls of HMS *Victory* and HMS *Royal Sovereign* at the time of Trafalgar, while others were completed after the war for commercial owners. Almost half these ships were still available in 1939 for naval use in the Second World War, almost all of them being in commercial service in the meantime, mostly with the fishing industry.

One of the 167 'Strath' class trawlers had a rather different, but long and varied peacetime career under private ownership. Originally named HMS *Samuel Green*, she was completed in July 1919 by John Brown (Marine) Limited at Greenock, sold by the Admiralty and given the name *Ocean Rover*, briefly taking up duties as a fishing trawler. In 1920 she was resold to racing driver Kenelm Lee Guinness, rebuilt as a yacht complete with luxury accommodation and painted white; there remained little resemblance to a trawler. Guinness is known to have taken two of his cars to Sicily aboard the ship.

In 1925 *Ocean Rover* was sold to the Duke of Leeds and renamed *Aries*. Resold again in 1928 she reverted to her former name *Ocean Rover* for her new owner Major Sir H K Newton. In 1934 she was owned by Sir Alfred L Goodson and in 1939 she became the property of James Napier of Old Kilpatrick. She was requisitioned in November 1939 as a torpedo recovery vessel eventually being released and sold to F D Fenton in 1949 with the new name *Ocean Mist*; she was based at Cowes. By 1954 she had been completely refitted as a modern luxury yacht and ownership passed to F G Mitchell of Peterborough.

In 1960 *Ocean Mist* was bought by J W Hobbs of the Great Glen Cattle Ranch at Fort William and after his death in 1965 was owned by his executors. After an extended lay-up on the Caledonian Canal at Banavie near Fort William, she was eventually bought by the Leith Steamship Company and taken to Leith in 1984 for conversion into a static restaurant. She was berthed at King's Wharf besides the Bernard Street Bridge. The restaurant closed in 2014 and the ship was abandoned at a berth in the Water of Leith. In 2019 it was proposed to convert her into a nineteen-room luxury hotel; work is in progress.

HMS *William Jackson* was a 'Mersey' class trawler fitted out in the Admiralty manner of the time with a 12-pounder gun mounted on a platform over the engine-room skylight abaft the funnel and there was a pair of depth-charge launchers right aft. She was built by Cochrane & Sons at Selby in 1918, and was equipped with anti-submarine hydrophone gear. On completion she was sent to Lerwick with the Northern Patrol. The normal routine was three weeks on duty and one

Ocean Mist (1919) at King's Wharf Edinburgh, no longer recognisable as the Great War Admiralty trawler HMS *Samuel Green*.

The Grimsby trawler *Evelyn Rose* (1918) was originally the 'Mersey' class HMT *William Jackson*. She stranded in 1954 with the loss of fifteen men, almost all from Fleetwood and Blackpool.

week in port, and sea duties tended to be monotonous with only rare contact with submarines. *William Jackson* was sold to Pickering & Haldane's Steam Trawling Company, Hull in 1921, renamed *Lord Byng* (H288) and converted by her builders for fishing duties. In 1929 she was sold to the Bunch Steam Fishing Company Limited, Grimsby and in 1936 to the Boston Deep Sea Fishing & Ice Company Limited, Fleetwood and registered as *Evelyn Rose* (GY9), still at Grimsby. In May 1940 she was hired for the Dunkirk operation and had to be beached at Margate on return with 150 soldiers on board. She was later used as a minesweeper.

Evelyn Rose stranded in the Sound of Mull on 31 December 1954 and quickly slipped into deep water. There were only two survivors out of a crew of seventeen men, all but one from Fleetwood and Blackpool. At the subsequent enquiry it was found that the skipper had misinterpreted the image on the radar screen and this led to the fatal navigational error.

Another example is HMS *William Westernburgh*, also a 'Mersey' class trawler, completed by Cochrane & Sons Limited at Selby in 1917. She was sold for commercial use in the fishing industry in 1932 and renamed *Lord Talbot*, sold again in 1938 and renamed *Star of the Realm*, recommissioned as the armed trawler *Nordstjörnan* in 1940 under the Norwegian flag, before reverting to *Star of the Realm* in 1948. She was then owned by William R Metaclfe of Dover and employed as a salvage ship, although she was registered at Falmouth.

HMS *John Felton*, another 'Mersey' class ship, went to the Fisheries Board for Scotland in 1921 as the fisheries research vessel *Explorer*. She had been built at Selby by Cochrane & Sons Limited in 1918 but was never commissioned. She was requisitioned in the Second World War as an examination vessel, and returned to fisheries protection again after the war until withdrawn and scrapped in 1955.

HMS *Isaac Arthan* (FY4297) was a 'Castle' class trawler that was sold in 1921 by her builders, Cook, Welton & Gemmell Limited of Beverley, for use as a trawler under the name *Amber*. In 1935 she was renamed *Ocean Harrier* and a year later she was sold to Malcolm Smith Limited of Aberdeen and given the name *Loch Buie*.

John Burlingham (FY3600) was a modified 'Castle' class trawler built by Cook, Welton & Gemmell in 1917. She served as a minesweeper. In 1920 she was sold to G D Sleight and became the Grimsby steam trawler *Rehearo* (GY329). She was requisitioned in the Second World War and was later returned to her owners and eventually sold for demolition in 1961 at the venerable age of 44 years.

A group of seventeen trawlers was seized in the White Sea in August 1918 or handed over to the British by the White Russians. They were all given 'Axe' names, *Battleaxe*, *Boneaxe*, *Bronzeaxe*, *Coalaxe* and so on. Seven of them were built for the Imperial Russian Navy in 1916 by Smith's Dock at Middlesbrough, one, *Poleaxe*, ex-*T19*, by Cochrane as a replacement for an earlier *T19* that was lost before acceptance. Others were built before the war as commercial vessels. All the surviving ships were sold for commercial service after the war apart from four of the Smith's Dock ships which were retained by the Admiralty. HMS *Poleaxe* became the Hull-registered trawler *Dorbie* and HMS *Ironaxe*, formerly *T22*, became the salvage vessel *Ironaxe*, based for many years at Aberdeen.

Admiralty Drifters

There were also many steel- and wooden-hulled drifters constructed for the Admiralty during the war. Commercial fishing trawlers were designed to tow heavy trawls, so they were easily adapted to tow minesweeping gear as the deck layout was readily suited to the task. Drifters were smaller, but were built to work in most weather conditions and designed to deploy and retrieve drift nets over the side. Most Admiralty drifters were equipped with steam engines but a few had 2-cylinder Bolinder hot bulb oil engines (which needed to be started with a blowtorch). Most of these little ships went to the fishing industry in the post-war years. A few went to the Ministry of Agriculture & Fisheries, including for example, their *Atmosphere*, *Blacknight*, *Marigold*, *Sunny Bird*, *William C Farrow* and *Mildred W Rawson* (later *June Rose*), and to the Fishery Board for Scotland, ships such as *Star Divine*, *Imbat*, *Cineraria* and *Jessie Watson*.

Patrol Vessel HMS *Argon*

Before the Great War coast guard work and fisheries protection was carried out by vessels owned by the Admiralty. One such was *Argus* (C75), later to become *Peninnis* of the Isles of Scilly Steam Packet Company Limited, as Grahame Farr reports in *West Country Passenger Steamers*:

> … in 1919 steps were taken to form the Isles of Scilly Steam Packet Company Limited, and in the early part of 1920 arrangements were made to purchase HMS *Argon*. This yacht-like craft had an interesting history, being built as a steam coastguard cutter, the *Argus*, in 1904, by Bow MacLachlan & Company, at Paisley, who fitted their own triple expansion engines. By service measurement she was 380 tons displacement, and had a speed of 12.4 knots, being armed with two 6-pounder guns. Her duties were those of fisheries protection …

During the war *Argus* was taken over by the Navy as a patrol vessel, her name being changed to HMS *Argon* to avoid confusion with another unit. Sold out of the service in the early part of 1920, she was bought by William Henry Ward of Woodford,

Before: The Admiralty Fisheries Protection Vessel *Argus* (1904), became HMS *Argon* in the Great War and served as a patrol vessel.

After: *Argus*/HMS *Argon* (1904) in civilian life as *Peninnis* after she was bought in 1920 by the Isles of Scilly Steam Packet Company and converted into a passenger and cargo ferry.

Essex, and was extensively renovated for passenger carrying. She was registered at Scilly, as *Peninnis*, in April 1920, with a gross tonnage of 219, and registered under the ownership of the local company in March 1921.

Peninnis was in trouble with the weather on more than one occasion as reported in the local press in 1925:

> At about 12 noon, when the *Peninnis* was only six miles from the islands, a heavy sea swept over the port bow, came rushing aft and struck the bridge with terrific force. For a moment the port side of the bridge was hidden under a mass of seething grey water. When, however, the little vessel shook herself free, a devastating sight met the eye. The port wing of the bridge was missing as well as some of the iron stanchions … Seeing this, the Captain [Captain McAllister] wisely decided to return to Penzance.

Peninnis was sold in 1927 to the Alderney Steam Packet Company, renamed *Riduna* and registered at Guernsey. She ran between St Peter Port and Alderney. Early in 1931 the company was taken over by the St Malo and Binic Steamship Company Limited, but the deal did not include *Riduna*. She was sold to shipbreakers in Plymouth where she arrived on 1 April 1931.

Another Fisheries Patrol Vessel was *Safeguard*. She was completed in 1914 and stationed at Queenstown as HMS *Safeguard* on duty as a patrol and examination vessel. She had two 3-pounder guns. After the war she was sold to Henry Ensor of Queenstown and converted into the salvage vessel *Safeguarder*.

'Kil' Class Patrol Boats and Other British and American Small Craft

There was a miscellany of smaller craft available to purchasers after the war. These ranged from harbour craft to patrol boats. Almost all of the small double-ended 'Kil' class patrol boats found commercial buyers after the war. They were typically less than 900 tons displacement, had a symmetrical profile and a funnel dead centre; they had a service speed of 13 knots. Most were sold to one of three brokers on 14 February 1920, and sold on by them to private and commercial buyers mainly in the UK, South Africa and India. Some had long commercial careers, a few lasting in service into the 1960s. Many of the ships were used as coastal cargo vessels, others as whalers and some even as private yachts, as George Ransom wrote in a letter to the editor of *Sea Breezes*, November 1979:

> The yacht *Foinavon* was built as one of the 'Kil' class patrol gunboats of the 1914-18 war as HMS *Kilmarten* by Smith's Dock Company Limited as their yard No. 749. Completed on June 12, 1919, she bore the Admiralty pennant number FY4062. Her naval service was only brief … She displaced 895 tons (670 tons gross) on dimensions 182 feet x 30 feet x 10 feet 6 inches and her triple expansion engines gave her an ihp of 1,400 and a speed of 13 knots. Her designed armament was one 4inch gun.

Sold out of naval service on 14 February 1920 to L Gueret & Company Limited of London, she was renamed *Mandrake* and converted into a cargo ship. She was converted into the yacht *Foinavon* in 1934 for the Second Viscount Chaplin. She was taken up for naval service again in October 1939 as an accommodation ship and was returned to her owner in 1945. In 1946 she was converted back into a cargo ship and renamed *Varafjell*, for D/S A/S Saga of Haugesund in Norway, and in 1947 she was sold to Swedish owner J E Samuelsson and renamed *Dixi* before arriving at the yard of C W Dorkin, Gateshead for scrapping on 5 December 1952.

Over 400 wooden-hulled submarine chasers were built for the United States Navy during the war. A large number of them were transferred to

France on completion. They were 110ft long with three shafts and three petrol engines that gave them a speed of about 18 knots and good manoeuvrability. Many of these little ships were sold after the war to commercial owners in the United States, some to new owners in the Caribbean. *A Dictionary of American Fighting Naval Ships* records that between 1917 and 1921 Joseph G Hitner, ironworks owner and shipbreaker at Philadelphia, bought large tranches of the ships. Although most of these were scrapped, many were also refitted for commercial use and resold. A small number went to the Panamanian register, for example, *SC283*, *SC286* and *SC288* were bought by the Colon Import and Export Company Limited in 1922, while *SC287* was bought in 1924 by the United Fruit Company of Panama City. One, *SC38*, was sold to Thomas Lee of Ipswich. A small number were converted for use as private yachts, for example, *SC98* and *SC227* went to the Florida Boat Company for conversion and *SC338* was converted by the Yacht and Motorboat Agency, Constantinople.

Over 500 small motor launches were built in North America during the Great War. Deployed on coastal work, many of them were shipped to the UK and used also in the Mediterranean and later in the Baltic. Many were sold as work boats and harbour craft while others went to private owners as seagoing motor launches or as houseboats. They were equipped with twin shafts and a pair of petrol engines and armament consisted of a 12-pounder gun just aft of two small hatches on the foredeck and forward of the navigating position.

One small American patrol boat, USS *Etenia*, was bought as she lay in British waters, converted into the motor yacht *Etenia* and registered at Cowes. In 1926 she was bought by the Northsea Steamship Company of King's Lynn from which port she offered a variety of seasonal passenger excursions as far afield as Huntstanton and Skegness. In mid-season her ownership was changed to Marine Traders Limited (manager Edgar Gargett) and her port of registration changed from Cowes to King's Lynn. For the following three summers, 1927 to 1929, she was based at Great Yarmouth offering sea cruises. Thereafter, she reverted to a private yacht under the ownership of Arthur L Nunnely of Kenton Middlesex. Her registration was cancelled in 1934, her fate unknown.

'X' Lighters

The concept of the landing craft originated in the Great War. A number of landing craft, principally the 'X' class lighters, which were also known as 'Black Beetles' or just 'Beetles', were built for service in the war. They were designed by Walter Pollock, the naval architect at James Pollock & Sons Limited of Faversham. The craft were the result of the need for a basic, shallow-draft powered 'landing craft' and many were equipped with a hand-operated ramp extending over a spoon-shaped bow, while others were completed as water tankers and later saw service as fuel tankers. The first batches, completed in 1915, were towed out to the Mediterranean in time to see service in the ill-fated Gallipoli campaign. This was an attempt to take the Gallipoli Peninsula and so allow Allied shipping access to Constantinople. Later, some took part in the Russian campaign in the White Sea. They were among the earliest small craft to be equipped with oil engines, twin engines and twin screws; the majority of the engines were the 'hot bulb' engine built by Bolinders of Sweden for whom Pollock was the British agent.

The spoon-shape bow was designed for running onto steep shelving beaches. The dimensions were length 105ft 6in, breadth 21ft, depth 7ft 6in and they had a light displacement of 135 tons. The hull shape was based on the typical River Thames lighters of the day, with a flat bottom over much of the length. It was of steel construction with riveted plates. Those which arrived in the Aegean were given additional 'K' numbers for troop carriers and 'L' numbers for water tankers. Some were subsequently sent to Mesopotamia and designated 'ML' for motor lighter.

Some remained in naval service but the majority were sold after 1918 and many saw long service as dry cargo and tanker vessels in the short-sea and estuarial trades, especially on the Thames and Medway. Typical was *X219* which became *Mountain Ash* and served a variety of owners, latterly Irish-registered, until she was scrapped in 1950 after being beached with engine trouble. Another, *River Loyne*, modified for commercial use in 1923, was being used to carry stone from the Penmaenmawr Quarry, near Conway, to Liverpool when she was lost on 8 December 1948.

Other examples include *X178* built by Swan Hunter and Wigham Richardson which was used at Portsmouth until 1929 when she became an aircraft transport vessel. In 1955 twin 90bhp 3-cylinder Crossley engines were fitted, and in 1966 she was bought by Bowker and King and renamed *Rutland*. *X64*, released from Admiralty service only in 1946, became *Cawarstone*, owned by Cawood Wharton. She was scrapped in 1950.

Another was *X57* which became *Peter P*, working as a motorised barge on the Thames between the wars. She ended her working career in 1999 when she was bought for use as a houseboat, with her former hold converted into living accommodation. *X81* became *Colin P* after the Second World War and later *Fence*. She was rebuilt

'X' class lighter *X28* (1915) working cargo at Sulva Point in 1915 with an array of other 'X' class beyond.

River Loyne (1915) was a former 'X' class lighter that was modified for commercial use when she was sold by the Admiralty in 1923.

One of three 'X' class lighters surviving today is *Spithead* (1915), originally *X44*. Note the spoon-shaped bow for running onto beaches.

in 1964 and acquired by the aggregates company J J Prior for use as a sand carrier. The depth of her hull was extended at this time, the bow remodelled and the wheelhouse changed, although she retained the aft engine room housing. In the 1980s the Island Transport Company Limited, of the Isle of Wight, had *Arreton* working to the mainland. She was the former *X211*.

Three 'X' lighters remain in various states of preservation in the United Kingdom:

- *X67*, now named *Brandram*, was built in 1915 by the Sunderland Shipbuilding Company and worked commercially between the wars. She was requisitioned as *C7* during the Second World War.
- *X44*, now named *Spithead*, was built by Osbourne Graham & Company Limited, of Sunderland in 1915. She was bought in 1921 by the James Dredging & Towage Company who used her until 1936. She was then sold to F W Horlock Ocean Transport Limited and deployed in the aggregate trade. During the Second World War, she was requisitioned by the Admiralty and was used as a fleet tender at Scapa Flow, thereafter returning to her previous owners and duties. Her last commercial use was as a dive/salvage vessel in the 1970s.
- *X8* was built by Sir John Lang, Sunderland and converted to a water tanker at Warrens, New Holland, Shipyard. Given the name *Tankard*, she was used as an auxiliary until sold out of service in 1921. She was sold in 1922 to Vauxhall Trading, Sheerness, and in 1955 to British Tanker Company, Sheerness. She was sold to Metal Trading, Swansea, in 1961 but was bought from them by G O Tate; her remarkable commercial life came to an end in the mid-1970s.

6

GERMAN NAVAL VESSELS – SOME CONVERSIONS AFTER THE GREAT WAR

A paragraph of the Armistice signed at Compiègne on 11 November 1918 stated that:

German surface warships which shall be designated by the Allies and the United States shall be immediately disarmed and thereafter interned in neutral ports or in default of them in allied ports to be designated by the Allies and the United States. They will there remain under the supervision of the Allies and of the United States, only caretakers being left on board. The following warships are designated by the Allies: Six battle cruisers, ten battleships, eight light cruisers (including two mine layers), fifty destroyers of the most modern types.

The subsequent Treaty of Versailles included the following Articles:

Article 181: After the expiration of a period of two months from the coming into force of the present Treaty the German naval forces in commission must not exceed six battleships of the *Deutschland* or *Lothringen* type; six light cruisers; 12 destroyers and 12 torpedo boats; or an equal number of ships constructed to replace them as provided in Article 190. No submarines are to be included. All other warships, except where there is provision to the contrary in the present Treaty, must be placed in reserve or devoted to commercial purposes.

Article 182: Until the completion of the minesweeping prescribed by Article 193 Germany will keep in commission such number of minesweeping vessels as may be fixed by the Governments of the Principal Allied and Associated Powers.

Article 189: Articles, machinery and material arising from the breaking-up of German warships of all kinds, whether surface vessels or submarines, may not be used except for purely industrial or commercial purposes. They may not be sold or disposed of to foreign countries.

The Treaty of Versailles was signed on 28 June 1919. It had become obvious that the fleet of ships held at Scapa Flow would all fall to the Allies under the prospective treaty, and thus, a week earlier and, contrary to Article 31 of the Armistice 'No destruction of ships or of materials to be permitted before evacuation, surrender, or restoration', the German flag officer, Ludwig von Reuter, ordered the entire fleet to be scuttled.

Instructions were then drawn up how to immobilise the remainder of the German battle fleet. For the most part this comprised distribution of some ships to Allied countries for breaking and some allocated eventually for further service. Sales of vessels for demolition or further use as mercantiles were handled by the Government to which the vessel had been ceded and handled by the same government agencies that would dispose of that country's own redundant warships. All sales of redundant German warships by Great Britain, for example, were thus registered in the Navy Sales Lists.

The Larger Ships

Germany was so short of merchant ships at the end of the war that a request was made to convert some of the military vessels, otherwise destined for scrap or for disposal at sea, into merchant vessels. Some of these conversions were quite remarkable and included reconfiguring two 'S' class destroyers as sailing schooners. Aidan Dodson and Serina Cant, in their book *Spoils of War*, explain:

> … on 13 February 1920 the German Foreign Office wrote to the NIACC [Naval Inter-Allied Commission of Control] asking for a ruling on the definition of 'breaking up'. Germany proposed that it be understood as 'so stripping such vessels of their characteristics as war vessels that re-construction of war vessels would be impossible', the intention being that such vessels could be used as the basis for merchant ships. This was referred to the Allied Conference of Ambassadors with a recommendation for acceptance, as it achieved the objec-

The coastal defence vessel *Ägir* (1895) seen in a contemporary lithograph by Hugo Graf, 1899.
(Public domain)

The *Großer Kreuser Victoria Louise* (1897) looking an unlikely candidate for conversion for use as a merchant cargo ship.

tives of the clause while also meeting a requirement under Article 189 that material arising from the breaking up of warships must be used for industrial or commercial purposes.

Article 181 allowed for surplus German warships to be devoted to commercial purposes, and a considerable number of minesweepers were sold for conversion to ferries or small cargo ships. In addition, a handful of larger vessels were rebuilt as merchantmen. The coast defence ships SMS *Frithjof*, SMS *Odin* and SMS *Aegir* [*Ägir*] became vehicle transporters, the boiler rooms and magazines being stripped out to provide cargo space, the original engines being replaced by a pair of 550 bhp ex-submarine diesels. They appear to have been successful in the new role, as *Frithjof* lasted until 1930 and *Odin* was not scrapped until 1935 [*Ägir* had been wrecked off the island of Gotland in December 1929].

Also, the old cruisers SMS *Gefion* and SMS *Victoria Louise*, lying at Danzig, were purchased by a local consortium to be converted to cargo ships, to provide employment in the former Danzig Imperial Dockyard and act as symbols of Danziger commerce, work being authorised by the local Allied authorities in May 1920. *Gefion* (renamed *Adolf Sommerfeld*) received a pair of 2,400 bhp diesels from the unfinished submarines *U115* and *U116* (building at Danzig), fitted in what had been her after engine room. Some components were salvaged from the battleship *Brandenburg*, also bought by the consortium, additionally donating material for *Victoria Louise*'s conversion to the similar, but steam powered SS *Flora Sommerfeld*; the battleship was then scrapped. Neither of the Sommerfelds lasted long in mercantile service, both ships being broken up in 1923.

The three coast defence ships – *Küstenpanzerschiffe* – were converted by Deutsche Werke at Rustringen in 1922 and 1923 and were owned by A Bernstein Company of Hamburg. They were initially deployed as vehicle transporters but they were later used as general cargo ships.

The converted cruisers were owned by Norddeutsche Tiefbaugesellschaft and managed by Danziger Hoch und Teifbau GmbH. Cargo space was divided between the former magazines as well as redundant machinery and boiler

The cargo ship *Frithjof* (1891) was formerly the *Küstenpanzerschiff* SMS *Frithjof*. She is seen working cargo at Helsinki, Finland, during her seven-year career as a cargo ship for A Bernstein of Hamburg. (Wikimedia Commons)

compartments following installation of the new engines, submarine diesels that provided a service speed of 11 knots.

Proposals were also submitted to convert a number of unfinished ships, including battleships, battlecruisers, destroyers and torpedo boats. Most were intended to be diesel-powered with engines from uncompleted submarines. In autumn 1920, options on the cruisers and big ships had been taken by the Deutsches Petroleumgesellschaft to be converted into oil tankers. However, despite approval by the NIACC, the proposals came to nothing and the larger ships were all demolished. None of the torpedo boats were ever converted to merchant ships.

Four destroyers were converted, each with new blunt bow sections and a new stern to accommodate the engine compartment aft, while the original midship boiler and engine rooms were adapted as cargo holds. There were two schemes, an engines-aft coaster and a four-masted sailing schooner. Dodson and Cant again:

> Two [destroyers] (*S178* and *S179*) had been building at Schichau, Elbing: following the removal of their bows, they had been moved successively to Danzig, then to Bremen, where they were both completed according to the sailing schooner scheme, and entered service with the Bremerhaven firm of F Kimme in 1921. The former *S178* became *Franziska Kimme*, passing through various hands until sold for scrap in Brazil in 1935. The ex-*S179* entered service as *Georg Kimme*, coming under the French flag in 1928 as *Zazpiakbat*, by 1932 adapted as a refrigerated trawler for employment off the Grand Banks of Newfoundland, still rigged as a sailing schooner. Laden with

cement, she was scuttled at Martigues, near Marseilles, on 21 August 1944; attempts to refloat her in 1945 failed.

The remaining pair were *Howaldtswerke* (H186) and the unnamed *H187*. They were completed as cargo ships in early 1921, under the names of *Hansdorf* and *Hoisdorf* respectively, and owned by Baltische Reederei GmbH of Hamburg. They were sold in 1924 to Aug. Bolten, Wm. Miller's Nachfolger and renamed *Dietrich Bohnekamp* and *Hermann Bohnekamp*. Renamed *Peryneas II* and *Peryneas* by their third German owner, Schroder & Fischer, the former *H186* went to a Brazilian owner in 1930 and was sold for scrap in 1935, and her sister passed to owners in St John's, Newfoundland in 1931 and to owners in British Honduras in 1933. She was wrecked on Mud Island, Nova Scotia, on 22 April 1933.

All the other remaining potential merchant conversions, from the summer of 1921 onwards, were abandoned and vessels scrapped. A decline in shipping demand meant that the reconstructions were simply no longer economically viable. Dodson and Cant:

> Four large submarine pressure-hulls were used to build self-propelled tankers at Germania's Kiel yard, although the costs appear to have been high. They employed the hulls of *U183*, *U184*, *U187* and *U188*, which they had been building at the yard, the first two forming the basis for *Ostpreussen* (1921), with her engines from another unfinished Germania submarine, *U129*. The other two hulls went into her sister *Oberschlesien*, whose engines came from *U130*. Of 3900 tons gross, the resulting vessels were 87.5 metres long overall, with a beam of 12.3 metres, and capable of 10 knots … They entered service with the Hamburg-based Hugo Stinnes-Rübeck Montan & Oelwerke AG, but were sold to Italian owners in 1927, *Ostpreussen* becoming *Caucaso* and her sister *Nautilus*. Both ships were lost during the Second World War, *Caucaso* (ex-*Ostpreussen*) being beached after being bombed by British aircraft off the Tunisian coast in December 1942, and *Nautilus* (ex-*Oberschlesien*), returned to the German flag as a naval replenishment oiler in July 1942 as *Languste*, was sunk by a British submarine off Sardinia that October.

One ship from the Austro-Hungarian forces was sold commercially – in 1920 the elderly river monitor *Szamos* became the dredger *Tivador* for owners in Budapest.

M Type Minesweepers

The German minesweeper force was reduced after Germany's obligation to clear minefields had been fulfilled. Seventy-five of the larger M type minesweepers were struck off the navy list between 1920 and 1922. They were equipped with twin fast-running triple-expansion steam engines supplied by two water tube boilers working under forced draught giving a service speed of not less than 15 knots. While many were sold for scrap others went for conversion to merchant ships. A large group were bought by Victor Boitin of Berlin for conversion for merchant duties and resold to overseas owners. The ships were *M1* to *M5*, *M13*, *M17*, *M20*, *M29* and *M30*.

M10 was sold in March 1920 to Hellenic Company of Maritime Enterprises, Athens and renamed *Aktion*. She was converted for use as a daytime passenger ship on inter-island services. In 1930 she was sold to Canadian National Railways and given the name *Prince William*. She was transferred shortly afterwards to Canadian National Steamship Company, Limited. *Prince William* was little used and spent much of the 1930s laid up at Prince Rupert before she was sold in March 1940 to Armour Salvage & Towing Company, Halifax. She was broken up in 1946.

M42 was sold to Norddeutsche Lloyd for use as a passenger tender and renamed *Nymph*. The following year she was bought by Camille Blanc of Nice and converted into a private yacht with the name *La Nymphe*. In 1924 her ownership passed to Vicomte Le Guales de Mezaubran. She was then sold to SA des Bains der Mer et du Cercle des Etrangers de Monaco in 1928 and subsequently requisitioned by the French Navy at the start of the Second World War as *AD204*. With the fall of France, she was used by Germany again as a tender under her old name *Nymph*. She was scuttled off Northern Italy in April 1945.

M72 became a tug on the Rhine under the name *Luwen 3*. She was sold to Hafen-Dampfschiffahrt in 1928 and employed as the ferry *Reichspräsident* at Hamburg. In 1935 she was sold to Blohm & Voss and named *Kranich* – she was employed as an aircraft recovery vessel and was operated by the Luftwaffe during the war. Thereafter she became a salvage vessel until sold for scrap in 1961.

A number of vessels were sold after the war for completion for merchant service. *M131* was launched in June 1919 and sold to Cia Uruguaya de Nav Ltda of Montevideo and converted into the passenger ferry *Carmelo*. She was employed on the Buenos Aires, Argentina, and Carmelo, Uruguay, ferry service. Her ownership passed to Cia Argentina de Nav Mihanovich Ltda of Buenos Aires in 1934 and to Cia Uruguaya de Nav Ltda also of Buenos Aires in 1935. She was broken up at locally in 1942.

M139 and *M140* were completed in 1919 as the passenger ferries *Helgoland* and *Hörnum* for HAPAG, the Hamburg America Line, for use on the local River Elbe and Heligoland passenger services and for tendering duties. *Helgoland* was sold to Norwegian shipowners Tonsberg & Hortens in 1922 and renamed *Tönsberg*, and sold again in 1931 to the Columbian Navy and renamed *Bogota*. She was struck from the navy list in 1946. *Hörnum* was sold to the Liverpool & North Wales Steam Packet Company of Liverpool and renamed *St Elian*. She was licensed to carry 528 passengers.

St Elian replaced *St Seiriol* which had been lost on minesweeping duties during the Great War (see Chapter 1). F C Thornley wrote of *St Elian* in his history of the Liverpool & North Wales company:

> She was a most useful addition to the fleet and opened up calls which had not been made for many years, namely, excursions to Bardsey Island from Llandudno, and also to Holyhead.

The former minesweeper *M140* (1919) seen leaving the Mersey as the Liverpool & North Wales Steamship Company's excursion steamer *St Elian*. (Courtesy Richard Danielson, Frank Thornley collection)

St Elian also made excursions to Blackpool as well as short sea trips from Llandudno, and for a short period took the principal sailing Liverpool to the Straits. To save time she travelled only as far as Beaumaris, passengers to and from Menai Bridge having to make the journey by bus.

St Elian was laid up shortly after the start of the 1926 season due to coal shortages caused by the General Strike; collieries remained closed between May and November. The ship resumed duties in 1927 and her last public sailing under the Red Ensign took place on 10 September from Menai Bridge to Liverpool. During the autumn *St Elian* was sold to Societa Partenopea Anonima di Navigazione of Naples, leaving Liverpool for Italy on 26 December 1927. As *Partenope* she was used on seasonal services from Naples to Sorrento, Ischia and Capri. Thornley again:

Partenope survived the battering which Naples received during the late war and the summer of 1944 found her again running on the same routes under allied control. She was painted grey and devoid of any masts but by 1946 she had been repainted and had then a black hull, green boot-topping, grey upper works, and grey funnel with a yellow and red band; the masts had not yet been replaced. In October of 1949 her name was changed once more, this time to *Ischia*, although she still remained with the same company.

In 1972 she was sold for use as a floating restaurant at Salerno with the name *Bucaniero* and was only sold for demolition in 2008.

M147 was converted on the stocks and launched as the engines-aft cargo vessel *Erna David*. Subsequent changes of ownership gave her the names *Principio*, then *Apollo*, *Principio* again, then *Zaragoza* and eventually *Tooya*. In 1938 she was sold to Bolec-Estudios e Inversiones Mineras, SA of Santa Rosalia, Mexico who renamed her *Korrigan IV*. As *Korrigan IV* she had obviously found her niche and she served her Mexican owners for the next 28 years; the ship eventually foundered in the Gulf of California in November 1966.

M151 was bought by Krull & Mais of Hamburg and completed as the *Kosmos I*, a cargo vessel equipped with an oil engine rather than the usual

Partenope (1919), formerly *St Elian*, arriving at Molo Beverello, Naples on 29 June 1935. (Courtesy Richard Danielson, Frank Thornley collection)

steam machinery. In 1925 she was sold to W M P Angione in Nicaragua and sold again in 1927 to the Standard Fruit and Steamship Company of Honduras. Between 1939 and 1941 and she was named *Inspiration* and she then became *Baranquilla* registered in Panama. In 1945 she went to the Mexican registry as *Presidente Madero*. She ended her career as *Florida* working for the Costa Rican company Hermanos Ayo from 1948. She was wrecked on a voyage from Puerto Cortes to Guadeloupe on 3 February 1964, having served an extensive civilian career.

M158 was completed for Nordeutsche Lloyd as the passenger tender *Grille*, based at Bremen. She was sold in 1922 to Vicomte le Gualès de Mezaubran, of Lucinière Castle, Pays de Loire, and renamed *Dinard*. She maintained the summer-only St Malo to Jersey service managed by France-Jersey Line until October 1931 when the Southern Railway took over the route. *Dinard* was then sold to the Colombian Navy in 1933 and renamed *Cordova*. There were many more examples, though not all were converted for passenger use.

FM Type Minesweepers

Coastal minesweepers of the much smaller FM type were just 135 tons displacement compared with the M type, which ranged from 425 tons to 506 tons. The first thirty-six of the FM Type were 141ft length overall and subsequent ships were 149ft overall; they were flat bottomed and the boilers were coal fired. Most of the FM type were struck off the navy list during 1919 and 1920, with just three kept for a few years as pilot boats. A few were sold to various nations and converted into small ferries and coastal cargo carriers.

About sixty of the vessels were converted for civilian use. Examples converted into passenger ships include *FM1* which was used as the ferry *Siegfreid* by O Karczinowsky at Königsberg from 1925 onwards. She was requisitioned as *HS29* in the Second World War and bombed at Gdansk. However, she was salvaged after the war and returned to her owner in 1947. The vessel was broken up in 1960. *FM3* was used as a tug until broken up in 1935. *FM5* became the Greek ferry *Georgios Galaos* in 1919, later renamed *Maria K* and *Maria Kalydon* until captured by the Germans and sunk in 1941. *FM25* became the German ferry *Bismarck*, based at Rostock in 1925 and two years later was renamed *Ålands Express* and later just *Express* when she was registered under the Finnish flag. She was then sold to Italian owners and renamed *S Constanzo Express* and based at *Trieste*, and then renamed *Gianpaolo I* by Nav a Vapore Municipalazzata, Trieste. She was broken up in 1954. *FM29* also became a ferry, initially at Stettin with the name *Westfalen* and later for Portuguese owners as *Montejense*. She foundered in 1958. *FM36*, completed in 1919, was one of a number of similar vessels sold to a Romanian bank. The bank sold them on, *FM36* then served as the Romanian

The minesweeper *M158* (1919) was converted for Nordeutsche Lloyd as the passenger tender *Grille* before becoming the France-Jersey Line passenger ferry *Dinard* in 1922 – she is seen leaving St Helier in the late 1920s.

ferry *Socrates*, until 1941, when she returned to German service as *Xanten*; she was eventually scuttled in the Black Sea in August 1944. *FM37*, *FM38* and *FM49* were based at Fiume in Italy (now Rijeka in Croatia) as the small ferries *Fiumana I*, *Fiumana II* and *Fiumana III* throughout the 1920s and 1930s. *FM50*, *FM54* and *FM55* were also sold for use as ferries in Turkey, Norway and Belgium respectively.

Submarines

Diesel engines from scrapyards dealing with German submarine pressure hulls were in great demand and attracted good prices. The perceived quality of German diesel engines had a lot to do with the premium prices, as did the ready availability of the engines at a time of shortages. Dodson and Cant again:

> Thus, in the first wave of sales of boats for scrap in early 1919, they [the engines] were sold separately from the hulls, albeit often to the same purchaser (the breaker who had to separate them from the hull in the first place). These engines regularly changed hands at prices close to those of the hulls to which they had originally belonged: for example, the Tyneside-based breaker Hughes Bolckow paid £2,000 for two engines from U9, while the rest of the boat only went for £475 more.
>
> The engines were then widely cascaded from the breakers' yards to specialist engineering subcontractors for refurbishment, which also provided employment for former naval crew with experience of working with diesels. They were then sold on at some profit, with £9,000 realised from the sale of four engines, two from U100 and two from U164, to Southend Corporation … . Southend's acquisition of these six engines [in total] for three sites at London Road Southend, Leigh-on-Sea and Thorpe Bay, formally opened in May 1922, received widespread publicity. Together, the three sites generated electricity to service the local tramway system, with the Leigh and Thorpe Bay termini at either end and the London Road depot at the centre of the system.

German submarine engines were acquired by a number of other local authorities to generate power, including Guildford, Harrogate, Wisbech and York in England, and Larne in Northern Ireland. They were also applied to a wide variety of other purposes, for example, in breweries, cement works even at the British Empire Exhibition at Wembley in 1924.

7

SECOND WORLD WAR CONVOY ESCORTS – CORVETTES, FRIGATES AND PATROL CRAFT

Great Britain's naval design programme for 1939 focussed on a convoy escort vessel which was capable of being built quickly, able to deploy anti-submarine equipment and cope with the heavy seas around the British Isles. Last but not least, the new escort vessel should be able to match U-boat speeds. The result was the 'Flower' class corvette.

Following the success of the Z Whalers in the Great War, designed by Smith's Dock Company at Newcastle and Middlesbrough, the same company was instructed to develop the larger whaler-type 'Flower' class in 1939. They were originally designated Patrol Vessels, Whaler Type but became the 'Flower' class because of the consistent ship nomenclature of names of flowers. They were designed for patrol minesweeping and anti-submarine duties in coastal waters and the Western Approaches. An article in *Sea Breezes*, September 1962, described them:

> With a length of 205 feet overall the vessels were fitted with a 4-cylinder triple expansion engine of 2,750 ihp and 185 rpm also designed by Smith's Dock Company, and two cylindrical boilers, giving a speed of over 16½ knots. These ships were able to operate in all kinds of weather. The first of the Flower corvettes was completed in 5½ months from the laying of the keel, and following vessels were completed at the rate of one every 3½ weeks.

Wartime pressures had the ships increasingly deployed on deep-sea convoy escort work. A larger successor was developed to assist in this role, the 'River' class frigate, with a length of 302ft and twin engines and boilers. Compared with the 'Flowers', the 'Rivers' had increased bunker capacity for the Atlantic convoys, a greater speed of 20 knots and increased range of 7,200nm. Finally, there was the 'Castle' class corvette which had a length overall of 252ft, twin triple expansion steam engines, and twin boilers to provide a speed of about 20 knots. Much use was made of prefabricated construction in all three classes of ship, and plans were replicated for use in Canadian, Australian and American shipyards.

Some 145 'Flowers' were eventually built in the UK and they, led by a few destroyers, formed the bulk of the escorting warships which fought the Battle of the Atlantic. Their short length and shallow draught made them uncomfortable ships to live in, even when they were modified, after the fall of France, to enable them to counter the extended range of the German U-boat 'Wolf-packs'. A fortnight of constant rolling and pitching on transatlantic convoy duty tended to exhaust all who sailed in them.

After U-boats demonstrated mid-Atlantic attack capability from French bases, construction of 'Flowers' was discontinued in favour of the 'River' class frigate, a larger ship and better suited for ocean escort work. 'Rivers' offered the size, speed and endurance of escort sloops using the inexpensive reciprocating machinery of corvettes. They were designed for North Atlantic weather conditions and included the most effective anti-submarine sensors and weapons. Sixty-seven were built for the Royal Navy and others for allied navies. Later in the war, shipyards too small to build 300ft long frigates were put to constructing an improved 252ft corvette, known as the 'Castle' class; larger than the 'Flower' class, some 'Castles' remaining in service until the mid-1950s.

One hundred and seventy-five 'Flower' class corvettes were commissioned into the Royal Navy and twenty-six 'Castle' class joined them. Many others were commissioned by allied navies. The war-built ships were supplemented by the existing fleet of escort ships built between the wars. The main class of these ships was the *Black Swan* class, which continued to be built into the war, but there were seven other classes, including the *Bittern* class of three ships, four ships of the *Shoreham* class, and the *Grimsby* class of thirteen ships which were also available for escort duties (see Chapter 8).

The service of all these little ships in combatting the U-boat menace cannot be overstated. That many of them also sustained substantial commercial activities after the war is a credit to their designers, builders and engine makers. They were treated roughly in the war, given inadequate maintenance, and some were in poor condition after the war. As a consequence, many of the 'Flowers', 'Castles' and 'Rivers' were scrapped or mothballed by the mid-1950s. By then most of the ships were not economically worthy of conversion and purpose-built shipping was also available at reasonable cost. Nevertheless, four 'Castles' were converted as second-generation weather ships in the late 1950s, clearly a cheaper option than building new ships.

'Flower' Class Corvettes

Many of the 'Flowers' were sold after the war to commercial owners and used in diverse roles including, of course, that of whale catcher. Whale catchers were at a premium at the end of the Second World War, Christian Salvesen Limited of Leith, for example, had sixty-three catchers in December 1941 but had only thirty-two at the end of the war. The whaling companies were put under pressure by the Ministry of Food to restart their operations after the war, and for many companies the solution was to purchase former naval ships for conversion to whale catchers.

Christian Salvesen bought seven 'Flowers' which were put into service in Antarctic waters (see Table 1), and another, HMS *Aconite* (K58), and completed for the Free French Navy (*Forces Françaises Libres* – FFL) as FFL *Aconit*, was purchased in 1960. She had been bought by United Whalers Limited, London in 1947 and renamed *Terje 11*, becoming part of the Hector Whaling Limited fleet, also of London, in 1953.

Table 1: 'FLOWER' CLASS CORVETTES CONVERTED TO WHALE CATCHERS BY CHRISTIAN SALVESEN

Name and pennant number	Renamed	Acquired	Scrapped	
HMS *Ranonculus* (K117)	Southern Lily	1947	1967	
HMS *Phlox* / HMS *Lotus* (K130)	Southern Lotus	1947	1966	Lost on delivery voyage to shipbreakers
HMS *Starwort* (K20)	Southern Broom	1948	1967	
HMS *Woodruff* (K53)	Southern Lupin	1948	1959	
HMS *Arrowhead* (K145)	Southern Larkspur	1948	1959	
HMS *Cyclamen* (K83)	Southern Briar	1948	1966	Wrecked off Jutland under tow to breakers
HMS *Carnation* (K00)	Southern Laurel	1948	1966	Served in Royal Netherlands Navy as HNMS *Friso*
HMS *Aconite* (K58)	Southern Terrier	1960	1967	Served in Free French Navy as FFL *Aconit*

Southern Briar (1940), formerly HMS *Cyclamen*, was one of eight 'Flower' class corvettes converted to whale catchers by Christian Salvesen Limited.

Other examples include HMS *Monkshood* (K207) which was sold in 1947 to Union Whaling Company Limited (A E Larsen, managers) and renamed *W R Strang*. She flew the Red Ensign until 1957 when she was renamed *Toshi Maru* and was sold in 1965 for breaking-up. HMS *Rhododendron* (K78) and HMS *Stonecrop* (K142) were sold to become the whalers *Maj Vinke* and *Martha Vinke* respectively, in the Dutch fleet of Vinke & Company.

HMS *Aubretia* (K96) was sold for use as a Norwegian buoy tender in 1948 and resold in 1951 to Andres Jahre & Company, strengthened for ice and renamed *Arnfinn Bergen* as a whaler. She was broken up in 1966.

Ian Ramsay describes an interesting application of two 'Flower' class ships, HMS *Sundew* (K57) which was lent to the Free French Navy as FFL *Roselys* shortly after she was commissioned in 1941 and HMS *Iris/Coriander* (K183), which became FFL *Commandant Detroyat* also in 1941:

I commenced my pupil apprenticeship in 1949 with A & J Inglis Ltd which from 1919 had been a wholly owned subsidiary of Harland & Wolff Limited of Belfast. At the end of the war Harlands had secured a contract to build the Whaling Factory Ship, *Balaena*, for United Whalers Limited, later Hector Whaling. Part of the contract was the provision of six whale catchers to support the factory ship and the contract for the construction of the catchers was transferred from Harland & Wolff to A & J Inglis Limited. The first two whale catchers, *Setter I* and *Setter II*, were based on 'Flower' class corvettes in that two redundant ships of the class were purchased and broken up (I think by West of Scotland Shipbreaking Company at Troon) in order to save the cast steel stern frame, the rudder, the propeller and shafting, the boilers, the triple expansion main engine and all the engine and boiler room auxiliaries. After refurbishment, these items were incorporated into the Inglis built hulls. *Setter I* ran successful trials on 18 October 1948 and achieved a maximum mean speed of 15.44 knots. *Setter III, IV, V* and *VI* were of Inglis design but fitted with owners' choice of Fredrikstad double compound, four-cylinder, steam engines supplied with steam from two water-tube boilers. *Setter III* ran successful trials on 13th August 1949 and achieved a maximum mean speed of 15.11 knots.

There are numerous examples of commercial conversions of 'Flower' class corvettes for other purposes and these include, for example, HMS *Anchusa* (K186), built by Harland & Wolff at Glasgow in 1941, and sold in 1949 to be converted into a fishing vessel. Given the name *Silverlord*, she was based mainly at Port Louis in Mauritius and was renamed *Sir Edgar* in 1954. She sank at her moorings at Port Louis during a cyclone in 1960 and was later salvaged and broken up. Another conversion into a fishing vessel was HMS *Loosestrife* (K105), built by Hall, Russell & Company at Aberdeen in 1941, which became the Faroese trawler *Kallsevni* in 1948. She was broken up in 1962. HMS *Azalia* (K25) was sold in 1946 to Soc. Anon Maritime et Commerciale of Panama and converted for merchant service as *Norte*.

Another example was HMS *Alisima* (K185), built by Harland & Wolff at Belfast and commissioned in 1941. She was decommissioned on 11 June 1945. In 1947 she was sold and reconfigured as the Greek-owned cargo ship *Laconia*. She was resold in 1950 to K Samartzopoulos of Piraeus and renamed *Constantinos S* and sold again in 1952 to D Efthimiou, Piraeus and renamed *Parnon*. The ship sank at anchor in July 1954 and was later raised and demolished.

One ship that spent much of the war in the United States Navy was HMS *Arabis* (K73)/USS *Saucy*/HMS *Snapdragon* (from 1945), a 'Flower' built by Harland & Wolff, Belfast and commissioned in 1940. She was converted for merchant service in 1947 for Cia de Vapores 'Albatros' SA and registered at Panama as *Katina*, and in 1950 was sold to Fareed Awad, of Latakia, Syria and renamed *Tewfik*. She was broken up in 1964.

HMS *Bergamot* (K189) was sold in May 1946 to the Greek government and converted for use as a passenger and cargo ferry with the name *Syros*. She was sold to Kavounides Shipping Company of Piraeus in 1952 and renamed *Delphini* and in 1955 she was given the name *Ekaterina*. She was withdrawn and scrapped in 1974. HMS *Mignonette* (K38) was also sold to the Greek government and converted for passenger ferry duties in 1947 as *Alexandroupolis*. She was wrecked on 30 November 1948 on passage from Lemnos to Piraeus.

Another 'Flower' class conversion was HMS *Clover* (K134), placed on the Disposal List in 1946 and sold on 17 May 1947 to Wheelock, Marden & Company Limited of London and renamed *Cloverlock*. She had been built by Fleming & Ferguson Limited at Paisley in 1941. In 1952 this ship was purchased by the Chinese government and converted in China back for use as a warship. She remained in active service until after 1967 but had been struck from the Navy List by 1972. In October 1946 Wheelock, Marsden & Company Limited also bought the *Shoreham* class sloop HMS *Fowey* (L15) and renamed her *Rowlock*. She was used commercially until 1950 when sold for breaking up at Mombasa. She had been built at the Devonport Dockyard in 1930.

HMS *Coreopsis* (K32), which was built by A & J Inglis Limited in 1940, was sold to Ealing Studios to play the role of HMS *Compass Rose* in the film *The Cruel Sea*, based on the book by Nicholas Monsarrat. The ship had just been returned from the Greek Navy and was found early in 1952 at Malta awaiting a tow back to the UK to be scrapped. She was towed back to Britain at the expense of Ealing Studios and taken to Plymouth where much of the filming took place. With the name *Compass Rose* still on her bridge the ship was resold in July 1952 for demolition at Sunderland.

There were many other commercial conversions of 'Flower' class ships not only from the Royal Navy but from allied navies as well. Some were sold for commercial use to diverse owners, many in South Africa, Greece and in Sweden. The ships went to the whaling and fishing industry, for use as cargo and passenger vessels as well as numerous niche activities such as research vessels, pilot vessels and even coast guard duties.

'Castle' Class Convoy Rescue Ships

Towards the end of 1943 the demand for convoy escorts had lessened with the declining threat from Nazi U-boats. However, there was an urgent demand for convoy rescue ships, not only to save lives of skilled men but also to boost morale in the Merchant Navy. To this end, five 'Castle' class corvettes were taken over at various states of fitting out and completed as convoy rescue ships. They were not ideal in the role because the sheer of the hull meant that only a small midships part of the ship was suitable for bringing small boats alongside. In the event they were only commissioned in the last few months of the war and were never able to demonstrate their worth as rescue ships.

Empire Shelter (1944) was one of five 'Castle' class corvettes completed as convoy rescue ships. She is seen at Malta in February 1949. (Wright & Logan)

The five convoy rescue ships were:

- *Empire Comfort*, launched as 1944 as HMS *York Castle* (K537) in September 1944.
- *Empire Lifeguard*, launched as HMS *Maiden Castle* (K433) in June 1944.
- *Empire Peacemaker*, launched as HMS *Scarborough Castle* (K536) in September 1944.
- *Empire Rest*, launched as HMS *Rayleigh Castle* (K695) in June 1944.
- *Empire Shelter*, launched as HMS *Barnard Castle* (K594) in October 1944.

They were all placed under civilian management with the City Line Limited (part of the Ellerman group of companies) on behalf of the Ministry of War Transport. Collectively the ships made twenty-one voyages between November 1944 until the end of the war; *Empire Shelter* made only three voyages but she was not commissioned until April 1945. The ships were returned to the Ministry of War Transport at the end of the war, placed on a variety of duties until they were all taken up as Army transports working in the Eastern Mediterranean. They were scrapped in 1955, *Empire Rest* being withdrawn earlier and scrapped in 1952.

'River' Class HMS *Halladale*

One of the better-known former 'River' class frigates was HMS *Halladale* (K417), which became the cross-Channel car and passenger ferry *Halladale* in 1950. She was completed by A & J Inglis Limited at Glasgow in 1944 and equipped with twin screws and turbine machinery. She was sold at Portsmouth in 1949 to Townsend Brothers Ferries Limited for £15,000 and towed to the Cork Dockyard Company at Rushbrooke, County Cork, for conversion into a passenger and car ferry with a stern loading door. Purchase was something of a lottery as the Admiralty would not allow prior inspection – in the event she was found to be in excellent condi-

Before: HMS *Halladale* (1944) was a 'River' class frigate, the largest of the wartime-built convoy escort ships.

tion. Furthermore, she was one of only six of the eighty-three 'River', 'Loch' and 'Bay' class frigates equipped with turbines, the remainder having triple-expansion steam engines.

The conversion cost £77,000 and included provision of high-quality accommodation for 368 first class passengers and space on the main deck for 55 cars. At the end of the work she was measured at 1,370 tons gross. There was a small, but intimate, dining saloon seating thirty-four. Many of the cars were stowed on the low after deck and protected by canvas screens although stowage continued forward along the main deck to below the bridge. *Halladale* was the direct successor to the old *Forde* (see Chapter 4) which retired at the end of the 1949 season and was dispatched to M H Bland & Company Limited at Gibraltar for ferry duties between Gibraltar and Morocco under the name *Gibel Tarik*.

Halladale, HMS *Halladale* as was, retained her original name under the Red Ensign, and entered service between Dover and Calais on 7 April 1950. She had received a bow rudder during the conversion for navigation astern at both Dover and Calais. On 10 April, however, she grounded in Calais Harbour and did not resume service until 9 May. Fit for 20 knots she was able to cross to

Calais in just over one hour, although her service speed was recorded as 17.5 knots. During her first winter lay-up a new deckhouse was added forward of the bridge. She operated a summer-only service, two trips per day, each year until November 1961, when she was withdrawn and sold for £42,000. Until 1951 all cars were craned on and off, but in 1951 provision was made at both Dover and Calais for stern loading and the Townsend dream of the roll-on roll-off ferry finally came to fruition. New linkspans were opened at Dover in April 1953 and *Halladale* immediately moved to these berths. During her tenure at Dover she acquired a reputation for rolling even in a moderate sea, and for some passengers one trip was enough! Others, however, adored the ship and she acquired quite a following with the motorist and coach traveller.

Her new owner in 1961 was W Rostedt, Turku, Finland and she was deployed on a service across the mouth of the Gulf of Bothnia between Turku and Norrtelje on the east coast of Sweden. She was renamed *Norden* and her passenger certificate was increased to 700 although she now only carried up to ten cars. Shortly afterwards she was resold to Partrederi Turist Expressen and given the name *Turist Expressen*, but late in 1962 she sold to Ferry Boats Margarita SA of Pampatar, Venezuela as *Ferrymar III*, surviving in this role until sold for demolition in 1973.

After: Townsend Brothers Ferries Limited's *Halladale* (1944) served as a vehicle and passenger ferry between Dover and Calais from 1950 until 1961.

Weather Ships

A number of 'Flower' class and 'Castle' class corvettes were converted after the war to serve as weather ships for the newly-formed International Weather Watching Service. The International Weather Watching Service was initiated in 1946, when the International Civil Aviation Organisation elected to maintain thirteen, reduced to nine in 1954, of the ocean weather stations established in the North Atlantic during the latter part of the Second World War. A report in *The Sphere* on 2 October 1947 under the headline '*Weather Observer* is ready for sea' announced the first British ship for the service:

> This former 'Flower' class corvette, built in 1941 and known as the *Marguerite*, is one of four ex-submarine hunters converted into ocean weather ships for the Meteorological Office of the Air Ministry. The *Weather Observer* is the first to be completed and, at the time of writing, she is preparing to take station off the west coast of Ireland. Altogether thirteen weather-ships will be anchored [sic] in the North Atlantic. United States, France, Holland, Belgium, Norway and Sweden are cooperating with Great Britain in the maintenance of a service which will provide weather reports to the Powers concerned, provide navigational aids for aircraft, take part in search and rescue services, and make oceanographical and other scientific observations. The *Weather Observer* has been fitted out at Sheerness. The crew of the *Weather Observer* consists of twelve officers, twenty petty officers and twenty ratings.
>
> The situation of the new Atlantic weather stations provided navigational aids for aircraft in flight, and make oceanographical and other scientific observations when practicable. Surface and upper-air observations will be made at frequent intervals, day and night, and the results transmitted to the Meteorological Office at Dunstable by radio. For upper-air observations, radio-sonde and radar will be employed. The ships will also re-transmit weather reports received from certain merchant ships.

Weather Observer was renamed by Philip Noel-Baker, Secretary of State for Air, at a ceremony held at Shadwell Basin London on 31 July 1947. W B Hallam describes the full British contribution in a letter to the editor of *Sea Breezes*, January 1972:

> The first British ocean weather ships were originally corvettes of the 'Flower' class, bearing the names and pennant numbers HMS *Marguerite* (K54), HMS *Genista* (K200), HMS *Thyme* (K210) and HMS *Snowflake* (K211). They were renamed *Weather Observer*, *Weather Recorder*, *Weather Explorer* and *Weather Watcher* respectively.
>
> The *Marguerite* was completed by Hall, Russell & Company, at Aberdeen in November 1940, and was of the original 'Flower' class with short foc's'le. She saw much service in the Indian Ocean. The *Genista* was a product of Harland & Wolff's Belfast yard in December 1941, and with the *Thyme* formed part of the escort group for the invasion of Madagascar in May 1942. Both corvettes served in the escort groups based on Durban, in company with my own ship HMS *Jasmine*. During the German U-Boat offensive of 1942-3 these corvettes, with others in the group saw much action. The *Thyme* and *Snowflake* were sister-ships which came from the Middlesbrough establishment of Smith's Dock Company Limited in October 1941.

The ships and their crews endured rough weather. In January 1951, *Weather Recorder*, some 400nm west of the Irish coast, had her steering gear damaged and her master Captain A W Ford had to con the ship with a loudspeaker so that two seamen at the emergency steering gear below decks could respond. But worse, on 11 January, a 40ft sea landed on the afterdeck where two crew members were working. They managed to cling on to what they could to avoid being washed overboard. Both were badly injured and needed hospitalisation on return to Greenock. The steel balloon observation compartment aft was crushed to the deck and one of the plates alongside the firemen's quarters was stove in.

The ships were registered under the ownership of the Air Ministry although ownership of the *Weather Observer* was retained by the Admiralty. The weather ships served 27 days at sea including six days to get on station and return home, the remaining 21 days were spent on duty. They each had 15 days at Greenock between trips when their crew went on shore leave. The upper works were painted in a garish yellowy-orange colour to make them visible to other shipping while the hulls were a more serviceable dark grey. Working in depths usually greater than 1,000 fathoms the ships had to be maintained on station by good navigation, generally steaming about 25nm a day to attain a point near the centre of their 210-mile square operational grid.

Between 1958 and 1960 the first-generation former 'Flowers' were replaced by four larger frigates of the 'Castle' class. *Weather Explorer*, ex-HMS *Thyme*, was sold to Chandris interests in 1958, renamed *Epos* and registered at Piraeus. She was sold for demolition in 1962. *Weather Recorder*, ex-HMS *Genista*, and *Weather Observer*, ex-HMS *Marguerite*, were both broken up in Belgium in 1961, while *Weather Watcher*, ex-HMS *Snowflake*, was scrapped at Dublin in 1962.

The four 'Castle' class conversions were HMS *Amberley Castle* (K386), built by S P Austin & Son Limited at Sunderland in 1943, and renamed *Weather Advisor* on conversion for her new duties; HMS *Oakham Castle* (K530), built by A & J Inglis at Pointhouse in 1944, became *Weather Reporter*; HMS *Pevensey Castle* (K449), built by Harland & Wolff at Belfast in 1944, *Weather Monitor*; and HMS *Rushen Castle* (K372), built by Swan Hunter & Wigham Richardson at Wallsend in 1943,

Before: The 'Castle' class corvette HMS *Amberley Castle* (1943) was converted for use as the weather ship *Weather Advisor* in 1960.

Weather Surveyor. These ships were all about 1,400 tons gross compared with the 'Flowers' which were about 800 tons gross. Unlike their predecessors they were painted in light colours as transatlantic shipping was then equipped with radar as its primary look-out at sea.

The first of the 'Castle' class weather ships, *Weather Advisor*, had previously been laid up in reserve at Penarth between 1953 and 1957 and was converted into a weather ship at Blyth. She was renamed at a ceremony on 22 September 1960 at the James Watt Dock, Greenock by Lady Sutton, wife of the director-general of the Meteorological Office. *Weather Advisor* started work in September 1960. She was again extensively refurbished and modernised with restyled superstructure in July 1976, by the Manchester Dry Docks Company, and renamed *Admiral Fitzroy*, after the first director of what later became the Meteorological Office. The ship was sold for scrap in 1982 and demolished at Troon.

HMS *Oakham Castle* was reduced to reserve at Devonport in December 1950. She was refitted in 1953, and laid up at South Shields. She was converted for weather-watching duties by James Lamont & Company at Greenock and on 16 May

1958 was renamed *Weather Reporter* by Lord Hurcomb. She was sold for scrap in 1977.

Weather Surveyor was commissioned on 21 December 1961. She was sold on 15 July 1977 and converted to a salvage vessel for Pound's Marine Shipping Limited without change of name. She was sold for demolition in 1983 at Hendrik-ido-Ambracht in the Netherlands.

Weather Monitor was converted at Blyth in 1961. She was upgraded in the same style as *Weather Advisor* at Manchester in 1976 and renamed *Admiral Beaufort*. She was withdrawn from service in 1981 and scrapped at Troon the following year.

The service declined in the 1970s as jet aircraft took to the Atlantic routes carrying sophisticated navigation and communication systems. From 1977 only *Admiral Fitzroy* and *Admiral Beaufort* remained in service as Britain's contribution to the weather-watching network. The network was terminated in 1980 when weather satellites became available.

Although very few Japanese naval ships were fit for sale for commercial service after the war, two Japanese Type B escort vessels, *Shiga* and *Ukuru* were adapted in 1950 to become weather ships. Renamed *Shiga Maru* and *Ukuru Maru*, the pair served in the Pacific. They transferred to the Japanese Maritime Safety Agency in 1954 as *Kojima* and *Satsuma*. Built in 1945 and 1944 respectively, the ships stood down in 1964. The former *Shiga* became part of an amusement park at Chiba City near Tokyo and was broken up in 1998, while the one-time *Ukuru* was sold for scrap in 1965.

Patrol Craft Escort

A batch of seventeen Patrol Craft Escort (PCE) were sent to Britain by the United States in 1943 under the Lend-Lease Act (a further sixty-eight were built for the United States Navy). They were built by the Pullman Standard Car Company of Chicago from 1942 onwards – the time to build a PCE was the same as that of building the carriages for one streamlined railway train! The ships were 185ft long, had twin diesel engines, a service speed of 13 knots and were manned by a crew of ninety-six men. They carried a range of armament including two depth-charge racks.

The ships were built in fourteen sections at the Pullman works then taken to the assembly slip four miles away by rail. Twelve vessels could be assembled at the same time, each launched into Lake Calumnet complete with oil engines and most fittings. The engine exhausts were discharged through the hull, there being no funnel. There were no scuttles either and all interior space was artificially lit. Royal Navy crews were enamoured of the ships; each officer had a comfortable cabin to himself and the crew had bunks rather than hammocks.

After the war the surviving PCEs that were decommissioned in British waters were sold to commercial interests mainly for conversion to passenger work, seven being destined for Norwegian coastal services as replacement for ships lost during the German occupation.

After: *Weather Advisor* (1943) was rebuilt as *Admiral Fitzroy* in 1976 and served until the weather-ship service was withdrawn in 1980.

Sideways launch of *PCE827* into Lake Calumnet at Chicago on 2 May 1943. (Pullman Standard Car Company)

The remarkable conversion of HMS *Kilchattan* (*PCE829*) into the overnight ferry *Stavanger*. (Mike Bent)

PCE827 and PCE829 became HMS *Kilbirnie* (BEC1) and HMS *Kilchattan* (BEC3) respectively. They were returned to the United States after the war. In 1946 *Kilbirnie* was sold to Det Stavangerske Dampskibsselskab of Stavanger, Norway, to be rebuilt as a coastal passenger ship. She was renamed *Haugesund*. She was refitted with a long after deck, and public rooms in both the forecastle and on the promenade deck. She was placed on the coastal service between Stavanger, Haugesund and Sauda. As time went on, she was modified to carry a few crane-loaded cars on the after deck. HMS *Kilchatten* was acquired in 1947 but was not refitted until 1950 when she adopted the name *Stavanger*. She was much more extensively modified, lengthened by 25ft, and she was also fitted with two continuous decks and a partial third deck. She was placed on the prestigious 'Night Route' between Stavanger and Bergen; she had a passenger certificate for 850 persons and offered 171 berths and space for crane-loaded accompanied cars fore and aft. The company also bought two Landing Craft, Guns for conversion (see Chapter 9).

In 1973 *Haugesund* was sold to Libera Navigazione Lauro SAS of Naples, Italy and renamed *Sicilia Ponte*. In 1982 she was resold to Fila Societa per Azioni, Italy and renamed *Tucalif*, and eventually sold for scrap in 1997. *Stavanger* was sold to Finnish owners and renamed *Kong Sverre* later becoming *Capri Corne*. She was scrapped in Finland in 1983.

PCE832 and PCE833, which became HMS *Kildwick* (BEC6) and HMS *Kilham* (BEC7), were sold in 1949 to S/A Investment (Fylkesbaatane i Sogne og Fjordane, Managers) of Bergen and renamed *Sunnfjord* and *Sognefjord* respectively. They were converted for coastal passenger use based at Bergen and employed on the Norwegian west coast services until 1982. *Sunnfjord* worked on the Norwegian west coast until 1973 when she was laid up at Bergen. In 1978 she was renamed *Sunnfjord II* and sold in 1983 but sank on the delivery voyage to Oslo. *Sognefjord* was sold in 1982 to Filmeffekt A/S of Oslo, Norway and renamed *Orion* and resold in 1984 to K/S Orion Film A/S of Bergen. She was laid up until 1987 then sold to Matkat OY of Helsingfors, Finland and in 1991 to Orion Risteilyt O/Y of Hamina, Finland and renamed *Orion II*. In 1996 she went to Jaako Mathias Eriksson of Honduras and was renamed *Orient Explorer*. She was for sale in 2019.

PCE830 was based at Gibraltar as HMS *Kilchrenan* (BEC4) on convoy and patrol duties along the West African coast. Decommissioned in 1947, she was sold to Hardanger Sunnhordlandske Dampskipsselskap, Bergen and converted into the small cruise ship *Sunnhordland* and for many years cruised the fjords between Bergen and Stavanger. In 1974, she was bought by the Partanen family of Kotka, Finland and was extensively upgraded and renamed *Kristina Brahe*. She was used for operatic-themed cruises along the Saimaa Canal on the border between Finland and Russia. She had sixty-four cabins for eighty passengers and two restaurants, a dance floor, a sun deck and a duty-free shop. She carried a crew of twenty-four. In August 2010 she was sold to the Saimaa Travel Network of Finland and renamed *Brahe* and resold in November 2016 to HSD Sunnhordland A/S, Stord, Norway and her name reverted to *Sunnhordland*. She is still in service.

PC828 was launched in May 1943 and became HMS *Kilbride* (BEC2). In 1947 she was sold to A/S Kristiansand Dampskibsselskab, Kristiansand, Norway and converted for use as a coastal passenger ship and with the new name *Jylland*, and later reconfigured as a car and passenger ferry. As such she could carry up to 650 passengers and twenty cars on her regular service between Kristiansand and Hertshals in Denmark. In 1967, she was sold to E Zammit of Valetta, Malta, and in 1984 sold again to Akdeniz Gemicilik of Kibtur, Turkey and renamed *Kibris* and later *Akdeniz*. In 1986 she went to Charterwall Maritima SA of Pireus, Greece and was renamed *Princess Lydia* and was sold for scrap in 1988 and broken up in Turkey.

The seventh ship to go to the Norwegians was *PC834* which came to the Royal Navy as HMS *Kilkenzie* (BEC 8). She was sold in 1948 to Giertsen & Co. A/S, Bergen and converted for use as a shelter-deck cargo ship under the name *Naddodd*. She was resold in 1952 to Southern Lines, Philippines and renamed *General Wright*. Resold in 1967 to the Sweet Line of Philippines she became *Sweet Sail*, until she was scrapped at Manila in 1978.

One ship went into Greek ownership for use as a passenger ferry. HMS *Kilmore* (BEC15) was sold in 1950 to Foustanos Brothers of Paxos and converted into the passenger ferry *Despina* for the Paxos and Corfu service. In 1969 she was sold to G Kousouniadis & Company and renamed *Evangelistria*. She was broken up locally in 1980.

Several other PCEs on Lend-Lease to the United Kingdom were bought for commercial service. Examples include:

– HMS *Kildary* (BEC5) and HMS *Kilmalcolm* (BEC10) were converted into the trawlers *Rio Vouga* and *Rio Agueda* for the Portuguese company Aveiro Fisheries. In 1979 *Rio Vouga* was sold for use as a cargo ship and renamed *Exportrader* under the Danish flag. In 1978 she was sold to Seasnipe Fisheries and renamed *Rio Star*.

– HMS *Kilhampton* (BEC9 became the cargo ship

The Finnish passenger cruise vessel *Brahe* (1943) was originally *PCE830* and later HMS *Kilchrenan*. She is still in service under the Norwegian flag.

The Kristiansand to Hertshals car and passenger ferry *Jylland* (1943) was originally the PCE HMS *Kilbride*, launched as *PC828*

Georgios F for Foustanos Brothers of Syra, under the Greek flag, until scrapped in 1970. She was used on a service between Greece and Suez to Madagascar.

- HMS *Kilmarnock* (BEC11) was sold in 1950 and converted into the cargo ship *Arion* for the Greek company P Skourletis. She was wrecked in January 1951 off the coast of Morocco.
- HMS *Kilmartin* (BEC 12) was sold in 1951 and converted into the cargo ship *Marigoula* for T Constantopoulos of Piraeus. She was sold for scrap in 1969.
- HMS *Kilmelford* (BEC13) was sold in 1949 and converted into the cargo ship *Aghios Spyridon* for Zacharis Brothers of Piraeus and in 1971 was sold to the St Matthew Shipping Company and renamed *St Matthew*. She was broken up in 1980.
- HMS *Kilmington* (BEC14) was sold in 1951 and converted into the cargo ship *Athinia* for N Gavalas of Larnaca, Cyprus, and she was renamed *Trias* on sale to Larnaca Navigation Company in 1955. In 1960 she was sold to the Greek company C S Pagoulatus & Company and renamed *Aghios Gerassimos*. She was only scrapped in 2007.

8

OTHER ESCORT SHIPS AND ESCORT CARRIERS

There were a number of classes of escort ships that came up for sale after the Second World War other than the wartime-built ships described in Chapter 7. Some had been built between the wars, while others were laid down as merchant ships but completed as escort aircraft carriers.

HMS *Enchantress*

After the war numerous corvettes and sloops were put up for sale at fixed prices, the Admiralty being conscious that bidding values would decline as the market became saturated. Many of the ships were old and worn out: some were not in a fit state for further use and were sold for scrap. One of the better-known vessels bought for commercial use was the *Bittern* class sloop HMS *Enchantress* (L56) which after the war became the luxury excursion steamer *Lady Enchantress*. She started work in commercial service in August 1947 running from Gravesend to Southend and Margate and towards the French coast every other day with two trips a week to the Goodwin Light Ship and the Kent coast.

Frank Burtt describes the ship in *Steamers of the Thames and Medway*:

> The *Lady Enchantress* … was laid down on 9 March 1934 as the *Bittern*, a naval escort vessel, at the yard of John Brown & Company at Clydebank. While under construction the original intention was abandoned and she was launched on the 21 December 1935, as an Admiralty yacht carrying the name *Enchantress*. The vessel cost about £150,000 when new minus armament.

She replaced the old HMS *Enchantress* as the Admiralty Yacht. This name had been carried by two previous Admiralty Yachts and also by three other warships. She was fitted out as a sloop and mounted three single 4.7in guns and was powered by oil-fired steam turbine machinery. HMS *Enchantress* had extensive accommodation built aft for the use of the Board of Admiralty. Following her commissioning on 8 April 1935 she

Before: The Admiralty Yacht HMS *Enchantress* (1935) complete with her accommodation deckhouse aft for the specific use of the Board of Admiralty.

attended the Silver Jubilee Review of the Fleet with the Admiralty Board embarked. When not in use by the Board she took part in local exercises, especially those involving submarines.

The new HMS *Enchantress* was the vessel by which the Duke of Windsor, formerly King Edward VIII, left Britain after abdicating the throne in December 1936. Edward boarded the Admiralty Yacht at Portsmouth on 12 December, and escorted by the destroyer HMS *Fury*, sailed to Boulogne, to board a train to Vienna where he arrived the following day.

HMS *Enchantress* was used primarily as a convoy escort during the war. Whilst employed on convoy duties around the Algerian coast she rammed and sank the Italian submarine *Corallo* off Bougie on 13 December 1942. She sustained extensive structural damage forward; temporary repairs were carried out at Gibraltar and the ship returned to the UK for permanent repairs to her bow section at a yard at Grimsby. She was then deployed at Freetown, Sierra Leone and later Gibraltar on escort duties. She was with the British Pacific Fleet in the China Sea and in the Pacific between August and December 1945. She was converted for this work into a Landing Ship HQ (Small). All armament except four 20mm anti-aircraft weapons was removed, and additional communications equipment was installed.

The ship finally sailed for home on 27 December 1945 and arrived at Portsmouth in March 1946 when she paid-off and was de-stored to await disposal. She was sold to The Three Star Shipping Company Limited, of Margate for £22,500 on 22 October 1946 and renamed *Lady Enchantress*. Of her conversion for merchant service as an excursion ship, Frank Burtt wrote:

> The work of conversion was undertaken by Messrs J I Thornycroft & Company, Southampton. The *Lady Enchantress*, which is painted white, has two masts, two main and one sun deck. Her main dimensions are as follows: length 269 ft by 37 by 15. She has a cruiser stern and is of 1,474 gross tons. The propelling machinery consists of four geared turbines.

After: The steam turbine excursion vessel *Lady Enchantress* (1935), port of registry shown as Ramsgate, seen in dry dock at Southampton while being prepared for her brief tenure at Torquay in 1950.

The cost of the conversion work at Thornycroft's yard at Woolston came to a total of £174,000; the result was a luxury excursion ship offering creature comforts not previously seen on the Thames. She made her maiden commercial voyage from Gravesend to Southend and Margate on 4 August 1947. *Lady Enchantress* carried out thirty-three trips in a short six-week season, and with a fare of only 7/6, undercutting the services offered by the General Steam Navigation Company by 5/- on the French coast cruise, she was extremely popular. But by mid-September 1947 she was swinging at a buoy off Gravesend.

An Illustrated History of Thames Pleasure Steamers reports as follows:

> Having been designed originally as the sloop HMS *Bittern*, the narrow beam of the *Lady Enchantress* gave her an unfortunate tendency to pitch even in the slightest sea. There was quite a number of passengers who were perturbed by the motion of the ship and would not contemplate a repeat booking. This made the ship's longer-term viability questionable.
>
> Six weeks was not nearly enough to begin to recoup the financial outlay and the ship was laid up at Gravesend in mid-September with virtually no prospect of a return the next season. Throughout 1948 she lay at Denton below Gravesend, but was eventually refitted at Southampton for excursion duties at Torquay, divided between long day cruises to Guernsey and shorter coastal cruises. She commenced service on 10 August 1950 and ended her career dramatically on 31 August with the radio message: 'Lady Enchantress position lat. 49° 50' north, long. 2° 45' west, forward boiler out of action, brickwork now failed. After brickwork now failed, refractory casing white hot, proceeding at about 40 revolutions almost stopped. Request tug to tow into port. Weather good at present, passengers comfortable.'

The steamer was towed back to Torquay by the Admiralty tug *Turmoil* (see Chapter 12). The pair arrived at Torquay the following afternoon. Her place at Torquay on the Guernsey and coastal excursions was taken the following year by P & A Campbell's *Empress Queen. Lady Enchantress* was eventually sold for demolition and arrived at Dunston on the River Tyne for breaking up in February 1952.

'Colony' Class Frigates

HMS *Papua* (K588) and HMS *Tobago* (K585) were built in 1944 by the Walsh-Kaiser Company at Rhode Island as USS *Howitt* and USS *Holmes* respectively. They were twin-screw vessels, built to merchant-ship standards, each equipped with twin sets of 4-cylinder steam engines (18½in, 31in and two 28⅜in cylinders with a 30in stroke) and capable of 20 knots. The ships were comprehensibly armed with American equipment including depth-charge racks and a British Hedgehog anti-submarine mortar. They were returned to the United States at the end of the war. They were then sold to a shipbreaker at Baltimore but resold in 1950 to the Khedivial Mail Line S A E of Alexandria. The frigates were converted for use as the passenger and cargo ships *Papua* and *Tobago*. They were measured at 1,300 tons gross and described in *Lloyd's Register* as 'classification contemplated'. They were used on services in the Red Sea and Eastern Mediterranean. Both ships were sunk as blockships in the Suez Canal in 1956.

Grimsby Class Sloops

A class of eight escort sloops, the *Grimsby* class, were built in the UK in the late 1930s. They had two 4.7in guns mounted one fore and one aft, a single anti-aircraft gun and four 3-pounder saluting guns. The ships had two sets of geared steam turbine machinery driving twin shafts which maintained a speed of 16.5 knots. Two of them were sold for commercial service. HMS *Leith* (L36) was launched in 1933 and served throughout the war as a convoy escort and later as a guard ship. She was sold in 1946 to become *Byron* and registered in Panama. In 1948 she was bought by the World Friendship Association, renamed *Friendship* and registered in Denmark. The Danish Naval Department bought her in 1949 and gave her the name *Galathea* after converting her

HMS *Leith* (1933), a *Grimsby* class sloop, was sold after the Second World War, becoming *Friendship* for the World Friendship Association and later used as a Danish survey ship. (Abrahams & Sons, Devonport)

into a survey ship. She undertook a major two-year assignment before she was withdrawn and sold for demolition in 1954.

HMS *Wellington* (L65) was launched on 29 May 1934 at Devonport Dockyard, Plymouth. During the war, she carried two 4.7in guns and one 3in gun as well as lighter anti-aircraft guns and depth charges, serving primarily in the North Atlantic on convoy escort duties. She was sold to The Honourable Company of Master Mariners in February 1947 and has been moored at Victoria Embankment, London ever since.

Immigrant Ship *Hellenic Prince*

The convoy escort and patrol vessel HMS *Albatross* was built by Cockatoo Docks & Engineering Company Propriety Limited at Sydney as the seaplane carrier HMAS *Albatross*. She was launched in February 1928 and commissioned the following year. She had twin screws with each shaft driven by two Parsons' turbines receiving steam at 220psi from four boilers. In 1933 she was placed in reserve having become incompatible with the new seaplanes that were being introduced at that time.

After five years in reserve, HMAS *Albatross* was transferred in 1938 to the Royal Navy to offset the

Before: HMS *Albatross* (1928), originally a seaplane carrier in the Royal Australian Navy, was used on escort duties in the Second World War and later as a Landing Ship (Engineering) for repairing landing craft off the Normandy beaches.

cost of purchase of the light cruiser *Hobart* by the Australian Navy. During the Second World War, HMS *Albatross* was based in Freetown, for patrol and convoy escort duties in the southern Atlantic, and was relocated to the Indian Ocean in mid-1942. From late 1943 to early 1944, the vessel underwent conversion into a Landing Ship (Engineering) and was used as a repair ship for landing craft and other support vessels off Sword and Juno Beaches throughout the Normandy Landings. She was torpedoed and disabled in October with considerable loss of life, but was towed back to England and repaired. From January 1945, she served as a minesweeper depot ship, but was decommissioned later in the year and laid up to await disposal.

In August 1946, HMS *Albatross* was bought by the South Western Steam Navigation Company Limited of Torquay and Bristol (owners of the Torquay excursion paddle steamer *Pride of Devon* and the former *Auk* class minesweeper HMS *Strenuous* as *Pride of the West* (see Chapter 14). She was registered as *Albatross*. The plan was to convert her into a luxury cruise liner and a start was made on the conversion including fitting luxurious cabin accommodation and a large dance floor. In the event funds ran out and, before much of the conversion work had actually been carried out, she was moored off Torquay with the new intention of using her as a floating nightclub. For this onerous duty she was renamed *Pride of Torquay*. In 1947, before the grand opening of the nightclub venture, the ship was resold to the Yannoulatos Group (a London-based Greek company) and taken to Barry in South Wales for conversion into an immigrant ship. On 14 November 1948 she was officially renamed *Hellenic Prince* in recognition of the birth of Prince Charles who was born on that day, in honour of his Greek heritage.

Hellenic Prince was registered at Hong Kong under the ownership of China Hellenic Lines Limited. She was converted at a cost of £200,000 into a passenger liner by C H Bailey Limited, Shipyards, Barry. The work overran badly and she was not returned to her owners until September 1949. She was then measured at 6,558 tons gross, with a passenger certificate for 1,200 persons. She could maintain a service speed of 17 knots.

Hellenic Prince was certainly no luxury liner. She had dormitories for up to twenty people, as well as some eight- and four-bunk cabins, all just with basic facilities, although all the accommodation had air-conditioning. The dining room seated 560 and doubled as the lounge, and there were also two cinemas. There was no sign of a dance floor or of any luxury accommodation of any sort. In the three bays of her hangar deck were three separate hospitals – one for men, one for women and an isolation ward for sick children who would most likely have come from a refugee camp.

Hellenic Prince was chartered by the International Refugee Organisation and used as an immigrant ship to work between various ports of embarkation in Europe to destinations in Australia and New Zealand. In December 1949, she disembarked 1,000 passengers at Sydney on her maiden voyage as an immigrant ship. However, conditions aboard were said to be cramped and uncomfortable and the ship acquired a poor reputation as described in this contemporary account:

> Passengers were required to work during the voyage, undertaking cleaning, cooking, mess room duties, and working in the boiler and machine rooms, with payment received in Woodbine cigarettes. Drinking water ran out

After: HMS *Albatross* (1928) was sold for commercial use in 1946 and was eventually converted into the immigrant ship *Hellenic Prince*, as seen here after her maiden arrival at Sydney in December 1949.

before the end of the voyage, although 'stubbies' of drinking water could be purchased from passengers working in the machinery room for one US dollar, and a freezer breakdown saw food perish. Passengers were refused permission to disembark at any of the ports of call, and when fresh food was finally brought on board at Fremantle, it went to the crew, not the passengers. Sea sickness was also rife as the ship was rarely level due to a malfunction with the pumps.

These conditions resulted in increasing passenger discontent which culminated in a hunger strike and the ship's master then accused the passengers of mutiny. A letter of complaint was drafted and signed by all passengers and sent to the International Refugee Organisation. On arrival at Bonegilla, they received news that the ship had been inspected and action was taken against the master and the company.

The master of the ship at that time was a former naval commander and discipline was key to his everyday life. He had little compassion for his passengers and when voyaging from the Middle East described his human cargo in what can only nowadays be described as the language of a racist. On one voyage, a group of French passengers who had been ticketed in Paris as 'Tourist Class' found themselves domiciled between two dormitories, men in one and women in the other. Demanding a refund, they left the ship at the earliest opportunity, the master blaming the agent at Paris for having misrepresented the ship!

The final duty of the former seaplane carrier was a charter to the British Government as a troopship, voyaging to Mombasa during the uprising in Kenya in 1953. *Hellenic Prince* worked briefly as an immigrant ship again until she was sold for demolition in 1954 and scrapped at Hong Kong.

Escort Aircraft Carriers – Port Line

Two fast cargo ships ordered by the Port Line Limited, London, were converted to escort aircraft carriers after they were launched. Each ship was capable of carrying up to 20 Fairy Swordfish or Sea Hurricane aircraft, and had a crew of 700. HMS *Vindex* (D15) was an escort aircraft carrier that was originally laid down as *Port Sydney*. The ship was redesigned and reconfigured at an early stage of construction and launched as an aircraft carrier in 1943. She had twin oil engines that provided a service speed of 16 knots. HMS *Vindex* escorted a number of the Russian convoys to Murmansk and later went to the Far East and Australia. Her active service complement, including Fleet Air Arm personnel, was nearly 1,000. P J Humphreys wrote in a letter to the editor of *Sea Breezes*, December 1971:

> In 1944, what were, I believe, the first seaborne experiments on rocket-assisted take-off gear, were carried out on aircraft flying from HMS *Vindex*. This equipment was thereafter in normal operational use. Shortly after VE Day she went to the Far East, and was one of the first ships into Hong Kong immediately after VJ Day, from whence she helped to evacuate British ex-internees to Australia.

On her return home from the Far East, she was placed in reserve and laid up in the Firth of Forth. Port Line was then given first option on purchas-

HMS *Vindex* (1943), a convoy escort carrier, showing few clues to her commercial pedigree.

Port Vindex (1943) was ordered by the Port Line and bought on the stocks to be converted into the escort carrier HMS *Vindex*. She was sold back to the Port Line in 1946.

HMS *Nairana* (1943), sister to HMS *Vindex*, was also returned to Port Line after the war and converted back for merchant service as *Port Victor*.

ing the ship from the Admiralty and they had her towed to the Tyne for conversion back into a merchant ship by Swan, Hunter & Wigham Richardson Limited, her builders. Removal of the flight deck alone involved cutting away several hundred tons of steel, while 222,000 buoyancy drums and 2,000 tons of pig iron ballast also needed to be taken ashore. The task of building her upperworks, deckhouses and other fittings for commercial service took longer than anticipated and after 18 months at the shipyard the vessel was christened *Port Vindex*. With just one pole mast and a handsome red and black funnel, there remained little evidence that she had once been a fighting ship.

Port Vindex, now a refrigerated cargo ship, commenced her maiden commercial voyage to Australia when she left London on 22 June 1949 under the command of Captain H Hamilton Smith. The Port Line nomenclature was the names of ports in Australia and New Zealand. An exception was made for *Port Vindex* in recognition of her exceptional war service. She served her owners until 1971 when she was sold for demolition at Kaohsiung.

Another incomplete hull, to be named *Port Pirie* and of the same specification as *Port Sydney*, was laid down by John Brown at Clydebank on 7 November 1942. In March 1943, this was also acquired by the Admiralty and adapted for use as an escort aircraft carrier by the shipbuilder. The ship was launched on 20 May 1943 as HMS *Nairana* (D05). She had an equally illustrious wartime career as her sister, serving in the Atlantic and the Arctic. HMS *Nairana* was allocated to Western Approaches Command on 25 January 1944 for trade protection duties. She was loaned to the Netherlands and renamed HNMS *Karel Doorman*, being recommissioned on 23 March 1946. The ship was returned to the Royal Navy in May 1948 and was immediately sold to the Port Line, eventually to emerge as *Port Victor*, a sister to *Port Vindex*. She was scrapped at Faslane in 1971.

Escort Aircraft Carriers – *Bogue* Class

A total of forty-five *Bogue* class escort aircraft carriers were built in the United States by Seattle-Tacoma Shipbuilding Corporation, Ingalls Shipbuilding and Western Pipe and Steel Company. They carried twenty-four aircraft and deck equipment included a catapult forward on the port side and nine arresting wires aft. There were two lifts down to the hangar deck. The carriers were built around the standard C3 type fast freighter hull. Eleven of the ships were retained in the United States Navy and the remainder went to the Royal Navy as part of the Lend-Lease arrangement. After the war the surviving ten ships in the United States Navy were retained in service and later scrapped, one group in 1961 and the remainder in the early 1970s.

The British contingent, known as the *Attacker* class and *Ruler* or *Ameer* class, were returned to the United States after the war. A few were sold for scrap in a damaged or irreparable state and the remainder were sold for conversion into passenger liners, or fast cargo and refrigerated cargo ships.

Perhaps the best known of the conversions were HMS *Attacker* (D02) and USS *Charger* (CVE30) which became the Sitmar Line's immigrant ships *Fairsky* and *Fairsea*. In February 1947 HMS *Attacker* was sold to National Bulk Carriers of New York who removed the flight deck and other surplus wartime fittings. In 1950 the hull was bought by Navcot Corporation within the Vlasov group of companies and renamed *Castel Forte*. Intended for use on the Sitmar Line's refrigerated cargo service to Australia, the project was abandoned and the ship laid up.

USS *Charger* was decommissioned at New York in March 1946 and sold in January 1947 to the Vlasov group. Unlike the other escort carriers which were equipped with steam turbine machinery, she had a single 12-cylinder oil engine geared to the propeller shaft; as such she was the only ship in the so-called *Charger* class of escort carrier. USS *Charger* underwent major rebuilding and emerged

Sitmar Line's immigrant ship *Fairsea* (1941) alongside at Melbourne. She was launched as *Rio de la Plata* but was completed as the escort carrier USS *Charger*.

as the modern-looking passenger liner *Fairsea*. She was managed by Vlasov's Italian Sitmar Line and registered under the ownership of the Alvion Steamship Corporation of Panama. Successive accommodation upgrades secured the vessel's long-term employment, mainly as an immigrant ship operating between Italy or the United Kingdom and Australia, and offering tourist class returns for new Australians to visit their old home.

In 1957, Vlasov secured a new charter from the Australian government which would allow *Castel Forte* to join the lucrative immigrant trade. She was then also converted for passenger carrying, much in the same style as *Fairsea*, given the new name *Fairsky* and also placed under the management of the Sitmar Line. One class (tourist) accommodation was provided for 1,461 passengers in 461 cabins over five decks. There were also seven staterooms forward on the sun deck. Comfortable public rooms were available, mostly on the boat deck and a lido area and swimming pool was situated aft. She commenced her first voyage south in June 1958, and worked as an immigrant ship for the next 12 years before being upgraded for use as a cruise ship. On 23 June 1977

Fairsky hit a submerged wreck near Jakarta and was beached. The ship was offered for sale by the underwriters but was later scrapped.

In January 1969, *Fairsea* was disabled by an engine-room fire near the Galapagos Islands bound for Panama and on to Southampton. The ship had 986 passengers and crew on board, but the sea was calm and the ship was towed safely to Balboa where her passengers were able to disembark safely. The damage was such that she was later sold for scrap.

HMS *Attacker* and USS *Charger* were not the only escort carriers to become immigrant ships. USS *Croatan*/HMS *Fencer* (D64) and USS *Glacier*/HMS *Atheling* (D51) were sold in 1947 to become the Italian immigrant ships *Sydney* and *Roma* respectively under the ownership of Achille Lauro Fu Giocchino & Company of Naples. The ships were converted into modern-looking and attractive passenger ships with first class accommodation on the boat deck and tourist accommodation of a high standard spread over three decks below. The ships were based at Genoa and sailed to Australia commencing in 1951. They also undertook occasional voyages to Canada, some from Liverpool. *Roma* was sold for demolition in 1966 and *Sydney*, after several subsequent ownerships under different names, was scrapped in 1975.

There were two more immigrant ships. HMS *Tracker* (D24) and USS *Jamaica*/HMS *Shah* (D21) were sold in June 1947 to Cia. Rio de la Plata de Nav. De Ultramar SA of Buenos Aires and

USS *Croatan* (1942) and USS *Glacier* were sold in 1947 and converted into the immigrant ships *Sydney* and *Roma* for the Italian Lauro Line. *Sydney* is seen here at Princes' Landing Stage, Liverpool, awaiting departure for Canada.

converted into the immigrant ships *Corrientes* and *Salta*. The ships were rebuilt at Newport News Shipbuilding and Dry Dock Company in Virginia. They emerged as handsome-looking ships with third class accommodation for 1,320 immigrants and were sold to Compania Argentina De Navegacion Dodero SA, the Dodero Line of Buenos Aires.

Corrientes and *Salta* served on the immigrant route between Genoa and Buenos Aires and in the 1960s continued as low-cost tourist ships. The management of the Dodero Line came under the control of the government after the coup d'état in September 1955. The ships passed to Flota Argentina de Navegación de Ultramar and then in 1962, to Empresa Lineas Maritimas Argentinas. Throughout these changes they continued on their run between Genoa and Buenos Aires uninterrupted. In August 1964 *Corrientes* had to disembark her passengers at Lisbon having been towed into port with engine failure. She was scrapped shortly afterwards. In December 1964 *Salta* was withdrawn with mechanical problems and was eventually broken up locally.

Ministerio de Transportes de la Nacion, Compania Argentina de Navegacion Dodero bought three more *Ruler* class ships in 1947 for conversion into fast cargo liners with limited passenger accommodation. USS *Delgada*/HMS *Speaker* (D90), USS *St Simon*/HMS *Arbiter* and USS *Vermillion*/HMS *Smiter* (D55) were bought in 1947 and renamed *Lancero*, *Coracero* and *Artillero* respectively. *Lancero* was scrapped in 1972 and *Coracero* in 1972. *Artillero*, later renamed *President Garcia*, was wrecked off Guernsey in July 1967.

Four escort carriers ultimately came under the Red Ensign as cargo liners. There was a reluctance on the part of the United States Maritime Commission to empower the British Merchant Navy after the war. Although Britain was able to buy numerous Liberty-type merchant ships, it only managed to acquire a handful of the superior

The Argentinian immigrant ship *Corrientes* (1942) was the escort carrier HMS *Tracker* until sold in 1947. She is seen here at Genoa in January 1961. (Giorgio Chiglione)

'Victory' ships and C3 fast cargo liners. Four of the latter were former escort carriers: USS *Estero*/HMS *Premier* (D23) which became the Blue Star Line's *Rhodesia Star*, USS *Winjah*/HMS *Reaper* (D82) became her sister-ship *South Africa Star*, USS *Perdido*/HMS *Trouncer* (D85) ultimately became Ben Line's *Benrinnes*, and USS *Willapa*/HMS *Puncher* (D59) later became *Bennevis*.

HMS *Trouncer* and HMS *Puncher* were returned to the United States Navy early in 1946. Put up for sale, both were bought by the Lancashire Shipping Company (Mollers Limited), stripped of their military hardware and flight decks and converted to merchant ships, HMS *Trouncer* was renamed *Greystoke Castle*, and HMS *Puncher Muncaster Castle*. Because of post-war steel shortages they were rebuilt using the superstructure of two damaged Liberty ships, *Ignace Paderewski* and *James Rumsay*, hence the unique profile of these two converted merchant ships.

The Lancashire Shipping Company's staple trade was the tramp market in the Far East. After the war this never picked up again and despite Moller taking an interest in the company the ships were disposed of or chartered out. In January 1954 the Shaw Savill & Albion Line chartered *Greystoke Castle* which was renamed *Gallic* and *Muncaster Castle* which became *Bardic*. Both ships were sold in March 1957 to the Ben Line while still under charter. The charter ended in

Ben Line's *Bennevis* (1944) was built as the escort carrier USS *Willapa* and came to Britain as HMS *Puncher*. She was sold for conversion to commercial service in 1946. (Author)

OTHER ESCORT SHIPS AND ESCORT CARRIERS

The escort carrier USS *Winjah* (1944) came to Britain as HMS *Reaper*, was bought by the Blue Star Line in 1947 and converted at a yard in Mobile, Alabama into the refrigerated cargo liner *South Africa Star*.

March 1959, and the *Gallic* was renamed *Benrinnes* and *Bardic* became *Bennevis*. Both ships were sold for demolition in Formosa in 1973 having enjoyed long and profitable commercial careers.

The Blue Star Line's *Rhodesia Star* and *South Africa Star* were both completed during the Second World War as escort carriers. *Rhodesia Star* was originally commissioned in 1943 as the escort carrier USS *Estero* and transferred to Britain as HMS *Premier* (D23), while *South Africa Star* was built as USS *Winjah* for the United States Navy by the Seattle Tacoma Shipbuilding Corporation, of Tacoma, Washington. She was transferred to Britain as HMS *Reaper* (D82). After her return to the United States she was sold to the Blue Star Line Limited in February 1947 and moved to the Gulf Shipbuilding Corporation, Mobile, Alabama, for conversion into a cargo liner. She entered service as *South Africa Star* in 1948; she was scrapped at Milhara in 1967.

HMS *Premier* was returned to the United States at the end of the war and converted to the cargo liner *Rhodesia Star*, also by the Gulf Shipbuilding Corporation on behalf of her new owner, Blue Star Line Limited. In 1967 she was sold to International Export Lines Limited, Bahamas, and renamed *Hong Kong Knight* operating between ports in the United States, Taiwan, Japan and Hong Kong. She was sold in 1974 and broken up at Kaohsiung, Taiwan.

The remaining *Bogue* class ships were all sold for merchant service:

– USS *Block Island*/HMS *Hunter* (D80) was sold in 1947 and renamed *Almdijk* for Holland Amerika Lijn of Rotterdam. She was retired in 1965 and sold for demolition. The *Ruler* class USS *Bastian*/HMS *Trumpeter* (D09) was also

The escort carrier HMS *Searcher* (1942), built on a standard C3 type hull, was converted into the Greek cargo liner *Captain Theo* after the war.

sold in 1946 to the Holland Amerika Liijn and renamed *Alblasserdijk*. She was sold to Greek owners in 1966, renamed *Irene Valmas* and was scrapped in 1971.

- USS *Hamlin*/HMS *Stalker* (D91) and USS *St Andrews*/HMS *Queen* (D19) became *Riouw* and *Roebiah* respectively for NV Stoomvaart Maarts 'Nederland' of Amsterdam and were sold in 1967 and 1966 for further service. The *Ruler* class USS *Bolinas*/HMS *Begum* (D38) and USS *Cordova*/HMS *Khedive* (D62) became *Raki* and *Rempang* respectively for the same company and they were sold on in 1966 and 1968.
- HMS *Searcher* (D40) was sold to the Greek shipping company J & A T Vatis and renamed *Captain Theo*. She was resold in 1962 to Tung Chao Yung and renamed *Oriental Banker*, later scrapped in 1976.
- The *Attacker* class HMS *Ravager* (D70) went to Sea Shipping Company Inc. (Robin Line) of New York (which was taken over by Moore McCormack Lines in 1957) and was renamed *Robin Trent*. She later became *Trent* and was scrapped in 1973. The *Ruler* class USS *Chatham*/HMS *Slinger* (D26) and USS *Baffins*/HMS *Ameer* (D01) were also bought by Sea Shipping Company Inc. and renamed *Robin Mowbray* and *Robin Kirk* respectively and were sold for demolition in 1970 and 1969.
- USS *Keweenaw*/HMS *Patroller* (D07) and USS *Breton*/HMS *Chaser* (D32) were sold to NV Vereenigde Nederland Sheepv. Maarts Den Hague in 1947 and renamed *Almkerk* and *Aagtekerk* respectively. *Almkerk* was sold in 1968 and registered as *Pacific Alliance* in Panama, and was scrapped in 1974, and the *Aagtekerk* was sold in 1967 for further service and scrapped in 1972 following fire damage.
- USS *Prince*/HMS *Rajah* (D10) and USS *Niantic*/HMS *Ranee* (D03) went to NV Koninklijke Rotterdamsche Lloyd and were renamed *Drente* and *Friesland* respectively, sold for further service in 1966 and 1967, and scrapped in 1975 and 1974.

9

LANDING CRAFT, TANK AND DERIVATIVES FROM THE SECOND WORLD WAR

The Landing Craft, Tank and various assault craft were developed from the X class lighter introduced in the Great War. The Landing Craft, Tank came in a range of different sizes and shapes to suit a variety of different purposes (see Table 2). The best-known classes were the Mark 3 and Mark 4 Landing Craft Tank, the latter being some 187ft long by 38ft broad and driven by twin diesels at just over 9 knots. Crew accommodation aboard the Mark 3 ships provided a cabin for the commanding officer, reasonable accommodation for other officers, but cramped quarters for the men. The Mark 4 ships provided better accommodation: a small wardroom with three bunks, two small wardrobes, a small folding table and a washbasin. The later Mark 5 design provided generally poor and cramped living accommodation.

J F B Jowitt wrote in *Sea Breezes*, July 1992:

The LCT had a wheelhouse which contained the wheel, the steering compass, an engine room telegraph and a voice pipe from the bridge, which was directly above it and which contained a compass, an engine room bell push, signal flag locker, a box for the Aldis lamp, the voice pipe to the wheelhouse and a chart table. The LCT was conned as any ship in the RN and every movement of the wheel and every engine order was given verbally by the CO …

Unlike most ships of comparable size and tonnage there was no power on the forecastle, but aft there were two screws, two rudders and a powerful capstan. With little draught forward, especially when light, handling the craft successfully required good judgement and a competent forecastle party. Going alongside with a brisk offshore wind required everything to go right for once the bow had drifted off there was nothing that could be done but to go out and come in again.

More than 800 Landing Craft, Tank took part in Operation 'Overlord', the D-Day landings on

Table 2: LANDING CRAFT, TANK OF THE SECOND WORLD WAR

	Built	Length (ft)	Breadth (ft)	Number commissioned
Mark 1	1940-1 in UK	152	29	30
Mark 2	1941-2 in UK	159	30	73
Mark 3	1942-4 in UK	192	30	311
Mark 4	1942-5 in UK	187	39	865
Mark 5	1942-4 in USA	117	32	470

6 June 1944, each capable of carrying ten tanks or other heavy armoured vehicles into battle. Operation 'Neptune' was the naval dimension of 'Overlord', the largest amphibious operation in history, in which more than 7,000 ships and craft of all sizes landed over 160,000 soldiers on the beaches of Normandy.

Wartime losses were high and included 160 Landing Craft Personnel (Large), 9 Landing Craft Infantry (Large), 9 Landing Craft Guns, 4 Landing Craft Support (Large), and 134 Landing Craft Tank; many of the losses were sustained on the Normandy beaches. Six Mark III Landing Craft foundered during the night of 18/19 October 1944 in a storm off Land's End, the little ships being bound for the Far East.

The numbering of the craft was not consistent and identifying which ship was which can be difficult. Lenton and Colledge in their book on landing craft note the difficulties encountered in their research with the numbering systems of such ships:

> The co-authors experienced the singular difficulty that, for some types of landing craft, they were unable to ascertain the complete range of numbers involved. The issue was further complicated by the fact that some types of landing craft were modified to perform other functions and were sometimes renumbered and, on other occasions, retained their original numbers … Similarly, craft received under Lend/Lease from the USA were by no means consecutively numbered.

The Landing Craft, Tank and associated vessels did not fare so well in the commercial world although a number of them were sold after the war for merchant service. They were occasionally deployed on exercises such as Operation 'Beef' which took place late in 1951 and which was intended to transport cattle to market from the beach on Lundy Island.

Type 4 Landing Craft, Tank

A number of Type 4 ships were sold and converted for inshore ferry and excursion work. A notably successful conversion was the Mark 4 *LCT828* which became the Isle of Wight vehicle ferry *Norris Castle*. Built by A Findlay at Old Kilpatrick in 1943, she was acquired by the Southampton, Isle of Wight and South of England Royal Mail Steam Packet Company in 1947. She was modified to carry 30 cars and 230 passengers. J I Thornycroft & Company Limited carried out the work at Northam, which included providing side vehicular access to the main deck in addition to retaining the bow doors and the provision of passenger accommodation aft. In 1952 she took over the cargo service to East Cowes with departures from Southampton at 9 am and again in the early afternoon. She maintained this schedule until 1962; the service was suspended briefly each year during the ship's annual refit period. *Norris Castle* served her owners well, albeit in sheltered waters, and was only retired when the second of the company's purpose-built vehicle and passenger ferries, *Osborne Castle*, arrived in service in 1962.

Norris Castle was sold for further service in the Mediterranean to Compania Maritima Santa Kynaki SA, renamed *Nereis* and registered in Panama. Shortly afterwards she was resold to D Filipopoulos and renamed *Aghios Dionisios*. In 2000 she was bought by Honduran owners and given the name *Galina S*. She was deleted from the register in 2001.

Four similar Mark 4 Landing Craft were converted for car and passenger ferry work across the Forth between Granton and Burntisland in Fife. The announcement of the new service coincided with government plans being made public for the new Forth Road Bridge, but with a proposed fare of 5 shillings per car on the new ferry service and a through fare on the Tay ferries to Dundee at 10 shillings the proposal appeared to be sound.

Mark 4 *LCT848* (1943) was converted for commercial use as a vehicle and cargo ferry in 1947 for the Southampton to Cowes, Isle of Wight, service operated by Red Funnel. She was renamed *Norris Castle*. (Ambrose Greenway collection)

The man behind the idea was John Hall, who already operated two former Fairmile launches (see Chapter 13). His options on the four LCTs were taken up and the vessels were brought to the Clyde for conversion by James Lamont & Company at Port Glasgow. Thirteen months passed before *LCT(4)673*, now also bearing the new name *Bonnie Prince Charlie*, ran her trials at the end of June 1950. She had been built in 1943 by Stockton Construction at Thornaby. The bow door had been welded up, bilge keels fitted, side loading doors installed with space for up to forty cars and substantial covered accommodation provided including a tea lounge and cocktail bar. The vessel could manage 12 knots and was equipped with the latest navigational aids including radar.

The new service was set to start on 1 August 1950 when the second conversion was to become available. Indeed, *LCT895* did arrive in Granton in mid-July and shortly afterwards received the name *Flora Macdonald*, for a while also bearing both her new name and old LCT number. She was completed in 1943 by P & W McLellan Limited at Paisley. She had been bought by Westholme Fishing Company of Milford Haven in 1949 and transferred to J Gibson Johnson of Hull without change of name from *LCT895*, before she was acquired by John Hull.

During the following winter the two remaining LCTs were converted, *Glenfinnan*, formerly *LCT1048*, arriving at Granton in December and *Eriskay*, formerly *LCT(4)668*, in January 1950. They were both completed in 1943 by P & W McLellan Limited. Alterations to the existing slipways were given as the reason why the service could not start and it was April before the long-anticipated schedule actually commenced with departures every 30 minutes.

The weather was poor, the crews inexperienced, the ships difficult to handle in cross winds and passenger numbers initially below expectations. However, by mid-summer the ships were generally well loaded on all but the very early and very late sailings. The Fairmile launch *Ulster Lady*, formerly owned by John Hall and now registered as owned by Forth Ferries Limited, acted as pedestrian overflow vessel and catered also for bicycles. Winter receipts barely covered costs and a reduced schedule was operated. Despite a good summer trade in 1951, losses incurred through the delayed start of the service and the poor winter trading conditions meant that the company's liabilities at the end of the year amounted to over £250,000, almost ten times the issued capital for the company. Ian Brodie wrote in *Steamers of the Forth*:

The first of the four vehicle and passenger ferries to be ready for Forth Ferries Limited was *Bonnie Prince Charlie* (1943), seen dressed overall ready for the start of the new Granton to Burntisland ferry service. She is still carrying her naval name on the bows: *LCT(4)673*.

Flora Macdonald (1943), formerly *LCT(4)895-50*, loading a small road tanker at the Granton slip at dusk.

On 14 October 1952 the Court of Session issued a warrant, at the instance of Granton Harbour Ltd. for unpaid harbour dues and arrested *Flora Macdonald*. The warrant notice was fixed to her mast and she was not allowed to sail. As *Bonnie Prince Charlie* was out of service awaiting repairs the company could not afford, the ferry had to be reduced to an hourly frequency. Six weeks later the company gave up its hopeless struggle and sailings were suspended after the 8 pm run on Friday 12 December. A campaign to gain Government support failed, and the official notice of abandonment was published in September 1953.

The four ferries lay at Leith until 1954 when they were towed out to India in pairs in the summer. On arrival they were stripped of their deckhouses and became ore carriers under the ownership of Timblo, Irmados, Ltda. of Goa, India, with the names *Surendra*, ex-*Bonnie Prince Charlie*; *Hemelata*, ex-*Flora Macdonald*; *Pracaxa*, ex-*Glenfinnan*; and *Prapida*, ex-*Eriskay*.

The Khedivial Mail Line S A E of Alexandria bought *LCT(4)675* in 1946 and converted her for passenger and cargo duties, measured at 438 tons gross, for use at Suez. She was given the name *Armant* but in 1953 she was sold and renamed *Hawamda*.

Other Mark 4 craft were converted for a variety of purposes. *LCT1052*, for example, was converted into a tanker in 1948 as the Norwegian-registered *Esso 5*, and *LCT399* became Risden Beazely's salvage vessel *Topmast 20* in 1966. Risden Beazely's *Topmast 16* ex-*LCT474*, and *Topmast 18*, were former Mark 3 landing craft that were converted for salvage work in the 1950s. The provenance of *Topmost 18* is uncertain although she was likely built on the Tees in 1943.

Landing Craft, Guns (Medium)

Although seventy-two Landing Craft, Guns (Medium) were ordered, only fifty-six were completed. *LCG(M)127*, *LCG(M)181*, *LCG(M)194* and *LCG(M)196* were all successfully converted for passenger use after the war. Three other vessels, *LCG(M)124*, *LCG(M)186* and *LCG(M)195*, were also adapted, with minimal structural alteration, into passenger excursion ships for use at Bournemouth. Originally equipped with two 4.7in guns and two 2-pounder pom-poms, a deep bottom tank allowed this type of vessel to sink almost to main-deck level to provide a stable base for gunnery. Ships of this class had a straight sheer except for a short rise forward, double chine and transom stern. There was a small deckhouse aft.

LCG(M)127 and *LCG(M)194* were bought in 1946 by the Stavanger Steam Shipping Company (Det Stavangerske Dampskibsselskab) and converted for passenger use in 1950 and 1953 respectively with the names *Sauda* and *Sand*. The conversion work was carried out at Haugesund and the ships were known as 'Sea Buses' with attractive and light passenger accommodation and room for cars on the flat after deck. The conversions were not identical and the gross tonnage of the two ships differed, *Sauda* being 295 tons gross and *Sand* 335 tons gross. The company also bought two Patrol Craft Escort for use as passenger ships (see Chapter 8).

LCG(M)181 (1944) was sold in 1948 and converted for use as the passenger excursion vessel *Rochester Queen* for the New Medway Steam Packet Company.

LCG(M)181 was converted in 1948 by J Bolson & Sons at Poole into the Thames summer excursion steamer *Rochester Queen* of 345 tons gross, for the New Medway Steam Packet Company. The aft deckhouse and all the side armour were removed and a large deckhouse was built amidships. Bulwarks with an attractive sheer were added complete with substantial belting around the entire hull. A false rounded stern was built to provide a length overall of 147ft. The deep tank and extra watertight bulkheads were removed during the conversion but the pumping equipment was retained for damage-control purposes. Three saloons were built into the hull and a navigation bridge, funnel and comprehensive lifesaving equipment added to comply with a Steam Certificate Class V.

The initial duties of *Rochester Queen* were on the Medway, Southend and Herne Bay service, and in 1953 she carried out local cruises from Clacton. In 1954 she took up the Strood to Southend service. Following the 1955 season she was sold to German owners who gave her the name *Hein Muck*, but she returned to the Red Ensign in 1961 when Commodore Shipping bought her for their St Peter Port to Alderney and Sark services, as well as excursions. She was renamed *Commodore Queen*, and her promenade deck was extended right aft. In 1970 her owners withdrew from the Sark and Alderney services and *Commodore Queen* was laid up at St Samsons, Guernsey and later moved to the Medway. In 1971 she was bought by Jersey Car Ferries Limited and renamed *Jersey Queen* with the intention of starting a new car and passenger service between Carteret and St Helier. Side-loading facilities were then cut into her to allow carriage of up to ten cars on the foredeck. A sprinkler system was suspended on spars over the open vehicle deck and the lifeboats were moved to the aft end of the promenade deck to make way for the cars. On 30 July 1972 *Jersey Queen* arrived at St Helier but was then refused permission to sail from Carteret and remained laid up throughout the season. In 1973 she did serve between Jersey and France for Jersey Car Ferries Limited but no cars were carried, and she was again laid up in 1974 moving to Poole in May. In December 1974 she was sent to

LCG(M)196 (1945) was sold and converted in 1947 for passenger duties with the name *Sark Coast*, running between St Peter Port in Guernsey and Sark. The service was withdrawn in 1948. (The Trustees of the H A Allen Collection)

West Africa, leaving Falmouth on 29 March 1975, to become a survey ship for K G Specialist Ships, of the Channel Islands. She was contracted to Decca Survey (West African Surveys) working from Port Harcourt, Nigeria.

LCG(M)196 was purchased by the newly formed Island Shipping Company, a subsidiary of British Channel Island Shipping Company (Guernsey) Limited in 1947. Renamed *Sark Coast*, she was intended for tourist traffic between St Peter Port and Sark. She was converted for commercial use by Camper & Nicholson at Southampton, but shortage of materials meant that she was not ready for her new duties until almost the end of the summer season. The ship was given a large deckhouse with a passenger saloon and tea bar. She retained her transom. The mainmast carried two derricks to handle cargo to adjacent hatches. The 1948 season was set to be a prosperous one with two other vessels on hand, the former Admiralty Motor Fishing Vessel *Herm Coast* and the old passenger steamer *Robina*.

Three Landing Craft, Infantry, Small that were modified for excursion duties at Bournemouth for the 1946 season before the big paddle steamers were available: *Bournemouth Skylark 5*, *Bournemouth Skylark 4* and *Bournemouth Skylark 6*.

However, after the latter collided with and sank *Herm Coast* off Sark in mid-season, *Sark Coast* was left to run the service alone. The company withdrew at the end of the year. *Sark Coast* was sent to lay up at Great Yarmouth, her ownership transferred to parent Coast Lines Limited in 1950. She was eventually sold in 1952 to Pedder & Mylchreest Limited of London who renamed her *Madinina* in 1953. In 1954 she went to Martinique until 1957 when she was sold to C L Tammis of St Vincent and used for inter-island work. In December 1963 she sank off St Vincent.

J Bolson & Sons, for the summer 1946 season, bought three more LCG(M) type ships early in 1946 to be adapted ready for the summer excursions trade. David Chalk in his book on Bournemouth excursion steamers states they were originally *LCG(M)184*, *LCG(M)185* and *LCG(M)186*, built by the Stockton Construction Company at Thornaby-on-Tees. The vessels were named *Bournemouth Skylark No 4*, *Bournemouth Skylark No 5* and *Bournemouth Skylark No 6* respectively, and were used on services to Swanage, Poole and Yarmouth, Isle of Wight.

Delays in refurbishing the larger paddle steamers of Cosens and Red Funnel ready for service, and silting at Bournemouth Pier, meant that the three former LCGs had the profitable early summer season in 1946 to themselves. They were licensed to carry 271 persons on local excursions with a Steam III certificate. Painted all-white, the only outward changes to the vessels were windscreens added to the top of the conning towers and lifeboats positioned abaft the bridge over the deckhouse. A port anchor and hawsepipe was provided with an anchor capstan on deck. Passengers had access to the open foredeck, refreshments were available at a kiosk on deck, and there was also a small saloon and toilets in the deckhouse.

They were offered for sale in August 1946, once paddle steamers were again available to call at the pier, but the three *Skylarks* served at Bournemouth until the end of the season. The ships were sold: the *Bournemouth Skylark No 4* to Ets Cauvin of Nice and renamed *Gallus*, and resold in 1965 to Fratelli Savarese fu Antonino, Napoli and renamed *Pompei*; *Bournemouth Skylark No 5* had two seasons in Jersey as *Dames Des Iles*, owned by Jersey Fishing and Boating Company Limited, and in 1948 she was resold to Iraqi owners without change of name; and *Bournemouth Skylark No 6* was sold to Det Nordenfjeldske Dampskibsselskab, Trondheim, Norway for use as the fishing support vessel *Skule Jarl*. She was later modified for use as a passenger and cargo ship with the name *Barge*, and was resold in 1953 to Alf Mortensen, Oslo and renamed *Svan*.

Smaller Landing Craft

Landing Craft, Mechanised (LCM) were small 35-ton displacement boats that could be slung on the davits of a mother ship. In early 1946 two small flat-bottomed LCM Mark 1 boats were brought into service at Portaferry to work across the entrance of Strangford Lough. *Shipping News*, 19 June 1946, noted:

> A short while ago Portaferry was in the public eye when the new ferry service to Strangford was inaugurated by *Lady Nugent*. This service should be a great boon to the people of the Lower Ards peninsula and the Strangford area, and as it will be able to handle motor-cars it will no doubt be much appreciated by motorists wishing to make the round of Strangford Lough.
>
> The new ferry or ferries will be the now familiar flat-bottomed landing craft, LCM 1 type, fitted with twin engines, and capable of accommodating about 36 passengers and two motor cars. Without motor cars they could probably take up to 80 or 100 passengers.
>
> The tide ebbs and flows very quickly through the narrow channel between Portaferry and Strangford (it runs sometimes at the rate of eight knots), but the new ferries with their powerful twin engines should be able to negotiate the crossing at all times of the tides and under any weather conditions. From the strength of this tide, the name Stong-ford, and hence by corruption, Strangford, is derived.

Sadly, the new car ferry service ended the following year with the capsizing of one of the ferries and the loss of one life and several animals. It was not until September 1969 before a car and passenger service was reinstated when the purpose-built *Strangford Ferry* was introduced by Down County Council. At Dublin, the *Larsen*, another former landing craft, was used for passenger excursions in 1946 and 1947. She was sold at the end of her second season to Greek owners but foundered some years later.

After the war, one of the landing craft built to work with the assault craft HMS *Fearless* was later sold into commercial service. *LCM(9)708* was built in 1967 by Richard Dunston Limited at Hessel. The commercial career of the vessel started under the ownership of Skye Marine Limited with the name *Drambuie*, and she later passed to Thorne Demolitions Limited and was eventually privately owned and based at Goole.

Landing Ship, Small – *Duchess of Holland*

The last conversion of a major Second World War unit for commercial service took place in 1970. The roll-on roll-off ferry *Duchess of Holland*, that served Norfolk Line between Great Yarmouth and Scheveningen, was originally the American Landing Ship, Small *LSM558*. She was built by the United States Navy Yard at Charleston, and was launched on 28 April 1945, having been laid down on 11 April. She was equipped with twin 16-cylinder engines constructed by General Motors which provided a service speed of 16 knots. This class of ship had a gun mounting forward over the bow ramp, the latter lifting upwards and inwards as the doors closed. The conning tower was three-

Before: The American Landing Ship, Small *LSM558* (1945), became *Viper* (L753) in the West German Navy in 1958. She is seen here on the left of a group of four similar vessels.

After: *Viper* (1945) was sold to Norfolk Lijn (L Remeeus), Norfolk Line, in 1970 and converted into the roll-on roll-off trailer ferry *Duchess of Holland*.

quarters aft on the starboard side of the ship allowing a long uncluttered open tank deck. *LSM558* was placed in reserve in June 1946 and eventually transferred to the West German Navy in September 1958 and given the name *Viper* (L753).

In July 1970 *Viper* was bought by the Norfolk Lijn (L Remeeus), Scheveningen, Netherlands. She was rebuilt as a commercial roll-on roll-off ferry at Boele´s Scheepswerven, Bolnes in the Netherlands, with accommodation for nine trailers and renamed *Duchess of Holland*. She was given new superstructure aft, to replace the former conning tower, complete with new crew accommodation. As such she served between Great Yarmouth and Scheveningen under the Dutch flag. In 1973 she flew the Red Ensign as *Oil Dragon* when purchased by Ocean Inchcape Company Limited, who used her as a production testing vessel. She was later laid up in the River Fal,

LCT7074 (1944) beached on a pontoon at Southsea on 24 August 2020, ready to be wheeled across onto the Promenade. She was then taken along the road to the D Day Museum at Southsea Common for display.

but in 1986 she was given a major refit and moved to Gibraltar as *Seacore Dragon* under the ownership of Vantage Shipping Limited. She was demolished in 1989.

LCT7074/ Landfall

The Type 3 *LCT7074* was launched on 30 March 1944 by Hawthorn Leslie at Hebburn. She served in Operation 'Overlord' in June 1944 at Normandy and was decommissioned in 1948. She was one of a class of 311 LCT Mark 3 ships which were capable of carrying ten 30-ton armoured vehicles and were 192ft long by 30ft beam. They were equipped with twin Paxman oil engines, although some had twin petrol engines, but both types were capable of 9 knots.

On decommissioning, *LCT7074* was presented to the Master Mariners' Club of Liverpool for use as a club ship and given the name *Landfall*. She was moored in Canning Dock. Much later she was converted into a floating nightclub, and in the late 1990s the vessel was acquired by the Warship Preservation Trust and moved across the river to Birkenhead. In January 2006, the Trust went into liquidation and the ship was left unattended; by April 2010 she had sunk at her berth. The craft was refloated on 16 October 2014 and moved to Portsmouth for renovation as *LCT7074*. She is now on public display at Southsea.

A press statement was issued to coincide with the ship arriving at Portsmouth:

> The importance of D-Day cannot be underestimated, the liberation forces which landed on the beaches at Normandy were a prelude to victory in Europe and this humble, but vital ship, played a significant role for the Royal Navy. Also, importantly her sheer size – a 600 ton ocean going vessel capable of carrying ten 30 ton armoured vehicles – challenges the common perception that landing craft were small assault craft.

10

LANDING SHIPS, TANK

The Landing Ship, Tank was a logical development from the Landing Craft, Tank. In June 1940, British Prime Minister Winston Churchill identified a need for a new breed of seagoing ship which could land tanks and personnel directly onto hostile beaches. By October, a prototype landing ship was already on trial. Churchill's demand for a ship which could carry sixty tanks was modified by the Director of Naval Construction to a design with a more modest but more practical capacity of only twenty-five tanks. The result, some 18 months later, was the Type 1 Landing Ship, Tank, commonly known as the *Boxer* class. Only three ships were built, all by Harland & Wolf at Belfast: HMS *Boxer* (F121), HMS *Bruiser* (F127) and HMS *Thruster* (F131). They had twin screws each driven by steam turbine machinery arranged amidships and the funnel was offset to starboard to leave a clear tank deck onto which thirteen 30-ton tanks could be loaded. The ships could also accommodate 193 troops. The vessels were 376ft long by 49ft breadth. The hull construction was a hybrid with longitudinal framing along the flat bottom of the ships and on the vehicle decks to provide strength for grounding onto a beach with a distributed load of tanks, while the sides of the hull were built with conventional transverse framing. The bows had additional strengthening to withstand the stress of beaching.

Before the first of the *Boxer* class was commissioned, America entered the war and the Lend-Lease Act was agreed. Under this Act it was arranged that Type 2 Landing Ships, Tank would be built in the United States; the Type 2 Landing Ship, Tank was 328ft long by 50ft breadth and built of all-welded construction and was designed to carry eighteen tanks, each weighing up to 30 tons. The minimum design draft at the bow was just 3ft 4in when unloaded and up to 7ft 6in when loaded. There was a ramp that allowed vehicles access from the tank deck to the main deck, with access to the tank deck through bow doors and a long retractable loading ramp. The Type 2 ships were driven by two 12-cylinder oil engines and could maintain a speed of 10 knots; a small number were equipped with triple-expansion steam engines due to supply problems with the oil engines. A total of 115 ships were transferred to Britain, of which 110 were retained as Type 2 Landing Ships, Tank. The remaining five were adapted for specialist duties, *LST81* and *LST82* were converted to Landing Ships, Emergency Repair, and *LST13*, *LST216* and *LST217* into Fighter Direction Tenders.

Brian Macdermott wrote in *Sea Breezes*, July 1992:

> Although the LST idea was British, the design was prepared by John Neidermair, of the US Bureau of Ships. Neidermair had a background in submarine design and this was put to good use in LSTs by devising a system of ballast tanks. For ocean crossings they would take on ballast giving them a draught of around 7 feet forward and 13 feet 6 inches aft. For beaching, the draught would be reduced to around 3 feet forward and 9 feet 6 inches aft …

The metacentric height (unloaded) was extremely high which resulted in heavy rolling with a short period – 20-25° roll was reported in a period of nine seconds. This heavy rolling, as with a following sea, often had the propellers racing as they came nearer to the surface of the sea and met less resistance to their thrust. With their shallow draught and extensive freeboard, they could be difficult to manoeuvre, particularly in high winds.

The war record of the Type 2 Landing Ships, Tank reads like naval history: Malta, Sicily, Baytown (Messina), Salerno, Anzio, and then out of the Mediterranean to Operation 'Overlord' on the Normandy beaches in which fifty British Landing Ships, Tank were used. The surviving Type 2 ships were all returned to the United States after the war.

An improved version of the Type 2, the Type 3 Landing Ship, Tank, was first commissioned in the spring of 1945. These ships had better accommodation and were constructed both in North America and in Britain to a higher specification than the Type 2 ships. The Type 3 vessels were driven by two steam reciprocating engines driving twin shafts, and they could manage in excess of 10 knots in favourable conditions. The engines had 18½in, 31in and 38½in-diameter cylinders with a 30in stroke, and were sourced from a variety of builders including the Canadian Pacific Railway, Angus Shops at Montreal. The ships were 347ft long and 54ft broad with a depth of 12ft, varying slightly depending on where they had been built, and they all had longitudinal framing, bottom and sides, similar to that of a modern tanker. Some of the ships saw action in the relief of Norway and Denmark and the invasion of Malaya. As time went on, the Type 3 ships were progressively laid up in the Clyde.

A major task at the end of the Second World War was the recovery of stores, vehicles and other equipment. In 1946 the Royal Army Service Corps civilian fleet adopted seven of the Type 3 Landing

LST3024 (1945) was one of the seven Landing Ships, Tank transferred from the Navy to the Royal Army Service Corps in 1946. She was named *Maxwell Brander*.

Ships, Tank from the Royal Navy. These ships flew the Red Ensign and were named after distinguished corps officers: *Evan Gibb*, *Charles Macleod*, *Maxwell Brander*, *Snowden Smith*, *Humfrey Gale*, *Reginald Kerr* and *Fredrick Clover*. The ships needed to be brought up to commercial standards, requiring refits and alterations as well as additional crew accommodation. In due course five of the ships sailed for work in the Middle East, and two of them were deployed to the Far East. An early task for two of the Middle East ships was the evacuation of Palestine. *Humfrey Gale* and *Evan Gibb* made fifteen voyages each between Haifa and Port Said with British vehicles and stores.

During the war the strategic importance of the landing ships had been displayed repeatedly. It did not require too much imagination to visualise a commercial role for the ships. The demands on merchant shipping were accentuated in the immediate post-war years by the shortage of vessels, and the lack of materials with which to construct new ones. One of the three Type 1 ships, HMS *Bruiser* was sold for commercial service after the war. A few of the older Type 2 Landing Ships, Tank found commercial buyers, despite their known weakness of construction and poor sea handling. Not so the

Type 3s, which were all nearly new (most completed in 1945) and which had not suffered the ravages and extremes of war.

Type 1 Landing Ship, Tank – the cruise ship *Silverstar*

The Type 1 ship HMS *Bruiser* was bought by a Belgian company in 1946 which planned to convert her into a cargo ship. She was renamed *Nilla*, but the conversion was later abandoned and the ship was offered for sale again in 1948. A prospective sale which fell through saw the ship renamed *Silver Star* and she was eventually bought in 1950 by Swiss businessman Vassile L Winkler and registered in Panama. In 1951 her registered owner became Compania Naviera Estrella de Plata SA of Panama and the ship's name was altered to *Silverstar*. Howaldtswerke AG, Hamburg was awarded the contract for the conversion of the ship into a luxury cruise liner as well as lengthening her by 22ft. The work involved the provision of 171 air-conditioned cabins for 420 passengers and two new funnels, the forward one a dummy. Anthony Cooke wrote in *Sea Breezes*, June 2020:

> There was a cave-like nightclub called La Grotta, complete with plaster stalactites. One of her other bars had tartan carpeting, and then there was the Can-Can Bar whose walls were covered in velvet. The other public rooms were a lounge with a dance floor, the inevitable smoking room, a card and writing room and a general-purpose lounge which contained an altar. There was a swimming pool forward of the bridge.

In 1952 the newly-commissioned *Silverstar* was chartered to Silver Star Line (Arnold Bernstein Shipping Company, Managers) and used for cruises from Washington DC, Charleston, Miami or New Orleans to the Caribbean, calling at Nassau, Havana and Vera Cruz as well as into the Atlantic to Bermuda. However, the United States authorities worried about the stability of the vessel and restricted her to Caribbean duties in the winter months. Once a year, at the end of the summer, she sailed to West Germany for her regular dry-docking. The charter ended in December 1956 and she then undertook one cruise for Caribbean Cruise Lines. She was sold in January 1957 to Flota Argentina de Navegación Fluvial, Buenos Aires and renamed *Cuidad de Santa Fe* and was initially used on the Buenos Aires to Montevideo ferry and later on the River Paraná between Rosario and Assunción. Following collision damage in 1965 she was laid up and later scrapped in 1968.

An advertising image for the luxury Caribbean cruise ship *Silverstar* (1941), built as the Type 1 Landing Ship, Tank HMS *Bruiser*

Type 2 Landing Ships, Tank

Two of the Type 2 ships, *LST365* and *LST386*, were bought for use as floating platforms for experimentation with freezing fish at sea. *LST365* was completed by Bethlem Steel Company, Shipbuilding Division at Quandincy, Massachusetts in 1943; *LST386* was laid down by the Newport News Shipbuilding & Engineering Company in June 1942 and commissioned into the Royal Navy in December 1944. Both ships were equipped with two 12-cylinder oil engines. *LST386* was one of a number of Type 2 ships converted for use as an aircraft carrier with a 216ft long makeshift flight deck and a recovery crane.

Both *LST365* and *LST386* were decommissioned in 1946, and sold to Fresh Frozen Foods Limited in 1947 and 1948 and registered in Glasgow with the names *Mowbray Road* and *Barnes Park* respectively. Fresh Frozen Foods was the trading name of Sir Dennistoun Burney who was experimenting with fast-freezing techniques to prepare and store fish taken from trawlers at sea. The house flag of the company was that of the racing colours of the company's chairman, Mowbray Road and Barnes Park apparently being two of his race horses.

In 1948 Fresh Frozen Foods was acquired by Christian Salvesen Limited of Leith, and the experimental work was continued aboard the converted *Algerine* class minesweeper *Fairfree* (see Chapter 14). Both the former LSTs were assigned to Seafreeze Industries Limited, Wakefield. *Barnes Park* was sold in 1951 and used for further trading under the name *Sant' Anna*. She was eventually broken up in 1973.

Mowbray Road was used in British and Eastern Mediterranean waters for fish processing and freezing. On a voyage from Southampton in early 1949 she suffered engine failure and had to put into Falmouth for repairs. Later in the year she was stripped of her freezing plant and chartered to British Railways for a period of 12 months. She carried standard unit load railway containers on wheeled flats on a daily service between Barrow and Belfast. Although a sensible development of roll-on roll-off traffic, there was insufficient inducement to retain the ship after her initial 12-month charter and she was returned to her owners. The unit load traffic reverted to the Heysham and Belfast overnight cargo service. In 1952 *Mowbray Road* was sold to the Indonesian Navy, and renamed *Adri I*. In 1968 she was sold back into the commercial sector as *Daliah*, then owned by the Moro-Laut Shipping Company, Jakarta, and was sold for demolition shortly afterwards.

A number of other Type 2 Landing Ships, Tank were also sold for commercial service, mainly to owners based in the Philippines and in the Middle East and a few also to American companies. Most of the remaining ships that survived the war were sold for demolition while some were sold or transferred to overseas navies for further service as transports.

Type 3 Landing Ships, Tank

A number of Type 3 ships remained incomplete on the stocks at the end of the war. While some were scrapped as they lay, the more complete hulls were offered for sale. *LST3030* was completed in 1947 as a single-deck herring oil factory ship for A/S Clupea (S Bartz Johannessen, Managers) of Bergen with the name *Clupea*. A group of five ships, *LST3004*, *LST3018*, *LST3023*, *LST3032* and *LST3039*, were completed as the cargo ships *Rio Tejo*, *Rio Minho*, *Rio Guadiana*, *Rio Mondego* and *Rio Duoro* respectively, for E G Fontes & Cia, Rio de Janeiro. The hulls were towed to Rio where the conversion work was carried out between 1949 and 1952. The ships were mainly used on a service between Trinidad and Rio. They mostly lasted in service until the mid-1960s.

A group of redundant Type 3 Landing Ships, Tank had an important commercial role after the war. The man with the commercial vision for the Type 3 LST as a roll-on roll-off ferry was Frank

Bustard. Formerly an employee of the White Star Line and latterly an army officer who had witnessed the early trials of the Landing Ship, Tank both at New Brighton and at Barrow Docks, Bustard was well aware of the commercial potential of these vessels. Forsaking his life-long ambition to introduce a Freddy Laker style no-frills transatlantic liner passenger service, Bustard obtained an initial three-year charter on three Landing Ships, Tank during the summer of 1946. The charter fee for each ship was a paltry £13-6 shillings per day! The young James Callaghan, MP, was instrumental in arranging the charter in his capacity as Parliamentary Private Secretary to the Minister of War Transport.

Delivery of the three ships took place at Tilbury, whereupon they were each put in the hands of the Ship Repair Department of Harland & Wolff for a three-week conversion ready for their peacetime role. During their refit, the wheelhouse was raised by one deck and enclosed, the separate engine rooms were interconnected, crew accommodation was improved and space was set aside for up to twelve passengers (vehicle drivers) in a saloon-cum-dining room that was shared with the ship's officers; there were no berths for other passengers available at that stage. New funnels, lifeboats and navigational aids were also fitted. Vehicles could be loaded through the bow doors onto the main (tank) deck, and access to the upper deck was via a steep internal ramp.

As a concession to Bustard's yen for the White Star Line, the compulsory 'Empire' names for Government ownership were followed by sympathetic second names: the *LST 3519* became the *Empire Baltic*, the *LST 3534* became the *Empire Cedric* and the *LST 3512* became the *Empire Celtic* (see Table 3). Gone was the drab grey livery of wartime and in its place were three smartly-painted ships with black hulls and a broad white riband, white superstructure and blue funnels

Empire Celtic (1945), formerly *LST3512*, was one of the three original chartered LSTs that were the foundation of Frank Bustard's Atlantic Steam Navigation Company Limited. Note the military deck cargo destined for Hamburg

with a black top and a broad white band. On the bow was the blue and white arrow logo adopted by the charter party, the Atlantic Steam Navigation Company.

The first voyage for the Atlantic Steam Navigation Company (named after Bustard's transatlantic liner ambitions) took place on 11 September 1946. *Empire Baltic* left Tilbury with a cargo of lorries destined for Rotterdam – duly discharged over the beach at Waalhaven where the bow doors promptly became stuck in the sand. Michael Bustard reports in the company history (Cowsill, 1990):

> Eventually, the bow doors slowly opened only to find that the bottom corners of the port door stuck in the sandy bottom of the beach. The hero of the day – a Mr Bottomley, one of the stevedores – called for a spade and jumping into the water fully clothed immediately began to shovel sand away over 1 metre below the surface of the water. Eventually the door freed itself, thanks, I suspect, more to the tipping of the ship than to his digging efforts; the bow ramp came down and the cargo of lorries was driven ashore – getting rather wet in the process. The whole operation took place in this rather desolate section of the port of Rotterdam against a skyline of heavily blitzed warehouses, and I well remember the only spectators of this historic occasion were some rather thin and hungry looking Dutch boys leaning on the handle-bars of their bicycles.

The inaugural four-day round trip to Rotterdam was followed by the introduction of a regular

LST3507 (1945) was modified as *Empire Gaelic* when she joined Bustard's fleet in 1948 when the new service started between Preston and Larne. From a company postcard which states on the back 'Continental Line Transport Ferry Service, operates regular services between Tilbury and Hamburg and Preston/N Ireland. For the carriage of all types of vehicles and containers.' (Transport Ferry Service)

service between Tilbury and Hamburg with departures every other day; the cargo comprised vehicles for the British Army of the Rhine. The service to Hamburg was maintained until 1955 when it was transferred to Antwerp. *Empire Baltic* hit a mine on 24 September 1949, despite following the swept channel; she was able to get safely to Emden where repairs were carried out. Winter ice damage to the bow doors was commonplace. A small amount of commercial traffic began to join the military cargo as time went on, but British licensing restrictions severely inhibited access for foreign commercial vehicles at home, and at that time the nationalised British Road Services and Pickfords had no interest in venturing overseas.

A new service to Northern Ireland commenced

Table 3: TYPE 3 LANDING SHIPS TANK IN COMMERCIAL SERVICE AND REGISTERED IN THE UK – ALL SHIPS COMPLETED IN 1945

Naval name	Merchant Name	Builder	Scrapped
Vehicle ferries chartered to Atlantic Steam Navigation Company			
LST3519	*Empire Baltic*	Canadian Vickers Ltd, Montreal	1962, La Spezia, Italy
LST3534	*Empire Cedric*	Vickers Ltd, Esquimalt, British Columbia	1960, Ghent, Belgium
LST3512	*Empire Celtic*	Davie Shipbuilding & Repair Co, Lauzon, Canada	1962, La Spezia, Italy
LST3010/HMS *Attacker*	*Empire Cymric*	Harland & Wolff, Belfast	1963, Faslane
LST3041	*Empire Doric*	Harland & Wolff, Govan	1960, Port Glasgow
LST3507	*Empire Gaelic*	Davie Shipbuilding & Repairing Co Lauzon, Canada	1960, Burcht, Belgium
LST3026/HMS *Charger*	*Empire Nordic*	Blyth Drydock & Shipbuilding Co	1968, Bilbao, Spain
Managed for Ministry of Transport on a commercial basis			
LST3042/HMS *Hunter*	*Empire Curlew*	Harland & Wolff, Govan	1962, La Spezia, Italy
LST3524/HMS *Trumpeter*	*Empire Fulmar*	Davie Shipbuilding & Repairing Co, Lauzon, Canada	1969, Singapore
LST3006/HMS *Tromsø*	*Empire Gannet*	Harland & Wolff, Belfast	1968, Singapore
LST 3038/HMS *Fighter*	*Empire Grebe*	Fairfield Shipbuilding & Engineering Co, Govan	1968, Singapore
LST3525/HMS *Walcheren*	*Empire Guillemot*	Harland & Wolff, Belfast	1968, Singapore
LST3523/HMS *Trouncer*	*Empire Gull*	Davie Shipbuilding & Repairing Co, Lauzon, Canada	1980, Santander, Spain
LST3510/HMS *Slinger*	*Empire Kittiwake*	Davie Shipbuilding & Repairing Co, Lauzon, Canada	1968, Singapore
LST3520/HMS *Thruster*	*Empire Petrel*	Canadian Vickers Ltd, Montreal	1968, Singapore
LST3015/HMS *Battler*	*Empire Puffin*	Barclay Curle & Co Ltd, Glasgow	1966, La Spezia, Italy
LST3033	*Empire Shearwater*	William Pickersgill & Sons Ltd, Southwick	1962, Ghent
LST3517/HMS *St Nazaire*	*Empire Skua*	Vickers Ltd, Esquimalt, British Columbia	1968, La Spezia, Italy
LST3504/HMS *Pursuer*	*Empire Tern*	Canadian Vickers Ltd, Montreal	1968, Singapore
Managed for Royal Army Service Corps on a commercial basis			
LST3021	Charles Mcleod	Lithgows Limited, Port Glasgow	1968, La Spezia, Italy
LST3037	Evan Gibb	Fairfield Shipbuilding & Engineering Co, Govan	1963, La Spezia, Italy
LST3001	Frederick Clover	Vickers Armstrong, Walker on Tyne	1966, sold, renamed *Pacific Pioneer*, 1968 Hong Kong
LST3509	Humfrey Gale	Davie Shipbuilding & Repairing Co, Lauzon, Canada	1961 Italy
LST3024	Maxwell Brander	Smith's Dock, Middlesbrough	1968, sold, renamed *Fedredge Isabel*, 1969 Hong Kong
LST3009	Reginald Kerr	Harland & Wolff, Belfast	1966, Hong Kong
LST3028	Snowden Smith	Alexander Stephens, Linthouse	1964, sold, renamed *Eblano Primo*, 1969 Italy

in 1948. Rejected by the Mersey Docks and Harbour Board, the proprietors of the Atlantic Steam Navigation Company turned to the ports of Preston and Larne to support their new enterprise. The route was opened by *Empire Cedric* on 20 May 1948 after she had been converted at Belfast to carry forty-eight drivers. Less than a third of this complement was berthed; passenger berths were accessed from the open main deck – a long and sometimes wet and windy walk at night to the nearest sink or toilet. Loading at Larne was by means of a ramp installed by the army during the war, but at Preston part of a Mulberry Harbour pontoon unit was brought to Preston Dock and a bridge installed to link it to the quayside adjacent to the cattle lairage. *Empire Cedric* ran two round trips per week.

Initial cargo manifests included very few vehicles, but Frank Bustard's faith paid off as business eventually built up. *Empire Cedric* was joined on the service by *Empire Doric*, which took her first sailing from Preston on 26 October 1948 and *Empire Gaelic* which commenced on 6 January 1949, both ships having transferred from Tilbury. *Empire Cedric* inaugurated a new weekly service directly to Belfast on 15 January 1951, later increased to twice weekly, the other two ships running four round trips to Larne.

In 1952 the seven Landing Ships, Tank operated by the Royal Army Service Corps were placed by the War Office under the management of the Atlantic Steam Navigation Company. They all wore ASN company colours and were registered in London. These ships had been vested with the Royal Army Service Corps after the war and were given names of distinguished servicemen (see Table 3).

The fortunes of the company were enhanced in April 1953 when the Atlantic Steam Navigation Company was acquired by the British Transport Commission and many of the shares were subtly put into the name of the national haulier British Road Services. This move brought an end to the British inhibition to allow UK commercial vehicles to venture onto the Continent. Two more Landing Ships, Tank were brought into the fleet in 1955: the *Empire Cymric* formerly HMS *Attacker*, and the *Empire Nordic* ex-HMS *Charger*. These ships were converted by Harland & Wolff at Govan.

With the Suez Crisis in the latter part of 1956, the remaining ten Landing Ships, Tank were taken out of reserve and also entrusted to the management of the Atlantic Steam Navigation Company. Each of these ships was given an 'Empire-bird' name and full company colours. These were the *Empire Curlew*, *Empire Fulmar*, *Empire Gannet*, *Empire Grebe*, *Empire Guillemot*, *Empire Gull*, *Empire Kittiwake*, *Empire Petrel*, *Empire Puffin*, *Empire Shearwater*, *Empire Skua* and *Empire Tern*. The total complement of seventeen ships were now managed on behalf of the Ministry of Transport, and were sent to bases at Malta, Aden and Singapore. This meant that the commercial roll-on roll-off service between Preston and Northern Ireland had to be suspended on 17 August 1956 with the entire fleet sailing to Malta on 1 November.

Empire Gull was chartered to reopen the Tilbury and Antwerp service on 13 November 1956 and was followed by *Empire Baltic* on 13 January. *Empire Nordic* reopened the Preston and Larne route on 17 January 1957 with *Empire Cymric* and *Empire Cedric* joining shortly afterwards, while *Empire Gaelic* was back in service at Preston from 13 March. The spare ships were again laid up in reserve.

Management of one of the remaining ships, *Empire Shearwater*, was transferred to European Ferries Limited (a subsidiary of Townsend Brothers, Ferries Limited) in 1958. *Empire Shearwater*, completed in 1945 as *LST 3033*, had been laid up in the Clyde since 1951 along with a number of her siblings, and was recalled to service during the Suez Crisis. In 1958 Townsend Brothers, Ferries Limited's entire share capital was taken over by George Knott Industries; the new parent company took *Empire Shearwater* on charter from the Ministry of Transport, and had her adapted to run between the Eastern Arm ramp at Dover and an existing linkspan at Calais. The intention was to provide a daily return service for commercial vehicles at low cost in direct competition with the Atlantic Steam Navigation Company's service between Tilbury and Antwerp.

A new company, European Ferries Limited, was registered to look after the enterprise. The ship was taken to the Clyde for necessary work to bring her into line with commercial requirements and she was registered at Dover. She wore the George Knot Logo on her funnel, and first arrived at Dover on 12 January 1959 under the command of Captain W Allen. *Empire Shearwater* started the new commercial lorry service one week later, but after only six months was withdrawn and laid up in the Medway below Chatham. The concept was ahead of its time. Hauliers were reluctant to send lorries to the Continent through Calais, as the paperwork involved for loaded goods vehicles at French Customs was at best tortuous.

In 1960 *Empire Puffin* was chartered to, and managed by, K C Irving, St John, New Brunswick.

Empire Tern (1945) was originally *LST3504* and later renamed HMS *Pursuer*. She is seen at Malta in the colours of the Atlantic Steam Navigation Company.

During 1961 the Ministry of Transport transferred the management of the remaining ten military Landing Ships, Tank to the British India Steam Navigation Company. At the same time management of the seven Royal Army Service Corps ships was also transferred to the British India Steam Navigation Company, and the blue, white and black funnels were repainted in black with two white bands. Tasked by the War Office directly, the Royal Army Service Corps then had no further involvement with the administration of the ships. All the vessels were phased out shortly afterwards and sold for demolition apart from *Empire Gull* which transferred to the Royal Fleet Auxiliary (RFA) in February 1970.

The old Landing Ships, Tank in the Atlantic Steam Navigation Company's fleet, having provided sterling service, were slowly displaced by a new generation of purpose-built vehicle and passenger ferries. *Empire Cedric*, *Empire Doric* and *Empire Gaelic* were disposed of in 1960, *Empire Doric* having been laid up at Gare Loch since January 1957. *Empire Baltic* and *Empire Celtic* were returned to the Ministry of Transport during 1962 and spent much of the year laid up in the River Fal. They were dispatched to a shipbreaker's yard at La Spezia in the autumn, where it was planned to retain the midship sections of the ships for use as a floating jetty. By the end of 1963 only *Empire Nordic* remained with the Atlantic Steam Navigation Company.

Strangely, such were the commercial demands on the company during the rebuilding programme, that another Landing Ship, Tank was brought into the fleet even before *Empire Nordic* retired. This was the *Baltic Ferry*. The Landing Ship, Dock *AMD1* also came into Atlantic Steam Navigation Company ownership as the passenger and vehicle ferry *Celtic Ferry* (see Chapter 11).

In February 1970, *Empire Gull* was the only remaining Type 3 Landing Ship, Tank, under the Red Ensign, all the others having been sold or scrapped. When transferred from British India

Empire Nordic (1945), formerly *LST3026* and later renamed HMS *Charger*, is seen approaching Preston Dock on the River Ribble in August 1966. (Author)

management to the RFA her crew were recruited at Hong Kong and many of these men stayed with the ship after the change of management. She operated in the Mediterranean until August 1970, when she was sent to Sunderland for a major refit. After that she was used mainly on the Marchwood to Antwerp shuttle service for the British Army in Europe, or occasionally used on the Liverpool to Belfast runs for the troops in Northern Ireland. Chris Puxley described *Empire Gull* in her RFA days in the Mediterranean (http://www.historical-rfa.org):

> I flew from Heathrow to Cyprus, along with a few other RFA officers, to join the *Empire Gull* which was berthed at Famagusta. She looked very different to the normal RFA's we were all familiar with. This rather squat vessel had a black hull, white superstructure and a buff coloured funnel. The accommodation inside was very basic, painted pale green and the fittings were fabricated in thin steel plate, rather than the wood or Formica type materials that we were used to. She had two engines and propellers, which made her quite manoeuvrable. Her cargo space consisted of a large rectangular shaped tank deck, with doors at the bow, above which was the vehicle deck which had a ramp that could be lowered to the deck below and a cargo hatch served by derricks mounted on a pair of samson posts. Troop dormitories ran along either side of the tank deck. A stern anchor enabled the ship to haul herself off a beach or away from a landing stage after having discharged or loaded her cargo.

Empire Gull, the last of her kind, was eventually laid up at Portsmouth in 1978 and sold to Spanish breakers in March 1980.

Landing Ships, Logistics

The successor to the Landing Ship, Tank was the Landing Ship, Logistics of the 'Round Table' class. The first was *Sir Lancelot* (L3029). In December 1961 the following announcement was made: War Office Military Supply Ship:

> A 6,000 ton ocean-going twin screw military supply vessel has been ordered by the MOT from the Fairfield Shipbuilding and Engineering Co. Ltd. at Govan, who are to develop the final specifications of the ship,

Empire Gull (1945) completed as *LST353* and later renamed HMS *Trouncer*, was transferred to the RFA in February 1970 and adopted the livery seen here.

which is expected to cost about £1 million. Building will start around February 1962 and the ship is expected to be in service late in 1963 or early in 1964. The design calls for a fast troop and vehicle carrier capable of discharging onto beaches. She will have bow and stern loading facilities for tanks and military vehicles, ramp loading hatches, cargo handling cranes and provision for carrying and launching pontoons. A helicopter will be carried aft, and on completion she will have a Merchant Navy crew and will be managed by the British India Steam Navigation Co Ltd.

In March 1963 it was announced that tenders were to be invited for a further two vessels at a cost of £2 million each and would be part of an eventual class of five or six ships, all of which would be named after Knights of the Round Table. The final three vessels were ordered in April 1965, and in December 1968 it was announced that as from January 1970, the management of these six vessels, as well as that of the LST *Empire Gull*, would be transferred to the RFA.

Of the six vessels one, *Sir Galahad*, was lost in the Falklands War in June 1982, and only one, *Sir Lancelot*, was sold for commercial service. She was purchased in June 1989 for £339,500 by Lowline (Rambler) Limited (Lowline Ltd, Managers), London and renamed *Lowland Lancer*. Until then Lowline was better known as an offshore support contractor. *Lowland Lancer* was intended for a new passenger and vehicle ferry service between Weymouth and Cherbourg under the banner Westward Ferries. She commenced in June 1990 with significantly upgraded accommodation for 500 passengers, 200 cars and up to 18 commercial vehicles. She was scheduled to depart from Weymouth at 11 pm every night, and return the following day. The service was terminated in December 1990 ostensibly because of adverse time slots allocated at Cherbourg, a dispute that started with the French authorities during the summer months. Loadings up until then had been reasonable and the ship had been operated at a profit.

In mid-January 1991 *Lowland Lancer* was chartered as relief for the new St Helena mail ship, aptly named *St Helena*, which had broken down on her maiden voyage south in December 1990, so putting her out of commission while she received a new engine. *Lowland Lancer* made a single voyage from Cardiff to St Helena and on to Cape Town. She in turn broke down at Ascension where she was forced to lay over for nearly two weeks while engine repairs were carried out. *Lowland Lancer* was not very well received with her poor cabin accommodation and separate dormitory berths for men and women. At the termination of the charter she remained at Cape Town and was later converted for use as an offshore casino, under the banner of Southern Offshore Leisure taking passengers out beyond the three-mile limit. In October 1992 she was purchased by the Government of Singapore, Department of Defence, for use as a Transport in the Singapore Navy and renamed *Perseverance*.

LANDING SHIPS, TANK   113

![ship image]

Following a variety of other roles, she was eventually broken up in Bangladesh in 2008. The 'Round Table' class was succeeded by the 'Bay' class of four amphibious dock landing ships.

Lowland Lancer (1963) was built as the lead ship, *Sir Lancelot*, of the six 'Round Table' class Landing Ships, Logistics and was bought for commercial service in 1989. (Mike Lennon)

The present-day successor to the LST and the 'Round Table' class ships is the 'Bay' class amphibious Landing Ship, Dock. *Mounts Bay* (2004) is one of this class of four ships. (Author)

11

UNITED STATES NAVY AND ROYAL CANADIAN NAVY VESSELS AFTER THE SECOND WORLD WAR

Nothing the size of or larger than a destroyer was sold for commercial service either by the United States Navy or by the Royal Canadian Navy. The Americans tended to scrap the smaller vessels that were unserviceable and keep the remainder in the Reserve Fleets, while some ships were sold to overseas navies, notably Brazil and other South American states, as well as some other nations. Most of the smaller ships sent to Britain under Lend-Lease were sold, many for commercial service (see Chapters 7, 8, 10, 12 and 14). With the exception of Landing Ships, Tank (see Chapter 10) the largest vessels from the United States Navy that were bought for conversion for merchant service after the Second World War were 'Flower' class corvettes. Much of the Canadian fleet was sold for scrap after the war, many ships being unserviceable, while there was little commercial interest in the others. Some of the Canadian vessels continued their military careers under the French and Dutch flags, while the largest ships that were sold for merchant service were 'River' class frigates.

United States Navy

USS *Action* (PG86), was the lead ship of the *Action* class patrol boats. This class were 205ft long and 33ft broad, and had a deep draft of 14ft. They were equipped with four gun mounts and twin depth-charge tracks and had a crew of ninety. USS *Action* was laid down as CN-304 on 6 January 1942 by Collingwood Shipyards Limited, Collingwood, Canada; she was launched as HMS *Comfrey* on 28 July 1942 and then commissioned into the United States Navy in November 1942 as USS *Action*. In 1948 she was sold to Jonassons Rederier, Helsingborg, Sweden, with no change of name and converted into an engines-aft cargo ship with three hatches served by four derricks. There was no resemblance of her former military appearance.

Action was resold in August 1951 to J Presthus, Bergen, Norway, and renamed *Arne Presthus*. As such she traded mostly to southern Europe until sold in 1967 to Orri Navigation Lines, Jeddah, Saudi Arabia and renamed *Star of Marium*. In 1972 she was transferred to Fontana Shipping

The Norwegian cargo ship *Arne Presthus* (1942) shows no resemblance to her former self as the patrol boat USS *Action*. (SkyFotos)

Company of Cyprus as *Star of Beirut*, reverting to her former owners as *Star of Rawiah* early in 1972. On 6 April that same year she stranded near the Ashrafi Light near Suez on passage Suez to Safaga and was declared a constructive total loss. Given that the ship started life as a wartime patrol boat, she enjoyed a fruitful commercial career lasting 24 years.

Another example of a useful commercial career was that of USS *Brisk* (PG89), launched as the modified 'Flower' class corvette HMS *Flax*, and which was also designated as an *Action* class patrol boat in the United States Navy. She was sold to Tuxen & Hagemann of Copenhagen in 1947 without change of name, and converted into a cargo ship with holds forward of the bridge in a similar manner to *Arne Prethus*. *Brisk* was sold in 1951 to International Trading Corporation, registered in Liberia and renamed *Ariana*. Between 1954 and 1963 she traded as *Arvida Bay* for two further owners while she was still registered in Liberia, and she was then renamed *Zaida* and registered in Honduras. She was deleted from the register in 1999.

An *Action* class patrol boat that also provided valuable commercial service following conversion for peacetime duties was USS *Haste* (PG92). She was sold in 1949 to Carlo Cameli of Genoa, Italy and converted for use as a passenger ferry with the name *Porto Azzuro*. She was sold in 1950 to SA Navigazione Toscana of Leghorn, Italy, retaining her name, and was later withdrawn from service in 1971 and scrapped. The few other corvettes in the United States Navy were either lost to enemy action, sold to other nations as fighting ships after the war or scrapped.

A number of the small *PC842* class Patrol Craft Escort were sold to commercial interests both immediately after the war had ended and again in 1970 when ships were released from the Reserve Fleets. All the surviving vessels of this class sent to Britain under Lend-Lease were sold for commercial use, seven of them as passenger ships working on the west coast of Norway (see Chapter 7).

The United States built and maintained nearly 200 minesweepers. There were five classes of minesweeper: *Auk* class, Auxiliary Motor Minesweepers, *Hawk* class which were bought from commercial owners and returned after the war, *Lapwing* class and *Raven* class.

The *Auk* class displaced 890 tons on average, and were between 220 and 225ft in length. They had diesel-electric machinery and could make 18 knots for brief periods. The ships were equipped with one 3in gun, two 40mm Bofors guns, and eight 20mm Oerlikons. Twenty of the *Auk* class were transferred to the Royal Navy as the *Catherine* class, three were sunk in action, and seventeen were returned to the United States after the war. Most of these were sold to Greece and Turkey to continue their military careers. None of the seventy-five *Auk*s retained by the United States Navy, was sold commercially after the war. However, USS *Vital* (AM129) which was transferred to the Royal Navy was sold in 1947 and converted into the passenger excursion ship *Evening Star* and later renamed *Pride of the West* (see Chapter 14).

Auxiliary motor minesweepers were small wooden-hulled vessels originally designated yard minesweepers (YMS) which kept the YMS designation after being re-classified as auxiliary motor minesweepers. About 480 ships were built, many going to the Royal Navy under Lend-Lease. After the war most were dispersed to foreign navies or placed in reserve, while others were scrapped. Several were sold out of reserve to commercial owners, USS *Albatross* (YMS80/AMS1), for example was sold in 1959 to become the fishing vessel *Dorado* owned by Dorado Inc. based in New Jersey; USS *YMS268* was also sold in 1959 becoming the fishing vessel *Weems* for Standard Products Company Inc. of Virginia, she ended her days as a cargo boat in the Caribbean. USS *YMS470* was sold in 1959 to General Motors Defense Research Laboratories at Santa Barbara for use as a research boat. Another, USS *Swan/PCS1401*, was sold out of reserve in 1963 for use as a survey ship for Marine Exploration Company of Miami.

USS *YMS328* is still in service. She was sold in 1948 to Harold Jones of Vancouver and converted for use as a yacht with the new name *La Beverie*. Max Wyman of Seattle purchased the yacht in 1956 and renamed her *Wild Goose II*. In 1962, she was bought from Wyman by the actor John Wayne for US$116,000 and the ship was put through a major programme of renovation and upgrading. Wayne changed her name to *Wild Goose*, and kept the ship for the last 17 years of his life. She could berth twelve passengers and had a crew of six. Richard Nixon and Ronald Reagan were among the many guests entertained aboard the ship which Wayne described as his sanctuary and proudest possession. *Wild Goose* featured in the 1963 film *Skidoo* starring Groucho Marx, and the 1967 film *The President's Analyst*, in which the yacht became a Canadian spy ship. The vessel is still in use; owned by Hornblower Cruises of Newport Beach, California she is now available for short dinner cruises. The yacht was listed on the National Park Service National Register of Historic Places in 2011.

Forty-nine *Lapwing* class minesweepers were built towards the end of the Great War, and many of them served through the Second World War. They were equipped with triple-expansion steam engines and could maintain 14 knots. A few were sold after the war to commercial owners and some were scrapped, but most remained in service into the 1950s.

The *Raven* class comprised just two ships, USS *Raven* and USS *Osprey*. Only the former survived the war and she was placed in reserve and later used as a target and sunk.

In 1941, the United States Navy requisitioned a number of trawlers and tuna clippers for coastal defence work. They were designated as Auxiliary Minesweepers. Surviving vessels were returned to their owners post-hostilities.

A large number of 110ft-long wooden-hulled

John Wayne's *Wild Goose* (1942), her hull constructed from Douglas fir, was commissioned as *YMS328*, and is seen in her current guise as a day cruise ship based at Newport Beach, California.

submarine chasers, the *SC497* class, were built in the war as successors to the similar ships built in the Great War (see Lambert and Ross, 2018). They were twin screw with a pair of high speed 2-stroke diesel engines that provided a speed of 21 knots. A number of the ships were transferred to France on completion and permanently transferred towards the end of the war or immediately afterwards; some also went to Russia, China, Philippines and Norway. *A Dictionary of American Fighting Naval Ships* lists the vessels and their post-war disposal. A group of the ships were transferred to the United States Coast Guard post-war as 'Air' class air-sea rescue cutters. As with their Great War counterparts, most of the commercial sales were to companies in the United States although some were sold overseas for conversion for use as fast passenger launches and in various support roles. Probably the best known of them all was *SC1013* which was taken inland to become the sightseeing boat *Mount Independence* on Lake Champlain, which lies between the states of New York and Vermont. *Mount Independence* was bought by a private owner in 1989.

Some led surprisingly long commercial careers, mainly as fish packers and fishing boats. The fish packers included *SC504*, bought in 1946 by Parks Canning Company of Seattle and renamed *Pacific Laurel*; she foundered in 2006. Another was *Moonlight Maid* owned from 1951 by Murray Suthergreen of Seattle, formerly the Coast Guard cutter *Air Cormorant* and built as *SC536*; she foundered off the Alaskan Coast in 2012. *SC1039* was another fish packer after the war with the name *Norking* and based in British Columbia; she was advertised for sale in 2013. *SC715* went to the Coast Guard and later became the fishing vessel *Cape Pine*; she is still in service as a charter boat. *SC772* became the Coast Guard cutter *Air Mallard* after the war but was sold in 1948. After several name and owner changes she is now available as the party fishing boat *Lady Godiver* based at Scappoose, Oregon.

Cape Pine (1942) was built as *SC715*, decommissioned in 1946 and after service as an air-sea rescue cutter became a fishing boat. She is still in service as a charter boat. (Ronan Oger)

The *SC1466* class ships had twin screws and were powered by petrol engines which were readily sourced as the war progressed. Many of the ships were transferred to the Soviet Union on completion in 1944. Most of the surviving vessels were sold into friendly foreign navies although a few were sold to commercial companies for adaptation for a range of uses mainly in inshore waters. They were not as popular as the *SC497* class because their petrol engines were expensive to maintain and offered poor fuel efficiency; most of those in commercial operation were sold for demolition in the 1950s.

Many of the support vessels and rescue tugs were decommissioned and sold immediately after the war. While some went to overseas navies and governments, several of the rescue tugs and other vessels were bought commercially. For example, USS *Satinleaf* (AN43), a net layer built in 1943 at Washington, was sold in 1949 to the Quebec and Ontario Transportation Company Limited, Montreal and renamed *Rocky River*. In 1952 she was bought by Foundation Maritime, renamed *Foundation Josephine II* and converted for salvage work. She was sold to Sumarah R V, Halifax, in

The salvage ship *Foundation Josephine II* (1943) was one of many United States Navy auxiliary ships sold after the Second World War and was originally the net layer USS *Satinleaf*.

Before: USS *Pima County* (1945) at Albert Edward Dock, North Shields after being towed across the Atlantic from Philadelphia under the ownership of the Atlantic Steam Navigation Company. (Press photo, *Shields Gazette*)

1960 and given the name *North Star IV* and employed in survey work, but foundered during a hydrographic investigation in 1961.

The United States Navy *LST 1080* was built in 1945 at Ambridge in America and was renamed USS *Pima County* in 1955. Ten years later she was bought by the Atlantic Steam Navigation Company (see Chapter 10) for conversion into a commercial vehicle ferry. The ship was towed to Newcastle as reported in the *Shields Gazette*, 29 July 1965:

A former American Tank Landing Ship, which is to be converted into a vehicle ferry, arrived in the Tyne today after a 3,300 mile tow across the Atlantic from Philadelphia. She is the 3,591 ton *LST1080*, which has been bought by the Atlantic Steam Navigation Co. of London and renamed *Baltic Ferry*.

The company which operates roll on-roll off vehicle services between Preston and Larne and

Tilbury and the Continent, is inviting tenders for the conversion and the vessel has been berthed at Albert Edward Dock, North Shields, for inspection by any interested shipyards.

As the *Baltic Ferry* has been brought to the Tyne, there are hopes that a yard on the river – or at least one in the North East – will get the conversion contract.

Smith's Dock at Middlesbrough won the contract and converted *LST1080* into *Baltic Ferry* (at last company ownership allowed the 'Empire' names in the fleet to be dropped). The attraction of the new ship was that *LST1080* had been partially rebuilt with a completely new superstructure and new oil engines. As *Baltic Ferry* she could carry twenty-five commercial vehicles but had no passenger accommodation; she started between Felixstowe and Antwerp on 12 April 1966, but her main role was to help to develop the wheeled freight and unit load traffic between Preston and Belfast. However, as a stopgap, she only lasted in service with the company until 1968 and was then laid up at Barrow. She was next chartered to British Rail who put her in service between Stranraer and Larne from June 1970 alongside the car and passenger ferry *Caledonian Princess* which had only limited capacity for commercial traffic. She was sold in 1972 to Federal Offshore Services in Canada and renamed *Sable Ferry* working in the Hudson Bay area, and resold in 1978 to become *Nickel Ferry* for Worldwide Ship Sales. She was destroyed by fire off El Salvador on 1 December 1979 and broken up as she lay in shallow water.

In August 1966, with five newly-built vehicle and passenger ferries in operation, the Atlantic Steam Navigation Company acquired at auction yet another former American naval ship, the amphibious Landing Ship, Dock, USS *LSD 11*, once HMS *Northway*. She had been built at Newport, Virginia in 1944 and had spent much of her life laid up.

The Landing Ship, Dock was an amphibious assault craft with a dock aft of the machinery space that could be flooded by ballasting down the stern of the ship. The dock could carry two Landing Craft, Tank that could be dispatched to a hostile shore with vehicles and stores. Eight such ships were built for the US Navy comprising the *Ashland* class. These were succeeded by the *Casa Grande* class comprising seventeen ships of which four were sent to the Royal Navy under Lend-Lease.

After: *Baltic Ferry* (1945), ex-*LST1081*, ex-USS *Pima County*, seen leaving Stranraer on charter from Atlantic Steam Navigation Company Limited to British Rail in August 1970. (Author)

The four ships transferred to Britain were HMS *Eastway*, HMS *Highway*, HMS *Northway* and HMS *Oceanway*. After the war two were transferred into the Greek Navy, and one, *Highway*, was sold for demolition. HMS *Northway*, however, was laid up in the reserve fleet as *LSD11* at James River, Virginia. Completed at the Bethlehem Fairfield Shipyard in 1943, the ship was twin screw with each shaft driven by a triple-expansion steam engine with cylinders of 24½in, 37in and 70in diameter with a stroke of 48in. Oil-fired boilers supplied steam at 250psi. On D-Day HMS *Northway* had carried forty-six heavily-loaded DUKW amphibious trucks to Juno Beach arriving in the early evening of 6 June 1944. She returned to the Solent later that evening ready for further trips to the beaches.

In August 1948 *LSD11* was sold to Atlas Metals Corporation and subsequently resold to the Amherst Steamship Corporation and given the name *Jose Marti*. At this stage her gross tonnage is recorded in *Lloyd's Register* as 7,176. In 1956 *Jose Marti* was sold to the West India Fruit and Steamship Company, renamed *City of Havana* and flagged out to Liberia. This company was formed in 1946 to provide a reliable freight and boxcar service between the United States and Cuba with rail connections for through consignments of railway boxcars at either end. The company also owned a train ferry which ran to New Orleans. *City of Havana* was considerably reconfigured by her new owners with extensive passenger accommodation and a new main deck over the original dock which was now available for vehicles loaded over the original stern ramp. The passenger vehicle ferry ran alongside six roll-on roll-off freight ferries that plied between Stock Island near Key West and Havana. The tourist advertising slogan of the company was 'Drive your car to Cuba':

> If you are touring in your own automobile, you may drive from Miami via US Highway #1, to Stock Island two miles before you reach Key West. Turn left at the sign and drive your car aboard the ferry *City of Havana*. The escalator will take you from the car deck to the passenger

Before: Amphibious Landing Ship, Dock HMS *Northway* (1944), one of four similar ships transferred from the United States Navy to Britain under Lend-Lease.

After: *City of Havana* (1944), ex-*LSD1*, was a vehicle and passenger ferry owned by West Indies Fruit and Steamship Company running between Key West and Havana.

deck where you may enjoy a day cruise aboard the largest passenger ship operating between Florida and Havana. Tour the enchanted, historical tropical island of Cuba via the paved 700 mile Central Highway traversing the island from east to west.

One of the freight ferries, *Grand Haven* dating from 1903, was sold in 1960 because of a decline in trade due to the deteriorating relationship between the United States and Cuba. The company reported that it had been hard hit by loss of business and the absence of tourist traffic. In August 1961 the service was closed, the company having put *City of Havana* on the market along with her four consorts and the train ferry at the beginning of June.

In 1962 *City of Havana* was bought by the Federal Republic of Germany with the intension of converting her back to an amphibious Landing Ship, Dock, her original ballast tanks still being intact. The plan came to nothing and *City of Havana*, now renamed *LS1*, was berthed at Bremerhaven and used as a military accommodation ship until her facilities were condemned. The ship was put up for auction at Kiel in 1966 and bought by the Atlantic Steam Navigation Company against a bid of US$1.5 million.

LS1 was towed to the Tyne and entered Palmers' Shipyard at Hebburn for yet another phase of rebuilding. The ship's accommodation was gutted and completely refurbished with berths constructed for fifty-five drivers and passengers. The relatively new main deck aft was removed and replaced by a new strengthened deck capable of carrying unit loads, but she retained her original triple-expansion steam engines. Her gross tonnage was remeasured at 5,556 and she emerged as *Celtic*

Converted again: *Northway* converted into the vehicle and passenger ferry *Celtic Ferry* for the Atlantic Steam Navigation Company in 1966.

Ferry, having taken her trials in mid-February 1967, looking smart in her new colours but with a squat and square bridge front.

Celtic Ferry was used on the new Felixstowe to Rotterdam service as a stopgap to help develop the trade alongside new purpose-built tonnage. She was later put on the service to Antwerp alongside the newly built *Cerdic Ferry*. *Celtic Ferry* was left to maintain the Felixstowe to Antwerp service alone when *Cerdic Ferry* moved to Southampton, but by 1972 the passenger accommodation aboard *Celtic Ferry* had been closed off to all but a few lorry drivers and she was essentially used for cargo only. She was withdrawn from service later in 1972 and laid up at Barrow awaiting sale. She was sold towards the end of 1973 for demolition at Hamburg. Her final form as a freight ferry was so completely divorced from her original configuration as an amphibious assault ship that few of her passengers ever made the connection.

Royal Canadian Navy

One of the Canadian 'River' class was HMCS *Stormont* (K327) which had been built by Canadian Vickers Limited at Montreal and was commissioned in 1943. She was sold in 1947 for conversion to a merchant ship, and four years later *Stormont* was bought by the Greek shipping magnate Aristotle Onassis for US$34,000. In 1951 the vessel received a $4 million facelift at Keil to become the luxury yacht *Christina*, named after the owner's daughter. The ship emerged complete with a full-sized swimming pool with a tiled mosaic bottom which at the touch of a button rose to deck level to become a dance floor, an elegant spiral staircase and nineteen luxury staterooms. The guest list included the great and the good, and ranged from Winston Churchill, who thought the young John F Kennedy was a waiter aboard ship, to Marilyn Monroe and Frank Sinatra, plus of course, the opera singer Maria Callas, Aristotle Onassis' onetime mistress. In April 1956 the ship was made available for the wedding reception of Prince Rainier III of Monaco and the Hollywood star Grace Kelly.

Christina Onassis inherited the ship on the death of her father in 1975. In 1978 she gave the *Christina* to the Greek government for use as the presidential yacht. *Christina* was renamed *Argo*, but in government ownership she was not properly maintained and was eventually declared unseaworthy. In 1998, *Argo* was purchased by Greek shipowner, John Paul Papanicolaou, and under the new name *Christina O* the ship was completely refurbished and put back into service as a luxury yacht. She remains in service and is now a luxury yacht available for private charter in the western Mediterranean offering seventeen en suite luxury cabins and a host of deluxe amenities.

HMCS *Orkney* (K448), another 'River', was sold in 1947 to Israeli owners and converted for the less glamourous use as an immigrant ship under the name *Violetta*. The ship was instrumental in taking displaced Jewish refugees to Haifa until in 1949 she was taken over by the Israeli Navy, re-armed and given the name *Mivtah* (K28).

Two more 'Rivers', HMCS *Waskesiu* (K330) and HMCS *Kokanee* (K419), were both built at Esquimalt by Yarrows Limited and launched in 1943. They were sold to the Indian Government Hooghly Pilot Service in 1950 and converted for use as pilot cutters with the names *Hooghly* and *Bengal* respectively. The ships were stationed at the head of the Bay of Bengal providing pilots for the difficult and long passage up to Calcutta. They replaced *Andrew* and *Lady Fraser* which together had provided 85 years of service to the port of Calcutta. *Bengal* was renamed *PV Bengal* and the *Hooghly* became *PV Houghly* in 1956; the pair was sold for demolition in 1965.

Three more Canadian 'Rivers', HMCS *Stone Town* (K531), HMCS *St Stephen* (K454) and HMCS *St Catherines* (K325), were converted for use as weather ships in the Pacific. Of these HMCS *Stone Town* was taken out of service in 1968 and was sold to private owners for conversion into a fish processing vessel.

Seven of the Canadian 'Flower' class corvettes were sold to the Venezuelan Navy after the war

The luxury charter yacht *Christina O* (1943) was originally commissioned as HMCS *Stormont* and later became Aristotle Onassis' yacht *Christina*.

and smaller lots went to other nations. The Canadian 'Flowers', not loaned from the Royal Navy, amounted to well over 100 ships. Of these, some thirty-four were sold after the war for merchant service as whalers and small cargo ships. Examples of merchant-ship conversions include HMCS *Arvida* (K113) built by Morton Engineering & Drydock Company at Quebec and commissioned in 1941. *Arvida* was paid off on 14 June 1945 at Sorel, Quebec. She was sold and converted into the cargo ship *Arvida*, and resold in 1950 to Empresa Nacional 'Elcano' of Cadiz and renamed *La Ceiba*. In 1957, she was renamed *Rio Samo* and reported broken up in Spain in 1987. Another was HMCS *Baddeck* (K147), sold in 1947 to become the passenger and cargo ship *Rushbrooke* and renamed *Efthalia* for charter to W H Muller & Company before she was sold in 1948 to Haji Abdullah Alireza & Company of Jeddah and renamed *Yousuf Z Alireza*. She served as the Saudi Arabian Coast Guard cutter *Radwa* between 1955 and 1965. Another was HMCS *Barrie* (K138) which in 1947 became the Argentinian merchant ship *Gasestado* owned by the Argentinian Government (Flota Mercante del Estado, Buenos Aires) and in 1959 was again converted for use as an Argentine Navy survey ship with the name *Capitán Cánepa*. She was scrapped in 1972.

A number of the ships became whalers, several owned by Balleneros Limitada SA of Puerto Cortes in Honduras. These included HMCS *Brantford* (K218) which became the whale catcher *Olympic Arrow*, HMCS *Parry Sound* (K341) which became *Olympic Champion*, HMCS *Pictou* (K146) which became *Olympic Chaser*, HMCS *Smiths Falls* (K345) which became *Olympic Lightning*, and HMCS *Trillium* which became *Olympic Runner*. In addition, the company also had the former USS *Might* which became the whaler *Olympic Explorer* and USS *Intensity* which became *Olympic Promoter*. They were all later transferred to the Japanese flag.

An interesting conversion took place as part of the Fairfree stern trawler experiment, which started in 1946 using a converted yacht for experiments on the Clyde. Following successful trials, a larger ship was bought by experimenter and inventor Sir Charles Dennistoun's Fresh Frozen Foods Limited for £5,000. His company was sponsored by the Ministry of Food. The larger ship was HMCS *Coppercliff*, built in 1944 at Toronto, Canada, transferred to the Royal Navy and renamed HMS *Felicity* (J369). She was an *Algerine* class minesweeper, 225ft long with a beam of 35ft, and twin shafts powered by triple-expansion steam engines. She was taken to Fairfield Shipbuilding & Engineering Company Limited at Glasgow and partially rebuilt with a stern chute similar to that of a whale factory vessel. One boiler was removed to provide additional machinery space, speed no longer being a critical requirement. Alterations were completed in October 1947 and the ship emerged from the shipyard with the name *Fairfree* (GW19). The name derived from her conversion at the Fairfield yard and that she was acquired almost free of charge – the spare boiler having been sold for £3,000 to an Edinburgh brewery.

After fishing trials off the west coast of Scotland, Fresh Frozen Foods Limited, *Fairfree* included, was bought by Christian Salvesen of Leith in 1948 and given the new number (LH271). Two former Landing Ships, Tank owned by Fresh Frozen Foods were sold (see Chapter 10). After 12 months trialling and testing both the deck gear and the fast-freezing equipment that had been installed, *Fairfree* was re-engined with a pair of oil engines built by Mirrlees, Bickerton & Day. Voyages were undertaken to the Faeroe Islands, Iceland and Newfoundland Grand Banks while the ship generally discharged her frozen catch at Grimsby. She was laid up at Leith in September 1951, the experiment deemed a success while her owners planned three larger purpose-built ships, *Fairtry*, *Fairtry II* and *Fairtry III*. The pioneer of the stern-loading trawler, *Fairfree* was eventually sold for demolition in 1957.

12

ADMIRALTY FISHING VESSELS AND TUGS, SOME EXAMPLES

Motor Fishing Vessels

The Second World War saw another major construction programme of fishing vessels to the order of the Admiralty. These were all equipped with oil engines and were termed Motor Fishing Vessels (MFV). There were four separate classes ordered by the Admiralty, each defined by the length of the hull (see Table 4).

All the MFVs were equipped with a single 0.303in machine gun. Two hundred and thirty-eight of the *MFV1* class were built in the United Kingdom, seventy-nine in South Africa and twenty-five in Australia. The *MFV601* class were built in the United Kingdom apart from ten which were constructed in Bermuda. Both the *MFV1001* class and the *MFV1501* class were all built in the United Kingdom.

MFVs were usually bought by the fishing industry at the end of their naval careers. After the Second World War, by way of example, those that were registered in Lerwick alone included:

- *MFV130*: *Edwin Halsall* (FR3) then *Golden Acres* (BF336 later LK45). sold out of industry 1967.
- *MFV327*: *Responsive* (LK45 later PD28).
- *MFV1100*: *Scotch Queen* (FR241 and later LK331), sold as diving vessel in 1985.
- *MFV1104*: *Arran Corrie* (A275), later *Ocean Reaper* (LK64), sold out of industry 1975.

MFV60 (1943) was one of the 65ft-long *MFV1* class fishing boats commissioned by the Royal Navy from 1942 onwards.

Table 4: CLASSES OF MOTOR FISHING VESSEL BUILT IN THE SECOND WORLD WAR

Class	Built	Displacement tons	Length (ft)	Breadth (ft)	Number completed
MFV1	1942-6	50	65	18	342
MFV601	1943-6	29	50	17	227
MFV1001	1943-6	114	76	20	209
MFV1501	1943-6	200	97	22	72

- *MFV1234*: *Southern Cross* (LH185 and later LK39), later *Xmas Morn*, *Isle of Skye*, sold out of industry 1985.
- *MFV1504*: *Betty Lesley* (LK497), later *Boston Mosquito*, *Mosquito*, *April Diamond*, scrapped 1975.

Many vessels laid down towards the end of the war were cancelled or completed for commercial owners after the war had ended. In the latter case, although the hull was allocated an MFV number, the vessel may never have taken up that number. As a consequence, registers of many of these ships may recognise that the vessel was originally ordered by the Admiralty, but do not record the allocated MFV number. The dimensions of the vessel, however, reveal the MFV class.

A few of the ships were converted for passenger use. One of the *MFV1* class became a Clyde ferry in 1955 when she was sold out of service to Walter Roy Ritchie. She had been built as *MFV137* by Kris Cruisers Limited at Isleworth and was commissioned in 1944. Ritchie had her converted for use as a passenger ferry, with specific attention given to the watertight subdivision of the ship and remedial action where gribble worm had bored into the hull timbers. Renamed *Granny Kempock*, she served between Gourock and Helensburgh and latterly between Gourock and Kilcreggan until withdrawn and sold in 1979. Her original Kelvin diesel engine maintained a service speed of 9 knots.

An MFV, erroneously described by Duckworth and Langmuir as being built as *MFV1003*, was built by J Bolson & Son Limited at Poole in 1945. She was sold after the war to J W Bett of Cellardyke, Anstruther, in Fife, and given the name *Irene Julia* (KY 159). Equipped with a Bergius oil engine, her wooden hull was 61ft long by 18ft beam indicating that she was one of the smaller *MFV1* class of ship and not one of the 76ft-long *MFV1001* class vessels. Almost certainly she was one of a number of *MFV1* class ships ordered from Bolson on 10 March 1945 which were allocated the numbers *MFV437* through to *MFV442* but completed as merchant ships in 1946 and 1947 for the fishing industry.

In July 1955 *Irene Julia* was bought by David MacBrayne Limited, and refitted at Greenock. The fish hold was converted for cargo stowage and the former crew accommodation and small deckhouse adapted for passenger use. She was renamed *Loch Toscaig*. She took her inaugural sailing for MacBrayne in May 1956 running between Kyle of Lochalsh and Loch Toscaig, with morning cruises from Kyle during the summer. She held a passenger certificate for thirty-six persons. In April 1964 she transferred to the Oban and Lismore service.

Loch Toscaig was retired and laid up to await sale in 1974. In November 1975 she was sold to Mr Gerrard of London and was later used for fishing trips based at Gourock. On 29 December 1978 she sank in a gale at Gourock after drifting against the passenger ferry *Juno*. She was raised and beached, and was eventually demolished in September 1986.

MFV1003, often mistaken for *Loch Toscaig* in later life, was one of the 76ft-long *MFV1001* class.

MFV1086 (1944) was typical of the 76ft-long *MFV1001* class fishing boats commissioned from 1943 onwards, slightly larger than earlier designs to enable more equipment to be carried.

She was built by John Noble of Fraserburgh in 1942 and was sold for commercial use in 1951. Renamed *Pre-eminent*, she was used for fishing under the ownership of J M Lovie Snr. & others at Fraserburgh until 1964. She was then converted to a cargo ship with the name *Isle of Canna*, reverting to fishing in 1969 when she was based at Stornoway. Another of the *MFV1001* class, *MFV1195*, went to the Secretary of State for Scotland in 1947 as the fisheries protection vessel *Clupea*. She was sold in 1969.

Of the 50ft boats, *MFV613* was ordered in December 1942 and completed in May 1944 after which she was based at Portsmouth. She was sold in 1948 to Trinity House and renamed *Burhou*, and used as a pilot and work boat around the Channel Islands. She was one of the longest-serving boats for Trinity House; *Burhou* was sold into private hands in 1989 and renamed *Cornish Maiden*. Between 2002 and 2005 she was used as a floating shop at Erith in Kent and is now on the National Register of Historic Vessels.

A number of MFVs were gifted to the Sea Cadets. *MFV1023*, for example, was based at Exeter for the Sea Cadets for many years.

Naval Trawlers

The much larger naval trawler or HMT was built primarily for inshore escort duties, and built in large numbers in the Second World War. They were designed to Admiralty standards along the lines of a traditional fishing trawler with a single gun mount forward. The Admiralty also requisitioned over 200 commercial trawlers for military service during the war. The HMT came in a variety of shapes and sizes:

- *Basset* class – 460 tons, 12 knots, 33 men.
- 'Tree' class – 530 tons, 11.5 knots, 35 men.
- 'Dance' class – 530 tons, 11.5 knots, 35 men.
- 'Shakespearian' class – 545 tons, 12 knots, 35 men.
- 'Isles' class – 545 tons, 12 knots, 40 men.
- 'Admiralty' class – 600 tons, 14 knots, 35 men.
- 'Portuguese' class – 550 tons, 11 knots, 30 men.
- 'Brazilian' class – 680 tons, 12.5 knots, 40 men.
- 'Castle' class – 625 tons, 10 knots, 32 men.
- 'Hills' class – 750 tons, 11 knots, 35 men.
- 'Fish class' – 670 tons, 11 knots, 35 men.
- 'Round Table' class – 440 tons, 12 knots, 35 men.
- 'Military' class – 750 tons, 11 knots, 40 men.

Most of the trawlers were surplus to requirements after the war. They were bought for use by the fishing industry and for a range of other purposes. For example, Mr William Radcliffe Metcalfe bought HMS *Basset* (T68), lead ship of the *Basset* class, in September 1947. Renamed *Radford* and registered at Guernsey, she was put on a passenger and cargo service between Weymouth and Alderney in August 1948 working under the banner Radcliffe Channel Island Shipping Company of Weymouth and Guernsey. The company was founded in 1948 with the objective of serving Alderney and Sark.

HMS *Basset* was the first of the Second World War 'Dog' class armed trawlers, affectionately referred to as 'Dog Boats', and was completed by Henry Robb at Leith in 1935. She had a displace-

Before: HMS *Basset* (1935) lead ship of the *Basset* class Admiralty trawlers, was sold after the war to become a passenger and cargo ship running between Weymouth and Alderney with the name *Radford*.

ment of 461 tons with a length overall of 150ft and beam of 27ft 6in. She had a top speed of 12 knots and a crew complement of around thirty-five. She was initially armed with a 4in gun forward and assorted machine guns.

Radford served the Channel Islands until December 1949 when the company withdrew from the trade. The main business of its owner was marine salvage based at Dover and it was for this purpose that she was then employed.

The 'Isles' class trawler HMS *Neave* (T247) was built in 1942 at Beverley by Cook, Welton and Gemmell Limited, specialists in trawler design and construction. A total of 145 'Isles' class ships were built, with dimensions 164ft by 27ft 6in width by 10ft 6in deep. They were equipped with one 12-pounder gun and three 20mm anti-aircraft guns. The triple-expansion steam engine provided a cruising speed of 12 knots. HMS *Neave* served throughout the war until she was sold in 1952 to British Wheeler Process Limited of Liverpool and converted for use as a tank cleaning vessel with the name *Tulipbank*. She was one of three 'Isles' class naval trawlers purchased at the time for similar conversion, the others being named *Tulipglen*, built in 1942 as HMS *Procher* (T281), and *Tulipdale*, built in 1945 as HMS *Lingay* (T423). *Tulipglen* and *Tulipdale* were both sold for demolition in 1965 while *Tulipglen* was sold in 1965 to Elderslie Tank and Boiler Cleaning Company and again in 1975 to Beacon Cleaning Services (Scotland) Limited, eventually being sold for scrap in 1979.

HMS *Crowlin* (T380) was another of the 'Isles' class and one of thirty-two which went to Norwegian buyers after the war. She was completed in February 1944 also by Cook, Welton and Gemmell Limited. She had a long and varied

After: *Radford* (1935) arriving at St Peter Port, Guernsey with passenger accommodation aft and a large hatch forward of the bridge. (World Ship Society Photo Archive)

The Norwegian coastal cargo ship *Argo* (1943) owned by Anglo A/S of Haugesund, and no longer recognisable as the former 'Isles' class trawler HMS *Gillstone*.

commercial career and was initially sold to Hans Hummelsund and sent to Hetlands Verksted at Stavanger for conversion into a cargo ship. Work stopped in March 1948, her owner having run out of funds. Express Service A/S managed by M Wangberg of Oslo purchased the vessel as she lay. In August she was delivered to her new owner as a refrigerated cargo ship complete with a second-hand oil engine but retaining her former name. Her owner went bankrupt in December 1950 and the ship was sold by the Den Norske Creditbank to the Frozen Food Corporation of Puerto Cortes.

Crowlin was found floating bottom up off Stavanger on 31 March 1954. Taken into Stavanger the ship was later righted when it was found there was no trace of the crew of sixteen men. Ownership reverted to Norway and following refurbishment and the removal of an aft deckhouse to increase stability she became the frozen fish carrier *Thermo* for Govert Grindhaug of Kopervik, Norway. In 1960 she flew the Bulgarian flag as *Chernomorez*, and in 1964 she became *Axum* under the Eritrean flag and was renamed *Dire Dawa* in 1977. She foundered off Massawa, Eritrea, in March 1977.

The 'Isles' class trawler HMS *Gillstone* (T355) became another Norwegian cargo ship. She was built by Cochrane & Sons (Shipbuilders) Limited at Selby in 1943. In 1946 she was sold to Leif Gran Kahrs of Bergen and named *Gillstone* and then sold to Anglo A/S of Haugesund in 1949 and given the name *Argo*. She was sold in 1962 to become *Freedom First* and was reflagged from Norway to Panama, in 1964 she was renamed *Glenrock*, in 1969 *Sea Enterprise* and in 1970 *Almirante*. She was scuttled as an artificial reef off the Florida coast in 1974 having provided 28 years commercial service.

One of the 'Dance' class trawlers, HMS *Quadrille* (T133), built by Hall, Russell & Company Limited at Aberdeen in 1941, was sold to Skips A/S Storhaug of Stavanger in 1948 and converted into the cargo ship *Elsa*. Her new owners equipped her with an oil engine made by British Auxiliaries. With three subsequent names and six subsequent owners the ship led a long and fruitful commercial career and was finally deleted from *Lloyd's Register* only in 1996.

The Secretary of State for Scotland adopted a number of the trawlers for fisheries protection duties in 1947. The 'Isles' class trawler HMS *Longa* (T366) retained her name, the 'Shakespearian' class HMS *Fluellen* (T157) became the research vessel *Scotia*, and the 'Tree' class HMS *Acacia* (T02) became *Vaila*. *Vaila* was wrecked at Loch Shell, Lewis on 1951 with the loss of five lives, while *Longa* and *Scotia*, the latter renamed *Scarba* in 1972, were scrapped in 1973. An 'Isles' class trawler, HMS *Annet* (T341), came to the Department in 1958 as *Ulva* – she was scrapped in 1972.

Many other ships were sold for commercial conversions, most into fishing vessels. Given the conditions under which these vessels were constructed, they were remarkably sturdy and well-built, many lasting in service through the 1970s and 1980s.

Fleet Tugs

Numerous tugs were built in the Second World War including harbour tugs ordered by the Ministry of War Transport which were given 'Empire' names. Some seventy-four civilian tugs were requisitioned in the Second World War, including sixteen 'Saint' class built in the Great War which, in the meantime, had been sold for merchant service (see Chapter 5). In 1938 the Royal Navy had also built four *Brigand* class rescue tugs built in anticipation of renewed war.

Orders were placed with Cochrane & Sons Limited at Selby in 1939 for twenty-one ocean-going Admiralty fleet tugs of the *Assurance* class. The *Favourite* class comprised twenty-three more ocean-going tugs which were built in the United States from 1942 onwards, equipped with diesel-electric machinery, and sent to Britain under Lend-Lease. There were also eight British-built motor ships of the larger *Bustler* class completed as the war ended. In 1944 six ships of the *Envoy* class started to be commissioned and in 1944 four wooden-hulled steamships of the *Director* class, built in the United States for Lend-Lease to Britain, were commissioned. Collectively the tugs were His Majesty's Rescue Tug Service and they flew the White Ensign, although the officers and crew were almost all Merchant Navy personnel signed on under T124 Articles and subject to naval discipline with the captain possibly, but not always, being the only regular Royal Navy officer. Many of the rescue tugs were based at Campbeltown for service with the Atlantic convoys.

The Admiralty sought to dispose of many of its larger tugs after the war. All the British-built ocean-going tugs were equipped with triple-expansion steam engines save the *Bustler* class which had twin oil engines driving two shafts that gave significant operational advantages over their steam-driven counterparts. The latter were ideally suited for the charter market and none were sold immediately after the war. The American Lend-Lease tugs of the *Favourite* class were returned to the United States in 1946, many then sold for commercial service. These were also commercially attractive as they were equipped with twin independent shafts each driven by a diesel-electric couple to provide a massive 1,700 brake horsepower.

Only one of the four surviving *Brigand* class tugs, HMS *Marauder* (W98), was sold for merchant service the others being sold for scrap in 1960. *Marauder* went to Collins Submarine Pipelines Limited of Southampton in October 1958 and was renamed *Emerson K*. In 1963 she was resold to Marine Diamond Corporation Limited of Cape Town without change of name. On 10 August 1965 *Emerson K* capsized at Cape Town while entering dry dock; condemned, she was scrapped locally in 1966.

Most of the sixteen surviving ships of the *Assurance* class were sold, some also chartered, for commercial service after the war had ended:

– HMS *Allegiance* (W50), was chartered to Whampoa Dockyard Company Limited, Hong Kong and renamed *Allegiance 2*. In 1954 she was chartered to Hong Kong and Whampoa Dockyard Company, Hong Kong (Mollers'

Towages, Managers) and renamed *Kowloon Docks*. On 1 September 1962 she foundered 100 miles from Hong Kong in a typhoon; there was only one survivor.

- HMS *Assiduous* (W142) was chartered to J D Irving Limited of Saint John New Brunswick. Irving bought the ship in 1961 and renamed her *Irving Tamarack*. She was sold for demolition in 1968.
- HMS *Diligent*, renamed HMS *Tenacity* in 1940 and renamed HMS *Adherent* (W18) in 1947, was sold to Swedish owners in 1962 and renamed *Hermes*. She was sold to RivTow Marine Limited in Vancouver in 1970 and renamed *Rivtow Viking*. She had two further owners based in Vancouver under the name *Canadian Viking*, and was deleted from the register only in 2010; HMS *Prudent* (W73) was renamed *Cautious* when she became a dockyard tug at Chatham in 1947. She was sold to MR Cliff Tugboat Company Limited of Vancouver in 1964 and renamed *Rivtow Lion* and sold again to RivTow Industries also of Vancouver in 1973. She was sunk as a recreational dive site at Nanaimo, BC, Canada, in February 2005.
- HMS *Dextrous* (W111) was sold in January 1947 to Overseas Towage and Salvage Company Limited, London, without change of name, and was sold to British Petroleum Tanker Company Limited in 1957, serving as *Zurmand* until 1966 when she was sold to Tsavliris Salvage & Towage Company Limited, Piraeus who later renamed her *Nisos Ikaria*. She was scrapped in 1969.
- HMS *Decision*, renamed HMS *Hengist* (W110) in 1948, was sold in 1965 to Tsavlirus Salvage & Towage Limited, Piraeus, Greece, to become *Nisos Crete*, and was broken up in 1972; HMS *Saucy* (W131) became *Nisos Chios* and was scrapped in 1971; HMS *Earner* (W143) became the *Nisos Rodos* and was scrapped in 1973.
- HMS *Frisky* (W11) was sold to the Kuwait Oil Company Limited, London in 1948 and renamed *Hasan*. Sold again in 1960, she was

Lead tug of the *Bustler* class, HMS *Bustler* (1945), seen without armament immediately after the war.

then renamed *Vernicos Marina* for service with NE Vernicos Shipping Company Limited of Piraeus and was scrapped in 1973.
- HMS *Griper* (W112) was sold to the Singapore Harbour Board in December 1946 as *Griper*. In 1962 she was sold to the Indonesian Government and renamed *Surabajah*. In 1970 she was resold to Perusahaan Negara Tundabara of Jakarta and renamed *Selat Surabajah* and was sold for demolition in 1991.
- HMS *Stormking* (W87) became the dockyard tug *Tryphon* in 1947 and was based at Sheerness. She was sold to Foremost Marine Transporters Limited of London in July 1957 and renamed *Melanie Fair*. She was resold in 1961 to Imprese Maritime e Portuali, Genoa, Italy and renamed *Toro*. She was sold for demolition in 1969.

The American-owned *Favourite* class ships were returned to the United States in 1946. They were mostly decommissioned and sold, their diesel-electric machinery being favoured by several towage companies in the United States and elsewhere. For example, HMS *Favourite* (W119) was sold to the New York tug company Mary Moran, Incorporated to become *Susan A Moran*, then *Eugene F Moran*, and in 1947 was again sold this time to Cia. Colonial de Navegacao of Lisbon and renamed *Monsanto*; while HMS *Masterful* (W20) became *Eugenie M Moran* in 1948 and was resold in 1960 and given the new name *Comanche*. HMS *Oriana* (W117) was sold in 1946 and given the name *Ocean Pride* for commercial service, renamed in 1947 as *Pan America* under the ownership of Gerald F Roberts of San Diego, California, and again in 1956 when she became *Zeeland* under the ownership of Mobil Oil Nederland NV, registered at Ijmuiden in the Netherlands. She was then equipped with up-to date fire-fighting waterjets and associated equipment.

HMS *Destiny* (W115) was sold to Mollers' Towages Limited, London in 1948 and renamed *Frosty Moller* and in 1950 became *Christine Moller*. She was sold again in 1951 to become *Oceanus*, owned by N/V Maats. Tot bet Uitvoeren van Scheepstranap & Beringswerken of Amsterdam and in 1953 was renamed *Gele Zee* on sale to L Smit & Company's Internationale Sleepdienst, Rotterdam. In 1963 she was sold to Loucas Matsas & Sons, Piraeus, renamed *Atlas*, and in 1975 she was sold again, this time to K M Corporation SA, Greece, and renamed *Atlas II*. In 1977 she was transferred to Guilan Production Company, managers Sachinis Shipping, Piraeus and was deleted from the register in 2010.

Other *Favourite* class ships sold for commercial use included HMS *Eminent* (W116) and HMS *Lariat* (W17) which were sold to the China Merchant Steam Navigation Company and renamed *Ming 105* and *Ming 108* respectively; they were later renamed *Ming 305* and *Ming 308*.

The Admiralty was reluctant to sell the *Bustler*-class ships. These were the only wartime-built fleet tugs equipped with a pair of oil engines and twin screws. However, it did charter them to commercial operators from time to time, to keep them in gainful employment. HMS *Reward* (W164) provides a typical example of the life of the *Bustler* class. One of eight similar ships to survive the war, the others being *Bustler*, *Samsonia*, *Growler*, *Hesperia*, *Mediator*, *Turmoil* and *Warden*, all built at Henry Robb's yard at Leith. *Reward* was ordered by the Admiralty to dimensions of 190ft long, 38ft 6in broad and 19ft deep, service speed of 16 knots, and of 1,100 tons gross. Her wartime complement was forty-two men. Like the other ships of the class she was built with two 8-cylinder British Polar oil engines. She was laid down on 6 April 1944, launched on 31 October and commissioned on 12 March 1945.

HMS *Reward* began her long career as part of Force 135 for Operation 'Nest Egg', the liberation of the Channel Islands in May 1945. She then sailed in a convoy which included her sister-ship HMS *Growler*. In November 1946 she took part in the rescue of the Liberty ship *Josiah P Cressey* when her engine room flooded and she had to be towed into Fishguard. In March 1947 she was involved in Operation 'Snow White', working with another of her sister-ships, HMS *Mediator,* to tow the floating dock *AFD35* to Malta, and in October of the same year she sailed from Portsmouth to Rosyth with HMS *Nelson*. In January 1951 she took part in the Home Fleet's Spring Cruise in the

HMS *Reward* (1945) started her career with the liberation of the Channel Islands. She was chartered to the United Towing Company of Hull in 1962 as *Englishman*.

Mediterranean and in 1952 was laid up at Chatham, and later taken to Pembroke Dock. Active again in 1953, she was part of Queen Elizabeth II's Coronation Fleet Review at Spithead in June and the Home Fleet's Autumn Cruise from Invergordon, which included Operation 'Mariner', in September. She was then involved in the Home Fleet's spring training based at Tangiers in 1954 and helped to tow HMS *Agile* to Malta in 1960. On 1 May 1962 she was chartered by the United Towing Company Ltd. of Hull, and was renamed *Englishman* until she was taken over by the RFA and renamed RFA *Reward* in June 1963. In 1970 she was transferred to the Port Auxiliary Service and her name modified simply to *Reward*. That same year she towed HMS *Troubridge* to Newport, Gwent, to be broken up and in October 1972 she was placed in reserve. In January 1975 she was towed to Chatham for conversion into a Naval Patrol Ship and commissioned on 11 July at Port Edgar, Scotland, once again as HMS *Reward*. On 10 August 1976, she was involved in a collision in the Firth of Forth, between the two Forth bridges, with a German-owned container ship, *Plainsman*, in fog. HMS *Reward* sank as a result. Twenty days later she was raised by a civilian floating crane, *Brunel*, and later sold for demolition.

Lead ship of the *Bustler* class, HMS *Bustler* (W72) was sold in 1973 and renamed *Mocni* for Brodospas-Brodus Split, Salvage, Towage and Demolition Enterprises, Split, Yugoslavia, and later renamed *Smjeli*. She was sold for scrap in 1989. HMS *Samsonia* (W23) was chartered in 1947 to the Canadian Foundation Maritime Company and renamed *Foundation Josephine*; she was registered at Leith but was returned to the Admiralty in November 1952 with pennant number A218. In 1974 she was also sold to Brodospas-Brodus Split, Salvage, Towage and Demolition Enterprises, and renamed *Jaki*. She was laid up in 1979 and cannibalised to keep *Smjeli* at sea and was eventually broken up in 1987.

HMS *Turmoil* (W169) retained her own name while under lease to Overseas Towage & Salvage Company of London. She later served under the

HMS *Turmoil* (1945) seen while on charter to Overseas Towage & Salvage Company Limited, London, between 1948 and 1963, she was then laid up and sold to Greek owners in 1965.

Greek flag as *Nisos Kerkyra* and in 1975 was bought by Loucas Matsas and renamed *Matsas*, retaining her Greek registration. As a fleet tug HMS *Turmoil* hit the headlines on both sides of the Atlantic at Christmas 1951 when she put the tug's mate aboard the disabled and heavily listing American freighter *Flying Enterprise* so that he could help her master Captain Carlsen with the towline, all other crew and passengers having been rescued from the ship. Slowly *Turmoil* towed the stricken ship towards Falmouth only to abandon her before she finally capsized three days later. HMS *Turmoil* was also responsible for towing the excursion steamer *Lady Enchantress* and her passengers back to port after that ship's boilers had failed at sea (see Chapter 8).

HMS *Growler* (W105) was chartered in 1947 to Moller Towages Limited at Hong Kong as *Caroline Moller* and sub-chartered in 1952 to Hong Kong Salvage & Towage Company Limited as *Castle Peak*. She was returned to the Admiralty in 1954 and reverted to HMS *Growler* (A111). In 1958 she was chartered to the United Towing Company Limited of Hull and renamed *Welshman*; she was returned to Admiralty service at Devonport in 1963 (Secretary of State for Defence), and was renamed *Cyclone* (A 111). In 1977 she was laid up at Gibraltar and in April 1983 she was sold to Eagle Tugs Limited of Guernsey, (managers Shipmarc Limited, Mombasa) and renamed *Martial*. She was broken up at Karachi in 1985.

HMS *Enchanter* (W178) was one of six ships of the *Envoy* class built by Cochrane and & Sons at Selby in 1944 and 1945. In 1947 she was purchased by United Towing Company of Hull and renamed as yet another *Englishman*. She hit the news during Christmas 1952 when she was towing the elderly RFA steam tanker *Olcades* from Singapore Roads to Blyth. The tow was put in the charge of two canal tugs at Port Suez and an Egyptian pilot joined *Englishman* for the canal transit. John Hobbs wrote in *Sea Breezes* August 1957:

> An aside from an Egyptian on board the tug while in the canal to the effect that he believed the *Olcades* to be an unlucky ship was not given a great deal of attention though if he had rejoined the tug at the end of her voyage he would have found the crew unanimous in support of his comment.

Englishman lost the tow in a storm off Malta, then after the tow was recovered, *Olcades* caught fire after passing Gibraltar due to an oil lamp toppling over as the ship rolled, and again lost her tow in the North Sea on 31 January almost in sight of her goal. With the tug in pursuit she headed into particularly rough weather. Sadly, the bosun was lost overboard and another crew member seriously injured. The tanker went ashore at Bacton Gap, Norfolk, was refloated and finally delivered to Blyth. *Englishman* was eventually sold in 1962 to Suprema Naviera SA, renamed *Cintra* and registered in Panama. The first duty for *Cintra* was to tow a large tanker from Stavanger to the breakers yard at Santander. She was herself broken up in 1972.

HMS *Encore* (W179/A379), another *Envoy* class tug, was sold in 1967 to Selco (Singapore) Limited

Envoy class fleet tug HMS *Enchanter* (1945) was bought by United Towing Company of Hull and given the name *Englishman*; she was sold in 1962.

and renamed *Salvaliant*. In 1970 she was transferred to Selco (Panama) Limited Incorporated, and sold for demolition two years later. HMS *Envoy* (W165) was sold in 1965 to Lucas Matsas, Piraeus and renamed *Matsas*, becoming *Georgios L Matsas* in 1968. She was sold for demolition in 1973.

The four wooden-hulled *Director* class steam tugs were returned to the United States at the end of the war. Of these, HMS *Emulous* (W138) was sold in 1947 to Leopoldo Simoncini, Buenos Aires, renamed *St Christopher* and registered in Costa Rica. She was laid up in Argentina in 1954 following engine failure and rudder damage and beached and abandoned in 1957. HMS *Freedom* (W139) was sold in 1948 to Foundation Maritime, Canada and renamed *Foundation Francis*. In the mid-1950s she was laid up, stripped of equipment and abandoned. Foundation Maritime also bought the boom defence vessel HMS *Dragonet* (Z82), but not until 1961, and renamed her *Foundation Venture*. She was built in 1939 by the Blythe Shipbuilding & Drydock Company Limited. Foundation sold her for further service in 1973.

Army Tugs

During the Great War a number of small tugs were built for the Army. These were designed either for cross-Channel work towing barges to French ports, as single-screw vessels, or to work on canals and rivers on the Continent helping to move materials up towards the Front for which duty they were equipped with twin screws. The latter had no rise of keel and the draught was the same fore and aft, and they had two towing winches either side of the engine casing. They were all given the prefix 'HS' followed by a number. Most of them were sold for commercial service after the war, for example, the Manchester Ship Canal Company acquired a number of them as W B Hallam reported in *Sea Breezes*, June 1968:

> From the fleet of W J Reynolds & Co. of Plymouth two tugs were bought in 1926. They were built in 1917 by John Cran & Sommerville Ltd., Leith for the Government, bearing the numbers *HS30* and *HS31*. They were [single] screw vessels of 154 tons with a horse power of 450. They were renamed *Mount Manisty* and *Cadishead* for service with the Manchester Ship Canal Company who did not dispose of them until 1961.

When the surviving tugs of the Bridgwater Navigation Company came to the end of their days in 1926-7, they were replaced by four twin screw tugs which had been built in 1916-17 for the Government by the Lytham Shipbuilding Co., Ltd. for use on the canals of France, towing barges carrying supplies for the British Army. They were the *HS15*, renamed *MSC Manchester*, *HS16*, renamed *MSC Salford*, *HS17*, renamed *MSC Runcorn*, and *HS18*, renamed *MSC Ellesmere Port*. They were tugs of 144 tons with horse power of 400, and took over the old paddler work of towing barges between the Ship Canal and the docks at Liverpool.

Mount Manisty and *Cadishead* were sold for demolition in 1961 and 1960 respectively. *MSC Manchester* was sold for demolition at Passage West in 1961, and the three remaining small twin screw tugs were sold to Rea Limited of Liverpool in 1948, *MSC Ellesmere Port* becoming *Ellesgarth*, *MSC Salford Salgarth*, and *MSC Runcorn Rungarth*. They were subsequently sold for demolition between 1955 and 1957.

German Tugs

Three German naval tugs sent to Britain for disposal after the war were retained in service as harbour tugs by the Admiralty. The motor tug *Expeller* (ex-*Bora*), steam tug *Exhorter* (ex-*Ostpreußen*) and *Excluder* (ex-*Goldingen*) were retained in service at Chatham until 1967, Devonport until 1962, while *Excluder* was sold in 1950.

13

THE FAIRMILE LAUNCHES OF THE SECOND WORLD WAR: EXAMPLES FROM THE BRITISH ISLES

Of the order of 1,000 fast wooden launches were built to four basic designs during the Second World War (see Table 5). These small vessels are collectively known as Fairmile launches, as the original idea for them came from the Fairmile Marine Company in 1939 (see Lambert and Ross, 2018). The Type B version accounted for some 680 of the total number.

The Fairmile Marine Company Limited was founded by car manufacturer Noel Macklin with the objective of designing a fast patrol boat for use against enemy submarines in British coastal waters. The headquarters of the company was at Fairmile, Cobham in Surrey. Macklin gathered together a team of engineers and naval architects to optimise his design, but as an initial promised order from the Admiralty was delayed, he decided to have a prototype, the Fairmile A, *ML 100*, built at his own expense by the Woodnut yard in Bembridge, on the Isle of Wight. In July 1939, two months before the outbreak of hostilities, the Admiralty awarded Macklin a contract to build eleven Type A Fairmile launches.

The hull of the Fairmile A had a hard chine which made the vessels difficult to handle at speed in poor conditions. Nevertheless, the Admiralty was impressed with the concept and had a new design prepared with a more rounded hull form based on that of a typical destroyer; a contract to manufacture kits to this new design, the Type B Fairmile launch, was then awarded to the Fairmile Marine Company, the kits to be assembled at boat yards large and small. The kits comprised parts that were prefabricated at numerous inland, usually small, manufacturers, for example, furniture and piano workshops, to form sections of vessels. The kits were delivered to numerous small boatyards in six bundles each of which could be

Table 5: FAIRMILE LAUNCH TYPES AND NUMBERS

Numbers	Class	Type
100–111	A	ML (Motor Launch)
112–311	B	ML
312–335	C	MGB (Motor Gun Boat)
336–491	B	ML
492–500	B	RML (Rescue Motor Launch)
511–553	B	RML
554–600	B	ML
601–800	D	MGB/MTB (Motor Torpedo Boat)
801–933	B	ML
2001	F	MGB
4001–4004	B	ML
5001–5029	Modified D	MGB/MTB

transported on a standard 15-ton lorry. Construction from the kits was a rapid process.

The Type B Motor Launch (ML) had the engine-room hatch at main deck level with a large ventilator either side. The Rescue Motor Launch (RML) version had a small rescue cabin abaft the engine-room coaming with the main engine-room hatch on a raised deck.

The ships were designed as anti-submarine vessels to work with coastal convoys, and to protect inshore waters. They were fitted with sonar instruments, and the armament included twelve depth charges, a single 3-pounder gun aft, and twin 0.303in machine guns. The initial design had the vessels powered by three American petrol engines, supplied through Lend-Lease, but this was quickly reduced to just two engines due to supply problems. The twin-engine version had a top speed of 20 knots which allowed them to outrun any submarine. The bunkers carried up to 2,305 gallons of high-octane fuel to give a range of 1,500nm at a cruising speed of 12 knots. The destroyer-type hull provided good handling in most weather conditions, although care was needed with a heavy following sea.

Although the Type B lacked the higher speeds of the Motor Torpedo Boats and Motor Gun Boats, they were a great success in a variety of roles. Some were converted for use against a possible invasion by German forces from occupied France, while others had two torpedo tubes fitted as a replacement for the depth charges. When the threat of invasion was no longer realistic, conversions again took place. One of these was the minesweeper version for use in the Mediterranean and off the D-Day beaches. The Type B saw service under a variety of flags: United States, Canada, India, Australia, New Zealand, Norway, Netherlands, Free French and South Africa. Canada built Fairmile Type B launches to a slightly different design; the beam of the Canadian vessels was larger and the ships heavier. They were also constructed in New Zealand, Australia, Hong Kong, Singapore, South Africa, Egypt and Jamaica.

There followed a small number of gunboats of Type C and Type D. The Fairmile Type D had a larger hull than the Type B but the sea-keeping qualities were inferior. The ships were poorly ventilated and condensation caused wood rot in many vessels, some requiring steel braces to be fitted across the main deck. Nevertheless, a number of them were used in static condition by the Sea Scouts after the war. The Type B was easier and more economical to convert, being twin screw, whereas the Type D were quadruple screw.

Fairmile Type B *ML303* (1941) supporting the D-Day Landings, Operation 'Overlord', 6 June 1944.

The Fairmile Marine Company had expanded considerably as a supplier to the Admiralty. However, due to lack of capital, Noel Macklin negotiated an agreement to become a non-profit making commercial division of the Admiralty with responsibility for receiving orders for Fairmile launches, managing supplies of materials and supervising the construction contracts that were awarded. At one point, the company had a staff of over 500 employees who had to ensure that production times were kept to a minimum, that components were available and that subcontracting was spread out among a variety of companies which were least affected by the war effort and had the capacity to undertake the work.

Not surprising then, that a question was asked of the Fairmile Marine Company Limited in Parliament on 21 March 1944, as recorded in *Hansard*, Volume 398:

> Mr Liddel asked the First Lord of the Admiralty to what extent the Government are interested, directly or through nominees, in the affairs of the Fairmile Marine Company, Limited, and/or the Fairmile Engineering Company, Limited; what is their paid-up capital; what authority either of these companies has to act as agents for the Government; and whether they are authorised in any way to make arrangements in connection with post-war purchases or policy.
>
> Captain Pilkington replied: The Fairmile Marine Company, Limited, is a private company, with a nominal share capital of £1,000 in £1 shares, of which six only have been issued, all of which are held by Government nominees on behalf of the Admiralty. They act with full authority as agents and managers for the Admiralty in connection with the construction of certain types of small craft. The Admiralty are represented on the Board of the company. The whole of the company's production is for Admiralty account. The Admiralty has no interest in the Fairmile Engineering Company, Limited. The answer to the last part of the Question is in the negative.

The last part of the question was important because at the end of the war almost the entire fleet of Fairmile launches was put up for sale. The design life of the wooden ships was just five years, but many had already demonstrated that they were fit for much longer careers. About 200 of the little ships were bought privately for conversion to motor yachts while others were bought commercially for coastal passenger and excursion services, or as workboats, survey or diving vessels. In nearly all cases the petrol engines were removed before the ships were sold and the engines returned to the United States. They were replaced by more economical diesel units and the petrol tanks replaced by smaller-volume diesel oil bunker tanks. This reduced the top speed of the launches from 20 knots and a cruising speed of 16 knots to just 12 knots. Some were given only cosmetic modification while others were upgraded in all manner of ways to suit their new owners' requirements – perhaps the luxury motor yacht of the day was the most extensively refitted of all the vessels.

Modified Fairmile Type D or 'Dog Boat' SCC *Golden Hinde* (1944) moored on the River Dart for many years as a Sea Cadet Corps training base.

Excursion Duties

About thirty Type B vessels were bought by British coastal operators for seasonal use in the holiday trade and many of these are still fondly remembered in that role. These ships became familiar sights at numerous seaside resorts, offering full-day and part-day sea and river cruises. Some only stayed briefly in the excursion trade while others lasted in service for over 50 years, despite the five-year design life of the wooden hull. In all cases they were readily identified as a former Fairmile launch as both the bridge structure, which was usually retained, and the hull shape itself were quite distinctive. Many had new funnels built to take the soot from the diesel engines away from the decks and the passengers, whilst others had a small deckhouse built aft of midships. Stability requirements dictated that nothing else could be added and with a full complement of up to 250 passengers the ships were liable to roll even in a light sea.

J Bolson & Son Limited at Poole was instrumental in many conversions from naval ship to excursion boat. Bolson also operated excursion boats from Poole and Bournemouth and these resumed in 1946. Because of delays in refurbishing the larger paddle steamers of Cosens and Red Funnel, coupled with silting at Bournemouth Pier, Bolson converted three Landing Craft Guns into passenger excursion boats each with a passenger certificate for 271 persons (see Chapter 9). In 1948 the yard converted a Fairmile Type B launch for passenger use and named her *Channel Belle*. She was built by Johnson & Jago at Leigh-on-sea in 1944. Her certificate allowed her to carry 250 passengers on local cruises within sight of land. She was equipped with a pair of 6-cylinder Gray Marine Motor Company oil engines built in Detroit.

Bolson sold *Channel Belle* for £13,500 in November 1949 to The Mayor, Aldermen & Burgesses of the County Borough of Wallasey, her registered owners, who gave her the name *Wallasey Belle*. She was of 126 tons gross (118 tons below deck) and had been bought specifically for late night cross-Mersey passenger ferry duties as buses were then prohibited from the Mersey tunnel at night and the last train ran at about

Channel Belle (1944) was a converted Fairmile Type B launch employed in the excursion trade at Bournemouth until sold for use as a Mersey Ferry after the 1949 summer season.

midnight. *Wallasey Belle* was used during the summer of 1950 for cruising on the Mersey with a passenger certificate for 250. A popular venue was to cruise close in off Cammell Laird's yard to view the aircraft carrier *Ark Royal* on the stocks. The *Wallasey Belle* was laid up towards the end of 1950, and Wallasey Corporation sold her for £1,250 to Mr A P Martin of Heswall in November 1953. She was resold shortly afterwards for private use in Australia.

Typical of the commercial purchases of the Type B launch was that made by the Bristol-based Poole and Solent Navigation Company Limited which was founded for the purpose in 1948. Graham Farr explains in his book *West Country Passenger Steamers*:

> The first was named the *Matapan*, 127 tons gross, built at Oulton Broad in 1941; next the *Dunkirk*, 127 tons gross, built at Leigh-on-Sea in 1942, and then the *Anzio*, 96 tons gross, built at Plymouth in 1941 ... All were registered at Poole, where they were based for trips to places between Swanage and Isle of Wight. The *Matapan* and *Dunkirk* were sold to the Dorset Yacht Company Limited in 1951, and to J Bolson & Son Limited of Poole, in the following year. *Dunkirk* was again sold in 1960, for a yacht, and, after rebuilding, renamed *Zymoa*.

Matapan (1941), ex- *RML180*, was renamed *Poole Belle* in 1968 and served at Bournemouth throughout her civilian career.

The *Anzio* remained in the Bristol ownership until 1959, latterly running from Brighton, and was then sold to William Foreman. On 4 August in that year she began a service from Southend to Gillingham, with occasional cruises on the Medway, but various formalities, such as Trinity House insisting that she always carried a pilot, made her unremunerative. In 1960, with a Class VI passenger certificate for 198 persons, she began a four-times-daily service from Sheerness to Southend in the ownership of the Thames and Medway Navigation Company. Later some alterations to Sheerness harbour walls made it difficult for her to get alongside so the service was abandoned and she was put up for sale in the spring of 1964. She was sold to Michael Angelos, of the Greek shipping firm, and he spent £21,000 in converting her to a luxury yacht at Ramsgate. She left for Greece on 16 July, 1964, but had an engine explosion when off the Île de Batz, caught fire and sank. Her crew of four were saved and taken to Brest by a fishing vessel.

In 1963 *Matapan*, ex-*ML180*, was rechristened *Poole Belle*. She was licensed to carry 250 passengers with a Class VI passenger certificate. Her last service day at Poole was on 30 September 1976 with a return trip to Bournemouth Pier. She was sold in the early summer of 1977, renamed *Western Clipper* and intended for charter cruises in the Greek Islands.

Regarding *ML113* converted after the war for use at Falmouth, Grahame Farr again:

> ... built [by Tough Bros.] at Teddington in 1940, was purchased by the Blackpool Steam Navigation Company (1947) Limited in July 1948 and refitted as a passenger vessel of 119 tons gross, with two Gray diesels. Without ever using her in their home waters they chartered her to the Falmouth Boat Building Company, for the 1949 season, thus accounting for the

historic name *Pendennis*. She had a certificate for 134 passengers in Falmouth Harbour and vicinity, and proved a most popular vessel. She was for sale in 1951 and made her last local sailings at the end of the season.

She was bought by the Radcliffe Shipping Company and based at Brighton from 1951, operating cruises to Eastbourne.

An early set of conversions were three Fairmile Type B launches for Commodore Cruises Limited for use along the south coast of England for cruises, rather than short day excursions, between holiday resorts. The vessels were registered at London and later at Ramsgate and given the names *White Commodore* (ex-*ML445*), *Red Commodore* (ex-*RML537*) and *Silver Commodore* (ex-*RML499*) and entered service in time for the 1947 cruise season.

In September 1947 *Red Commodore* was chartered to Sark Projects Limited for use on the St Peter Port and Sark link. As Sark Projects collapsed at the end of the tourist season Commodore Cruises Limited took up the reins themselves the following year using *Red Commodore*, joined later in the season by her two fleet mates, the work being more lucrative than the former cruise ship duties. Another Fairmile B, *Gay Commodore*, joined the fleet in 1948 and was used on the south Coast of England but sold in 1948, later based at Harwich without change of name. *Red Commodore* was broken up in 1948. Commodore Cruises was awarded the contract to maintain the Sark service in 1950 when another Fairmile launch, *Fleet Commodore* (ex-*RML534*), joined the service. *White Commodore* was sold in March 1951 and broken up in 1952. From 1952 onwards, only *Silver Commodore* and *Fleet Commodore* remained at Guernsey and the port of

Fleet Commodore (1942) leaving St Peter Port Harbour for Sark. (The Guernsey Press Company)

The cruise ship *Red Commodore* (1942) seen in 1947 with a party of passengers on the foredeck and with a tall radio mast for communication while at sea. (World Ship Society Photo Archive)

registry was finally changed from London to Guernsey.

In September 1961 *Silver Commodore* was sold to Croson Limited of Poole (formerly Bolson but changed to Croson following a merger with Crosby in 1958). She was renamed *Swanage Belle* and in 1968 became *Wessex Belle*. She had a Class VI certificate for 250 passengers. In the early 1970s *Wessex Belle*, along with her consort *Poole Belle*, maintained the Bournemouth to Swanage ferry and fitted in short cruises from Bournemouth. Croson sold *Wessex Belle* in 1973 to Michael Brooks of Poole, and she was converted for the charter cruise market. The ship was arrested in September 1980 for Customs infringements at Majorca and was sold shortly afterwards.

Fleet Commodore finally left the Channel Islands in June 1965. Latterly she had been employed only on the Guernsey to Sark service operating between April and September but carrying up to 30,000 tourist passengers per year on day trips. The journey time from St Peter Port to Sark was about one hour.

In Scotland, John Hall had operated the former Scarborough pleasure steamer *Royal Lady* on cruises on the Firth of Forth in 1947 before selling her on to GSNC to become their *Crested Eagle*. He replaced her for the 1948 season with *Royal Forth Lady*, a Type B Fairmile launch that he had refitted by Vosper Limited at Portsmouth with a seventy-seat bar and a fifty-seat tea lounge upholstered in leatherette and moquette complete with fluorescent lighting – then a new innovation. She arrived at Granton in early June and made an inaugural trip on the Forth with sheep for Inchcolm Island. The public service to Inchcolm started on 9 June with departures from Granton every 90 minutes between 2 pm and 8 pm. Hall also bought a second Fairmile Type B which he also had converted by Vosper Limited and re-christened her *Royal Tay Lady*. He based her at Perth. The service along the lower reaches of the Tay was poorly patronised and she joined her sister on the Inchcolm service in August. Both ships lost their 'Royal' prefix at the request of the Lord Lyon during the season, becoming *Forth Lady* and *Tay Lady*.

In 1949 *Tay Lady* received a large deck house and was sent to Belfast to ply her trade as *Ulster Lady*. David McNeill in *Irish Passenger Steamships Part 1* described her:

> In the summer of 1949, Mr John Hall sent the converted Fairmile naval launch *Tay Lady* to Belfast. He renamed her *Ulster Lady* and used her for 'four shilling' cruises on the lough which went to Bangor on Saturdays. A cocktail bar, a snack service and background music were provided. After one season she left, and so ended the only post-1945 attempt to revive the 'Bangor Boat'.

In 1950 *Ulster Lady* was deployed on the Clyde and based at Greenock with a morning departure for Rothesay where she offered short cruises. In August 1950 both ships were sold to Forth Ferries Limited, a company set up by John Hall to run former Landing Craft on the Granton to Burntisland ferry (see Chapter 9). The *Ulster Lady* was used to supplement the new ferry service for passengers and cyclists. Meanwhile, *Forth Lady* maintained the Inchcolm service. With mounting debts the excursion ships saw little service in 1952 and were laid up in the Old Dock at Leith. *Ulster Lady* was sold to Regent Diesels Limited of Leeds for demolition in 1953; *Forth Lady* was converted into a yacht at Burntisland and used to provide seasonal yachting cruises on the Thames and later along the Devon coast.

RML525 was built by Frank Curtis at Looe in 1941. She was sold to Mr L S J Wilkinson of Inverness for £2,600 in February 1946, renamed *Lenrodian*, and converted for passenger use on Loch Ness. The ship was sold in 1950 and renamed *Fae-des-Iles*. A second Fairmile was bought by Wilkinson (she was either *ML188* or *ML234*) and converted at Inverness in 1949 as *Glenrodian*, but renamed *Island Princess* before she was commissioned as an excursion ship. She had been built by A M Dickie & Sons at Tarbert in 1941. She was chartered for use at St Helier from late August until the end of September, leaving Jersey on 1 October for Chichester Harbour. Thereafter she worked on Loch Ness and was not disposed of until well into the 1960s. *Lenrodian* and *Island Princess* were both registered at Inverness.

In 1956 the Cambrian Marine Line Limited of Liverpool put the former Fairmile Type B launch *Cambrian Prince* into service at Llandudno. Registered at Liverpool, she was built in Maldon by J Sadd in 1941 as *ML253*. In 1951 she was converted into the private yacht *Lepanto*. As such she had the lifeboat slung on davits over the stern. *Cambrian Prince*, with the lifeboat stowed amidships, operated short one-hour morning cruises, long afternoon and short evening cruises, Monday to Saturday, from Llandudno. On Sunday the long cruise took place in the evening. The *Cambrian Prince* commenced on 14 May 1956 with an inaugural cruise for guests of the owners; she moored overnight off Conway. She was sold to Devon Cruising Company of Torquay in 1957 becoming the *Kiloran II* with a Class VI certificate for 182 passengers. She remained at Torquay until November 1963 when she was sold to Cornish Sea Cruising Company of St Mawes, to operate five-hour cruises along the Cornish coast and into the Rivers Fal and Helford. She was owned by Kenneth Cooper of Paignton in the early 1970s, was sold to Captain Morgan Cruises of Valletta, Malta in 1972, still as *Kiloran II*, and was later in use at Tunis until 2001.

The Western Lady Ferry Service between Brixham and Torquay was operated by a succession of former Fairmile Type B RML launches. Initially owned by Mr Edhouse, when the ships had yellow hulls, the fleet was sold later to John Perrett. The ships were easy to recognise because all of them, except *Western Lady II*, had the small rescue cabin abaft the engine-room coaming removed to make way for a deck shelter and tea bar.

The first ship acquired by Mr Edhouse was *Western Lady*, built in 1941 by William Weatherhead & Son of Cockenzie, East Lothian. She entered service in August 1942 as *RML535* with the 63rd ML Flotilla, Plymouth Command, where she remained until 1944, later working from Appledore before returning to Plymouth. She was sold at Dartmouth in 1946, minus engines and equipped with a new pair of diesels. The Western Lady Ferry Service had her maintain the Torquay and Brixham route with occasional sea cruises and trips to the River Dart. She had a Class VI passenger certificate for 213 persons. In 1968 she was aground at Elbury Cove but was able to refloat without injury or significant damage. She retired from the Torbay services of Western Lady Ferry Service in 1980, spent much time laid up, eventually becoming a derelict at Galhampton on the River Dart.

Western Lady II was built by Austin's, East Ham and was commissioned as *RML542* in July 1942 with the 63rd ML Flotilla, operating out of Falmouth, Newlyn, Padstow and Appledore. She joined the Western Lady Ferry Service in 1947 to work alongside *Western Lady*. *Western Lady II* was chartered to run cruises from Custom House Quay, Dublin and from Dun Laoghaire in 1955 and was sold at the end of the season for use as a private yacht.

Western Lady III was built by Southampton Steam Joinery Limited in 1941 and commissioned as *RML497* in July 1942. She was stationed with 62nd ML Flotilla at Portland between 1942 and 1944. She was then transferred to Kirkwall in January 1944 on anti-submarine target-towing duties until August. She then joined the 69th Flotilla based at Felixstowe until eventually being sold off at Itchenor in 1947 and entering service with the Western Lady Ferry Service between Brixham and Torquay in that same year.

Western Lady III (1941), ex-*RML497*, entered service between Brixham and Torquay in 1947. She was the last Fairmile Type B launch in passenger service in the UK, operating as *The Fairmile*.

Western Lady III had a Class VI passenger certificate for 208 people. She was withdrawn from the Torbay fleet at the end of the 2006 season, but returned to service from Swanage for Fairmile Classic Cruises in August 2007 running five cruises along the Dorset coast daily, apart from Tuesdays when she took a day trip to Yarmouth (Isle of Wight). Services recommenced in 2008, but the company ran into financial problems in September and extensive work was needed to extend her passenger certificate. In June 2009 *Western Lady III* was bought by the Greenway Ferry and entered service that summer as *The Fairmile*, operating between Torbay, Dartmouth and Greenway. In December 2015 she was acquired by the National Museum of the Royal Navy at Hartlepool.

Western Lady IV was built by Solent Shipyard Limited, Lower Swanwick, and commissioned as *RML526* in August 1942. Stationed initially with the 63rd ML Flotilla at Falmouth, she then transferred to the 61st ML Flotilla based at Newhaven and later Plymouth as an ambulance. After the war, she was sold for conversion into a private yacht and renamed *Anbrijo*. She was used as a ferry between Gibraltar and Tangiers from 1947 until 1949 when she was arrested by the Admiralty Marshal for non-payment of harbour dues. The ship was auctioned at Fowey in 1949, bought by Western Lady Ferry Service and renamed *Western Lady IV*. She was converted for excursion duties at Millbay Docks in Plymouth and given seating above and below the main deck and a certificate for 175 passengers, later increased to Class VI for 205 persons. She served until 2007 when she was sold to private owners, Tony & Kim Medri. They used her as a seagoing home until the vessel was moved to Rye in Sussex where she sank in 2019 and was later demolished.

Another former Fairmile Type B launch that was used at Torquay for many years was the *Pride of Paignton*, completed in 1942 as *RML492* by Aldous Successors, Brightlingsea. She was owned by the South Western Steam Navigation Company Limited, registered at London, and offered three cruises daily with a Class VI certificate for 212 persons.

Bambo, owned by Hedley Jennings Shipping Company, Limited, of Dawlish, also traded out of Torquay from 1949. She was built in 1940 as either *ML131* or *ML139* at the Looe shipyard of Frank Curtis and was registered as *Bambo* at London on 12 August 1948 with a recorded gross tonnage of 95. She sported an uninviting black hull and had a plain funnel with a narrow black rim.

In the afternoon of 2 June 1951, *Bambo* was in collision at Torquay with the open dinghy *Lanice*. *Lanice* was hit aft by the bow of the overtaking *Bambo* about three-quarters of a mile from the harbour entrance, was overturned and sunk, with

The Fairmile Type B launch *Bambo* (1940), commissioned as *ML131* or *ML139*, was bought by Hedley Jennings Shipping Company Limited and traded out of Torquay from 1949 until she was wrecked in 1952.

the death of two lady passengers, although the man in charge of the dinghy jumped overboard before the collision and survived. Captain Owen Thomas, in charge of *Bambo*, was admonished for shaping a course too close to the dinghy at the subsequent enquiry. *Bambo* was herself sunk in the River Dart above Kingswear in 1952; there was no loss of life. The Hedley Jennings Shipping Company, Limited was dissolved but business continued under the title Herbert Jennings and Son.

Merrie Golden Hind was based at Ipswich in 1948 and at Torquay in 1949 under the ownership of Bertram W H Fordham. The ship was registered at Ipswich. She had been built as *MGB346* in 1941 by Risdon Beazley at Northam Bridge. In 1949 she was used at Guernsey for a short charter to the Radcliffe Shipping Company. She was again in service at Torquay in 1950 but was chartered for use in Dublin Bay for the 1951 and 1952 seasons. However, late in 1952 *Merrie Golden Hind* was reported wrecked at Bullock Harbour in Dalkey, Dublin.

ML162 was built in 1942 by A M Dickie and Sons at Bangor, North Wales. She shot down six enemy aircraft, took part in the sinking of a submarine, and was highly commended for her role in the D-Day invasion. After the war, *ML162* was transferred to the Royal Netherlands Navy where she continued in service for a further two years. John Knight bought *ML162*, and converted her at Great Yarmouth for excursion duties with the name *Golden Galleon*. In 1950 she worked from Lowestoft but she moved to Great Yarmouth in time for the 1951 season. Initially she carried out sea trips but found her niche operating into the River Yare and exploring the Broads with two-hour cruises to Reedham, Burgh Castle and Breydon Water. For this she had a Class V certificate for 247 passengers and offered a tea room and lounge. She was registered under the ownership of Pleasurecraft Company, Great Yarmouth and was managed by J E Knight in later years. *Golden Galleon* was broken up on the River Yare in 2006.

Eastern Princess (ex-*MGB347*) came to Great

An advertising card for *Southern Princess* (1941), ex *RML293*, which worked from the Britannia Pier at Great Yarmouth in 1948.

Yarmouth in 1945 under the ownership of Southern Coastcraft Limited. She was one of three similar boats, the others being *Southern Princess* and *Western Princess*, all owned by Reginald Fligg. *Western Princess* and *Eastern Princess* operated out of Great Yarmouth and *Southern Princess* initially out of Lowestoft, but was based at Great Yarmouth for the 1948 season. All three offered sea trips, the Great Yarmouth boats to view the seal colony at Scroby Sands.

Southern Princess was built in 1941 by the Dorset Yacht Company at Hamworthy as *ML293*. She was put up for sale in August 1945 and bought by Southern Coastcraft Limited to be converted in time for the 1946 season as an excursion ship. Her career as an excursion ship was short-lived and she was leased to the Humber Conservancy Board in 1949 as a survey vessel with the name *E P Hutchinson*. She later flew the Dutch flag and with collision damage returned to the Red Ensign to lay up at Bristol. She was then renovated and used as the Naval Cadets base at Bristol. She later moved to Hooe Lake at Plymouth but by 2004 was reported to have been 'disposed of'. *Western Princess* was also sold at an early stage but *Eastern Princess* continued under the ownership of Southern Coastcraft. The company was taken over by the Yarmouth and Gorleston Steamboat Company in 1964.

In 1968 *Eastern Princess* was used on river cruises, and no longer offered the Scroby Sands seal trip. She was used on the Thames in 1971 by Meridian Line Cruises and was then licensed to carry 227 passengers with Class V and Class VI passenger certificates. She operated seasonal charter cruises and ran from Tower Pier down river to Greenwich and on to Southend-on-Sea. She was sold in 1973 for service in Greece, based at Volos. Her commercial career ended in 2006.

ML309 was built by J W & A Upham of Brixham in 1941. She was with the 61st Flotilla from 1942 to 1945, and was sent for disposal at Harwich in 1946. There she was bought by The Devon Star

River Lady II (1942) seen alongside Halfpenny Pier, Harwich, was owned by the Devon Star Shipping Company and operated river and sea cruises from Harwich and Felixstowe.

Shipping Company of Ipswich and used locally on the River Orwell for excursions in 1946. *River Lady* was replaced by *River Lady II* the following year when *River Lady* was sold to the Western Lady Ferry Service retaining her name. She was then used as a cruise and charter boat until 1970 and was then laid up. In 1973 she was used as a diving support vessel and was based at Plymouth as *Western Diver* until 1985.

River Lady II, 108 gross tons, which was converted at Brixham in 1946, ran the Orwell excursions from 1947 until 1963, latterly including coastal and river excursions from Felixstowe under the ownership of River Orwell Cruising and Ferry Service Company. After a brief period at Holyhead, she spent many years abandoned at Glasson Dock and by 1981 had become just *River Lady*, later a hulk on the mud at low water at St Georges Quay, Lancaster. She was subsequently moved to the beach at Silverdale and destroyed by fire.

During 1951 the former Fairmile Type B launch *John McLeod* operated out of Newhaven. She took afternoon cruises past Beachy Head to Eastbourne and westwards to Brighton. The ship moved to Gibraltar at the end of the season and was later renamed *Onset*. A sister-ship *Mae McLeod* also operated briefly on the south coast but was mainly used for charter work. She features in the 1953 film *The Steel Key*.

ML120 was bought in 1946 by John Baylay, then a hotel manager at Brighton. He renamed the vessel *Onetwenty* and had her towed to Shoreham to fit her out with new engines and accommodation suitable for charter cruises. The charter cruises were a success, some going to near Continental destinations, but ended after only two seasons when the owner pursued other interests. The vessel was laid up at Itchenor and was later used as a houseboat.

There were a number of other Fairmile B launches sold after the Second World War for commercial and private uses around the British Isles. These included *ML142/Tregarth*; *ML143/Gay Tulip*; *ML197/Cory 3*; *ML198/Cory 4*; *ML235/Pauline*; *ML252/Cheriton*; *ML344/Glen Tor*; *ML345/Warrior Geraint*; *ML347/Venturer*; *ML400/Dolphin*; *ML437/Mermaid*; *ML482/Walney*; *RML518/Commodore*; *ML600/Lady Penelope*; *ML913/Lulworth Castle*; *ML918/Lavender Lady*. These and others were applied to the excursion trade, survey work, diving support and a host of other uses. Many ended their days as houseboats; for example, *ML587* and *ML588* became the houseboats *La Contenta* and *Mary Lou* respectively.

The commercial career of the Fairmile Launch is a credit both to the designers of the ship and to the builders and kit manufacturers. Many holiday-makers at Great Yarmouth have a lasting memory of sitting under the awning over the main deck aft on a long bench on board *Eastern Princess*. There was little chance of visiting the tea room let alone try to get to the loo! Alongside before sailing, a photographer came on board and took family group pictures, row by row, the row in front being asked to bow forward so as not to obstruct the image! On return to the quayside two hours later, there was your photo ready for you to buy and take home. And how many seals did you see on Scroby Sands? Well, yes, there were a few ...

A powerful image of a Fairmile Launch: *Poole Belle* (1941) was commissioned as *ML180* and sold for use as the excursion boat *Matapan*, at Poole in 1948. She was renamed *Poole Belle* in 1963 and was sold overseas in 1977.

14

MINESWEEPERS AND OTHER SMALL VESSELS FROM THE SECOND WORLD WAR

Much of the design phase of the coastal forces vessels was undertaken in the four years prior to the outbreak of war. Successful designs concentrated on the motor torpedo boat, motor anti-submarine boat and the motor launch from work carried out by private companies, including British Power Boat Company, Vospers, and, of course, the Fairmile company.

British Power Boat and Thornycroft both produced prototype motor minesweepers, that from Thornycroft gaining favour with the Admiralty. One of the British Power Boat prototypes was lost in unfortunate circumstances in May 1966. She had become the yacht *Quesada* owned by a Campbeltown garage owner and was used for day charter cruises. On this occasion she had sailed from Rothesay to Campbeltown in poor weather when the engine failed east of the Davaar Light. The vessel foundered with the loss of eight of the eighteen men on board – there were only eleven life jackets on board.

Lenton and Colledge wrote about the motor minesweeper in their book on coastal forces:

> The MMS was the direct result of a weapon and counter-weapon: the magnetic mine, which required a non-magnetic 'sweeper, and the LL Sweep which permitted such a vessel to be of modest dimensions. The design details and construction were entrusted to Richards Ironworks who, despite their incongruous title, were wooden boat builders of wide experience. It was considerably larger than the prewar MMS which had only been designed with a view to sweeping contact mines, was capable of world-wide employment, and possessed the rugged reliability so essential to its arduous task.

Of the Harbour Defence Motor Launch (HDML), they wrote:

> Another successful Admiralty design was the round bilge HDML for patrol work in estuarial and coastal waters. It was of simple construction which enabled it to be built in yards abroad, not all of which possessed the facilities available in the UK, was easily maintained, and was a most sea-kindly craft. Capable of a wide range of employment it was in demand in every theatre of operations.

Bangor, *Ardrossan*, *Blyth* and *Auk* class minesweepers

The fourteen ships of the *Bangor* class were equipped with diesel engines driving twin screws providing a speed of 16 knots. The ships were 162ft in length and had a beam of 28ft. The *Blyth* class, of which nineteen ships were built for use by the Admiralty and Allied fleets, were 172ft long and were equipped with triple expansion steam engines and a pair of Admiralty-type boilers. The *Ardrossan* class had steam turbine machinery and the hull was extended again to 174ft; twenty-six were built. The three classes were used by the Royal Navy, the Royal Canadian Navy and the Indian Navy. The vessels had a shallow draft and tended to roll and pitch violently in rough weather. The *Auk* class were American-built ships propelled by diesel-electric machinery handed over to the Royal Navy under Lend-Lease. Twenty of the ninety-five ships built in this class came to Britain the remainder staying with the United States Navy (see Chapter 11).

Not many of the ships went into commercial service after the war. Many of the *Blyth* class with steam reciprocating engines and all the turbine steamers, which were expensive units to maintain, were scrapped after the war. Two *Bangor* class motor ships were transferred in 1946 to the Royal Air Force as Long-Range Rescue Craft, HMS *Bridport* (J50) and HMS *Bridlington* (J65) becoming HMAFV *Cawley* and HMAFV *Bridlington*. Both ships were constructed by William Denny & Brothers at Dumbarton in 1940. They served both military and civil aircraft rescue. Both ships were sold for demolition at Plymouth in 1959 and 1960 respectively, their roles having been taken over by long-range helicopters.

One *Blyth* class steamer that was bought commercially was the lead ship of the class. In May 1948, the Radcliffe Channel Island Shipping Company bought HMS *Blyth* (J15) for conversion for commercial use with the name *Radborne*. She had been launched at Blyth on 2 September 1940 and placed in reserve in 1946. As *Radborne*, she arrived at Guernsey in 1948 for conversion for service as a passenger and cargo ship to work between Guernsey and Weymouth; the work was never completed and she was laid up at Weymouth. She was sold in November 1952 and demolished.

HMS *Llandudno* (J67) was completed on 28 March 1942 by William Hamilton & Company Limited at Port Glasgow as an *Ardrossan* class turbine steamer. She was sold for commercial

The *Bangor* class minesweeper HMS *Bridlington* (1940) was one of two ships transferred to the RAF after the war and converted for use as Long Range Rescue Craft.

service after the war and renamed *Rorvick*, but she too was scrapped in 1952. All the other British *Ardrossan* class ships were sold for scrap after the war. That being said, two of the oil-engined ships of the *Bangor* class were sold to Norwegian owners in 1946 and served their owners until withdrawn and scrapped in 1961. A number of the *Blyth* class were only decommissioned from the Indian Navy in the early 1960s.

The *Auk* class minesweeper HMS *Strenuous* (J338), launched in 1941 as USS *Vital* (AM129), was sold in April 1947 and renamed *Evening Star*. She was the only ship of the class to be sold to a commercial owner. In 1949 *Evening Star* was resold to the South Western Steam Navigation Company Limited (of *Hellenic Prince* fame, see Chapter 8) and renamed *Pride of the West*. The intention was that she would be converted into a day passenger ship for use at Torquay, running excursions alongside the company's paddle steamer *Pride of Devon*. However, *Pride of Devon*, which dated from 1897, failed her survey before the start of the summer season in 1949 and was laid up at Southampton. With the paddle steamer later condemned, the company decided to cut its losses and put *Pride of the West* back onto the market, the conversion work barely having started.

There were no buyers and the ship remained laid up until sold for demolition in 1956.

Motor Minesweepers (MMS)

Over 300 MMS were built for the Royal Navy from 1938 onwards. Affectionately known as the 'Mickey Mouse Ships' they served a valuable role in making inshore waters safe. They were generally 119ft in length with a beam of 23ft, and were of wooden construction in order that they could deal with magnetic mines, some also carried a hammer slung over the bows on an 'A' frame to deal with acoustic mines. They had a single shaft and were equipped with a variety of different diesel engines which sustained a speed of about 12 knots. They carried two anti-aircraft guns.

One of the better known post-war conversions of the motor minesweeper was that of *MMS233* (J733) which became the passenger ferry *Loch Arkaig*, owned by David MacBrayne Limited. The *MMS233*, was built in 1942 by J Bolson & Son Limited at Poole. In 1947 she was renumbered as *MMS1733* and the following years was given the name *St David*, but reverted to just *MMS1733* in 1954.

MMS1733 was eventually put up for sale as lying on the Clyde in March 1958. She was acquired by David MacBrayne Limited in May 1959 destined for the Mallaig to Portree mail route. The ship was stripped to main-deck level by Jas. Lamont & Company Limited at Greenock and virtually all her fittings, including her engines, were removed and an aluminium superstructure, internal steel bulkheads and a new Bergius Kelvin engine were fitted. The passenger accommodation was completed by Timbacraft Limited at Shandon. In April 1960 the former minesweeper emerged as the MacBrayne passenger ferry *Loch Arkaig*. Of 179 tons gross, she had a winter Class II passenger certificate for 50 persons and summer Class III certificate for 234.

All ships, irrespective of their material of construction, be it metal, timber or even glass-reinforced plastic, obey the same laws of hydrostatics and hydrodynamics and if, like *Loch Arkaig*, they require a passenger certificate then they will have to comply with the requirements of a flag state regulatory authority (MCA in the UK) as described in Chapter 2. During *Loch Arkaig*'s conversion to a passenger-ship role she was fitted with new steel watertight bulkheads in order to comply with the compartmental sub-division requirements. Prior to this a statutory minimum freeboard would have been assigned and on completion of the conversion, the stability in all conditions of loading would have been calculated for subsequent approval.

Like all MacBrayne passenger and mail ships *Loch Arkaig* occasionally carried livestock and, as needs must, cars, as described by Sandy Ferguson in his book *From Burma to Barra*:

> The first time the mate informed me in Portree that we had two cars for Raasay, I thought he was taking the Mickey, then watched fascinated as we loaded the cars forward of the funnel onto the boat deck. This was done by using two long stout planks of wood. The tide was low at Portree and would be similar at Raasay, so the two planks were rigged jutting out from Portree Pier. The first car was driven carefully onto the boards, moving forward very slowly, until they began to tilt. The car then stopped while the outboard ends of the skids were pulled down onto the deck then the car continued its perilous forward descent until it came to rest on the vessel. The planks were then moved forward the required distance, and the operation repeated. At Raasay the opposite took place, with the planks first being on the ship and the car driving upwards to the tipping centre before driving on the level onto the pier. At times of high tide the reverse took place.

In 1964 *Loch Arkaig* took up the Mallaig–Small Isles service. For this route a samson post and

David MacBrayne's Inner Island ferry *Loch Arkaig* (1942), originally the motor minesweeper *MMS233*, was rebuilt from the main deck upwards when converted into a passenger and cargo ferry in 1959. (Author)

derrick was installed forward to handle cargo and a door cut in the bulwarks port and starboard to allow livestock access to the foredeck. Her Class III passenger certificate was reduced to 183 persons to compensate for the additional cargo deadweight she might now have to carry.

On 28 March 1979, *Loch Arkaig* sank at her berth in Mallaig Harbour. The timber hull had been breached by a projection in the quayside; patched and raised, she was towed to Port Glasgow where she was declared a constructive total loss and offered for sale. She was bought by Ship & Yacht Consultants Limited, of London and sold in 1980 to interests in the Middle East. She was reported to have sunk off Cadiz, in October 1985.

Christian Salvesen bought two motor minesweepers in 1948 for use as harbour service vessels to support their whaling interests in the Antarctic. These were *MMS372*, which was renamed *Southern Paul*, and *MMS378* which appropriately became *Southern Peter*. Both ships were built by Humphrey & Smith at Grimsby in 1944 and were each equipped with an 8-cylinder Crossley oil engine. It is believed that the pair sank at their moorings off the company's shore base at Leith Harbour in September 1964 when heavy snow on the upper works caused them to capsize.

Many other MMS were sold for commercial service after the war, there being no further use for them in the Navy. They were put to a variety of uses and many were maintained in gainful employment into the 1970s. A number of them were converted to trawlers. One, *MMS1039*, went to the French Navy as *D341* between 1946 and October 1947 and was sold in July 1948 to G D Claridge Limited of Grimsby for use as a trawler under the name *Guava*. Sadly, she went missing in the North Sea in January 1953.

There was also the smaller Yard Minesweeper (YMS) built in the United States and shipped to Britain as part of Lend-Lease. Eighty American YMS were ordered by the US Navy specifically for transfer to Britain. They were recorded on the Navy List as British Yard Mine Sweepers (BYMS) and numbered in a separate sequence from 1 to 80. Upon transfer to Britain, BYMS-1 to BYMS-80 were assigned the British pennant numbers *BYMS2001* to *BYMS2080*. Seventy more YMS were transferred to Britain shortly after completion and were also given BYMS pennant numbers.

As built, the BYMS were fitted out with a hot air heating system, an electric cooker, electric toaster, coffee percolators, a refrigerator, flushing toilets, piped hot and cold water, a distillation plant to convert salt water into drinking water for water fountains, proper bunks and some even had washing machines and dryers. The men assigned to these ships must have thought they were in heaven!

Radcliffe Channel Island Shipping bought *BYMS2001*, built by the American Car and Foundry Company at Wilmington, Delaware in 1942, and gave her the name *Radcliffe*. Now measured at 231 tons gross, she was used on St Peter Port to Alderney and Sark passenger services until December 1949 when the company withdrew from the route.

Radcliffe was renamed *Regency Belle* by Mr Radcliffe in July 1950 and deployed on excursion work from Brighton eastwards along the coast to Eastbourne. He sold the ship in January 1951 to S R Crowe, Torbay Cruising, and her ownership transferred to Torbay Cruising Company Limited in May 1955. She was acquired by Marine Salvage and Survey Service, Limited on 28 April 1964 and renamed *Regency*, passing to Overseas and General Brokerage and Finance Company, Limited in January 1966. On 19 September 1967 she sank off Wolf Rock, some 8nm off Land's End after a fire broke out in the engine room.

BYMS2026 was returned to United States' hands while laid up at Malta in 1946. In May 1949 she was bought by Joseph Gasan of Malta, who had secured the mail contract in 1947 for the ferry route between Marfa, in the north of Malta, and Mġarr on Gozo. The ship was converted to a passenger and cargo ferry and given the name *Calypso G*, entering service in March 1950. After

Radcliffe (1942), built as *BYMS2001*, seen leaving St Peter Port, Guernsey. She later became the Torquay pleasure boat *Regency Belle*. (World Ship Society Photo Archive)

Jacques Cousteau's research ship *Calypso* (1942) seen at Montreal in 1980. She was originally *BYMS2026* and was built at Seattle.

only four months on the route, Gasan sold *Calypso G* having received an attractive offer for the ship from millionaire and philanthropist Thomas Loel Guinness. After refitting as an exploration and survey ship with the name *Calypso*, she was leased to Jacques Cousteau for just one franc per year. The ship is currently being renovated at a yard in Turkey.

Admiralty Type Torpedo Recovery Vessels (TRV)

The Admiralty Type Torpedo Recovery Vessel was a class of eight small ships, characterised by a deep well deck. Two of them, built by G L Watson at Gainsborough, Lincolnshire, became the *Arrowhead* (TRV8) and *Channel Trader* (either TRV5, 6 or 7 – records are imprecise) and operated between South Coast ports or French ports and the Channel Islands for the Island Shipping Company Limited. This company was later subsumed within what is now Commodore Shipping Company Limited, itself a successor of Commodore Cruises Limited (see Chapter 13). *Arrowhead* was built by J S Watson (Gainsborough) Limited and completed in October 1946. The single screw was driven by a 6-cylinder oil engine made by H Widdop & Company Limited at Keighley. She started on Guernsey duties in 1950, initially on charter from the Ministry of Transport to Mr Williams, to run between Weymouth, Alderney and Guernsey; this lasted only a few months from January to June 1950.

Arrowhead was back in the Channel Islands in 1951 on charter to Commodore Cruises Limited. She returned in 1952 when *Lloyd's Register* gave her ownership as Ministry of Transport

Ile de Serk (1942) was originally ordered by the Admiralty but completed after the war as *TRV2*. She was chartered for use as a passenger and cargo ferry at Guernsey in 1950, eventually bought and renamed *Island Commodore* and later *Ile de Serk*. (Author)

(Commodore Cruises Limited, Managers), although she traded under the banner Island Shipping Company Limited of Guernsey. She was joined by *Channel Trader* in 1955. The *Arrowhead* was also chartered for a period for use between St Peter Port and Herm with accommodation for just twelve persons. Initially she was used more or less in her original form with an awning to shelter her passengers but in due course she acquired a small deck house aft. She foundered off Exmouth in February 1956. Shortly afterward *Channel Trader* was replaced by *Snider*, a naval stores ship, for 12 months until she too was replaced. *Channel Trader* passed to the Alderney Tramp Shipping Company Limited. She was wrecked off Cap de la Hague on 21 May 1959. The following day *The Times* reported:

> The British Ship *Channel Trader* (500 tons) bound from Portsmouth to Jersey, went aground late last night about 500 yards off Cap de la Hague, on the French Coast. There was a fog at the time, and it is thought that the ship's compass may have been affected by magnetic phenomena. The captain believed that he was east of Alderney. The crew reached St Gervain des Vaux by boat, and the British Consul in Cherbourg, Mr J W Foster, went there to see them.

Island Commodore (TRV2), built by Rowhedge Ironworks near Colchester, first arrived in the Channel Islands in June 1950 on charter from the Ministry of Transport to Commodore Cruises Limited. The company finally bought her in January 1955 and ownership transferred to Commodore Shipping Company with registration passing from London to Guernsey. Although she was ordered by the Admiralty and the keel was laid in 1942, she was not actually completed until after the war. She was 98ft long with a beam of 21ft and was of 195 tons gross, including 130 under-deck tonnage. Like other ships of the class, she was equipped with a 6-cylinder oil engine made by Widdop.

Island Commodore took one hour to get to Sark from St Peter Port and 2½ hours for passage to Alderney. She was licensed to carry 138 passengers. *Island Commodore* was sold to Sark

The preserved Torpedo Recovery Vessel *Elfin* (1933), formerly HMS *Elfin*, was latterly used as a tank cleaning vessel at Amsterdam. (Stichting tot Behoud van het Stoomschip)

Shipowners Limited in October 1969 and renamed *Ile de Serk*. Her ownership transferred to Isle of Sark Shipping Company in September 1977 and she was eventually withdrawn from the Sark

and St Peter Port service in November 1983. She was reactivated briefly in spring 1984 then sold to Reeferships Limited, British Virgin Islands, and put into service between Dominica and Guadeloupe as a passenger and cargo ferry registered at Road Bay, Anguilla. She was blown ashore and wrecked off Dominica in September 1989, the wreck was later towed out to sea and scuttled.

One pre-war steam TRV is preserved in Holland. Commissioned in January 1934 as HMS *Elfin* (T25), the ship was renamed HMS *Nettle* in 1941. Sold for scrap in 1957, she was resold in 1958 to de Amsterdamsche Droogdok Maatschappij (Amsterdam Dry Dock Company) and renamed *Droogdok 18* and later *TCA1*. She was used at Amsterdam as a tank cleaning vessel until withdrawn in 1985. The ship was subsequently adopted by Stichting tot Behoud van het Stoomschip, a Dutch preservation society and has been restored. Renamed *Elfin*, she is now based at Wormerveer.

Harbour Defence Motor Launches (HDML)

It was realised at the start of the Second World War that small launches would be needed for the protection of harbours and estuaries against submarines. It was stipulated that the boats should not exceed 72ft in length in order that they could be shipped abroad. They had a round bilge type hull, and were fitted with twin rudders to ensure manoeuvrability. Their displacement was about 54 tons and they were powered by two diesel engines, many the with Gardner 8L3 type, to give them a speed of about 12 knots; they were good seaboats. Later in the war they made long sea voyages to reach operational areas; they served in the Mediterranean, off the west coast of Africa and off Iceland.

A total of 300 HDMLs were built in Britain, 56 in the Dominions and 74 in the United States. Orders for these craft were placed with well-equipped yacht builders who were not involved in the Fairmile scheme. One of the ships, HMS

Medusa (ex-*ML1387*), is now owned and preserved by the Medusa Trust. She was built in 1942 by R A Newman at Poole.

The ships were ideal for conversion to inshore pleasure cruise vessels. The excursion ship *Pride of the Dart*, 58 tons gross, and built in 1944 as *HDML1396*, was bought by Torbay Cruising in 1947 to be converted for excursion work in 1948. She was later owned by the Western Lady Ferry Service and bought by Sunshine Cruises in 1990. She was equipped with Thornycroft Type RL6 diesel engines which she kept until 1971 when she was re-engined. Her career as a passenger boat ended when she hit Mew Rocks off the Dart estuary on 28 June 2002; *Pride of the Dart* was able to transfer her twenty-six passengers safely to two other boats and was then beached.

The excursion ship *Pride of the Dart* (1944), formerly *HDML1396*, showing her simple layout as she lies alongside at Torquay in the early 1960s.

Devon Princess, 91 tons gross, was another one-time HDML. She was completed in 1945, and was equipped with twin engines manufactured by Leyland, the Lancashire lorry manufacturer. She was bought and converted into a passenger excursion boat in 1949 by Hedley Jennings Shipping Company, later rebranded Herbert Jennings & Son. She was then based at Exmouth and offered excursions to Torquay, Brixham, Lyme Regis and to the River Dart. Herbert Jennings & Son, along with the *Devon Princess*, was acquired by Devon Princess Cruises (Mike Barrow) in 1973. During the 1970s *Devon Princess* was licensed to carry 130 passengers. In February 1988, whilst moored in the Exe Estuary, she was raided and sunk by vandals who stole valuable engine parts.

Not all the ships went to British buyers. HMS *Mastgat*, formerly *HDML1400*, was purchased by Wijsmuller of Ymuiden and used as a diving tender with the name *Sepia*. Built by Ekins at Christchurch, Dorset, *HDML1400* was completed in 1945 but rechristened as HMS *Mastgat* shortly afterwards. She was sold to the Royal Netherlands Navy in 1946 as a fast dispatch boat and reconfigured as a minesweeper in 1949. In 1956 she was converted again, this time as a diving support vessel, and it was in this configuration that she was sold for commercial use. Wijsmuller resold her in 1972 to Belgian owners.

Admiralty Pinnace/Motor Launch/Steam Launch

The original Admiralty pinnaces were built to the same design and construction as RAF pinnaces. The original design came from the builders Groves and Gutteridge of Cowes who completed the first RAF pinnace in 1938. The Admiralty version were known as Fast Seagoing Motor Boats (FSMB) or Torpedo Recovery Safety Boats (TRSB), or more simply as the 60ft Seagoing Motor Boat. They had a beam of 14ft, and a draught of just 3ft 4in and were of hard chine construction and built of mahogany. They were

Devon Princess (1945) was another former HDML, this one used for day excursions centred on Exmouth.

powered by three Perkins S6M diesel engines of 130hp which provided a speed of 17 knots.

There were several other types of pinnace and motor launch. One was the smaller 35ft pinnaces, hard chine boats fitted with twin Ford V8 engines which on trials achieved 21 or 22 knots, but only a handful were commissioned. There were also four fast motor pinnaces with twin Perkins P6 diesels capable of speeds of about 20 knots. The slow pinnaces were similar but fitted with a single Dorman engine and a Kitchen Reversing Rudder that provided a directional propulsion system in both the ahead and astern modes. The Kitchen Rudder consists of two slightly conical, semi cones that can be opened to give ahead thrust or completely closed to give astern thrust caused by the ahead thrust of the propeller reversing direction when it impinges on the closed semi cones. By turning the cones, as with a conventional rudder, a change of direction is obtained in either mode. With both cones partly opened, a neutral position results with neither ahead nor astern movement. The Clamshell thrust reverser on some aircraft jet engines works on the same principle.

Three 54ft-long launches were bought from the Admiralty by the Isles of Scilly Steam Packet Company after the Second World War. They were named *Kittern*, built in 1944 by Fox & Son at Ipswich, and *Tean*, built at Bangor in 1941, and in 1961 they bought the third, built at Rowhedge, and named her *Gugh*, she had been in commercial service for some years with the name *Fervent*. They were used on inter-island duties. The company previously bought a 48ft Great War naval pinnace in 1923. also for inter-island work. She was named *Ganilly* and was sold to Coast Lines for use as a tender at Falmouth in 1932, later dismantled in 1937. David MacBrayne also acquired an Admiralty launch when they purchased *Silver Crest* in 1949 and gave her the name *Craignure* ready to operate the Craignure ferry service. She could carry up to fifty passengers and was sold to Bruce Watt in 1964.

David MacBrayne had a former naval pinnace, *Vital Spark*, on charter from MacLean & MacRae between 1968 and 1972. She was a 52ft long Admiralty pinnace that was built in 1940 by James A Silver Limited at Rosneath. The hull was constructed with double diagonal teak over oak frames. MacLean and MacRae operated *Vital Spark* under contract to David MacBrayne, plying mainly between Kyle of Lochalsh and Toscaig.

From 1972 the service was operated directly by MacLean & McRae. This was a daily service carrying mail and passengers and ran for close on 20 years until *Vital Spark* was sold in 1987 to MacNab MacKenzie who operated her as one of several pleasure-boats from Ullapool to the Summer Isles. Three years later the boat was sold to Iain Morrison of the Isle of Mull who operated her between Ulva Ferry and Iona, Staffa and the Treshnish Isles from 1990 until October 1994. *Vital Spark* was then taken out of service and lay in a sheltered bay at Croig near Dervaig in Mull until December 1996 when the boat was bought by Jim Michie. In July 1997 she was taken inland to Loch Shiel and given the name *Sileas*. She now operates seasonal cruises on the loch whose length is otherwise largely inaccessible by road.

Numerous harbour launches were bought after the Second World War for use as workboats and passenger launches. J Bolson & Sons at Poole bought a 48ft launch in 1946 and named her *Skylark 1*. She was resold in 1948 for use on the River Fal as *Marina II* and was sold again to Cobbold & Weeks of Dartmouth in 1978. Bolson also bought four 36ft launches which also became *Skylarks*. All were disposed of by 1951, most for service on the Thames.

There were numerous steam harbour launches built during the Second World War. They were

Marina II (1944) formerly *Skylark I* was typical of the numerous harbour launches available for purchase after the war.

The former steam harbour launch *298* (1943) as *Nottingham Castle* at Cowes. She was later shipped to Canada.

Ivers Linje's passenger ferry *Christian Ivers* (1944), formerly the German M-Type minesweeper *M607*, ended her career working in the Mediterranean in the mid-1960s. (Kiel Korsör Linie)

just 60ft in length with a beam of 14ft and were equipped with a compound steam engine; most of the engines were built by railway company engineering departments. Many of these little steamships were sold after the war for use as work boats. However, they were expensive to maintain and to operate and few lasted long in civilian service.

Nevertheless, one of the former steam harbour launches survives to this day. Number *298* was built by Hancocks Shipbuilding Company at Pembroke Dock in 1943; her engine was a product of the Lancashire & North Eastern Railway's (LNER) Cowlairs Works at Glasgow. After the war she was sold to Machin, Knight & Sons of Southampton and renamed *Cresset*. They sold her in 1970 to the Imperial Tobacco Group which fitted her out for excursion work with a capacity of twenty passengers with the new name *Nottingham Castle*. Clearly an expensive marketing tool, she was again sold to John Coulter, Ken Fowler, Norm Wilton and Des Vaughn who shipped the vessel to Canada. *Nottingham Castle* was used by the Paignton House Resort on Lake Rousseau and when that company was sold *Nottingham Castle*, no longer paying her way, was abandoned and fell into disrepair. John Coulter sold her to Purves Marine of Sault Ste. Marie and she is currently being maintained and refurbished.

Conversions of Small German Vessels

Ivers-Linie (Paulsen & Ivers) of Kiel purchased the German M-Type minesweeper (*minensuchboot*) *M607* in 1949, and converted her into the passenger and cargo ferry *Christian Ivers*, and then also *M608* was similarly dealt with and was given the name *Harald Ivers*. They were used on the Kiel to Korsör (Denmark) ferry service. They were sold to Kieler Reederei in 1954 and chartered to J H J

Jensen of Tuborg. The pair were then rebuilt as roll-on roll-off car ferries, and equipped with new oil engines and renamed *Hanne Scarlett* and *Lille Scarlett* respectively. In 1957 they were sold to Skandinavisk Linietrafik of Gentofte without change of name.

In 1962 the one-time *Christian Ivers* was sold to Agostino Lauro of Naples and renamed *Salvatore Lauro* for ferry duties between Naples and Capri and Ischia. In 1957 ownership became Libera Navigazione Lauro SAS of Naples. She was re-engined in 1977. The passenger and car ferry *Salvatore Lauro*, the former Second World War M-Type minesweeper *M607*, was sold for scrap in 2006 but foundered on her way to the ship-breakers in Turkey.

Harold Ivers/Lille Scarlett was sold in 1962 to Ångfartygs Ab of Vaxholm, and resold in 1963 Christos S Pagouilas of Piraeus who gave her the new name *Elena P*. In 1976 she was laid up at Perama and eventually sold for demolition in 1982.

The former Norwegian *Laugen* class minelayer *Laugen* (NN05), built in 1917 and seized by the Germans in 1940, was sold in 1950 to A/S Mek. Verksted of Stavanger in Norway and converted into the passenger ferry *Rosenberg VI* and measured at 313 tons gross. She was scuttled in 1979. The former Norwegian *Gor* class minelayer *Tyr* was converted into the commercial ferry *Bjorn-West* in 1953. She was eventually reduced to static duties.

The German fast patrol boat *S97*, built in 1943, was bought by Windway Marine Services of Cardiff and converted for use as the houseboat *Raymen*; she was broken up in 2004. She had been ceded to Norway in 1949 and was decommissioned in 1962. *S130*, also built in 1943, was commissioned into the Royal Navy in 1945 as *MTBS130* and returned to the Federal Republic of Germany in 1957 as *UW10*. She was sold for use as a houseboat in 1991 and then bought two years later by the British Military Power Boat Trust and moored at Millbrook, Hampshire, and later in Cornwall.

Two German catapult ships were allocated for disposal to Britain, *Sperber* and *Friesenland*. *Sperber* became a floating crane at Wilhelmshaven and *Friesenland* was sold for conversion to a refrigerated cargo ship in 1950, serving under various owners until scrapped in 1969.

A number of former German naval vessels were used as accommodation ships in various ports until the early 1950s. Ships provided housing for port workers, demolition and construction gangs, local government offices and even a whole Police Department in one port. The accommodation ships became redundant as damaged and destroyed shore infrastructure was restored.

15

A VALUABLE ROLE FOR SURPLUS NAVAL VESSELS

There has always been a synergy between the Royal Navy and the Merchant Navy. A key role for the Royal Navy has always been the protection of trade routes to allow free passage of the nation's merchant ships and their goods. At times of war the Navy has been there to protect the merchantmen after corralling them into convoy formation. Many merchant officers and men transferred to the Royal Navy during hostilities and returned to their former civilian employers in peacetime, while Royal Navy officers and men were often stationed aboard merchant ships to serve in a variety of roles such as signalmen and gunners. This interaction assisted the success of redundant naval ships converted to a merchant role, particularly in post-war economic environments. These swords beaten into ploughshares were always considered worthy equals to purpose-built merchant vessels and, with few exceptions, the officers and men served aboard them with pride.

The conversion of naval vessels for commercial use has, over the years, been shown to fill significant gaps in the merchant service. This it has done at modest expense for the shipowner, allowing ships to be provided for trades such as passenger excursions that could not stand the cost of a new ship, especially with post-war inflated prices. Besides, the lead time to complete a new order was considerable in the late 1940s, when the shipbuilding industry was plagued by materials shortages and shipbuilding costs were increasing year by year. For example, the car and passenger ferry *Halladale* cost Townsend Brothers Ferries just £92,000, of which the majority was the cost of conversion from the Second World War frigate HMS *Halladale*. This financial outlay was at least half, if not a third, of the price for designing and building a comparable new ship. However, the life of a new ship was usually 25 years whereas the life of a former frigate, worked heavily in the war with little maintenance, was inevitably going to be less.

For the most part, the length-to-breadth ratio

The 1958 brochure for the car ferry *Halladale* (1944) serving between Dover and Calais.

Halladale (1944) was a good seaboat but did tend to roll, much to the consternation of some passengers.

of naval shipping was far greater than that of an equivalent-size merchant hull. That of *Halladale*, for example, was 8.2, whereas a comparable-sized ship such as the North of Scotland, Orkney & Shetland company's passenger ship *St Ninian*, completed in 1950, was just 6.2. The car ferry *Lord Warden* completed for British Railways' Dover to Calais service in 1952 was 6.1. This difference meant that narrow-beamed former naval ships, such as *Halladale*, tended to roll quite considerably in a modest sea, whereas the broader merchant hulls rolled less with a longer period. Besides, *Lord Warden* was equipped with Denny-Brown active roll reducing stabilisers

Forth Ferries *Glenfinnan* (1944) built as *LCT(4) 1048-50*, leaving Granton on 3 August 1954, under tow, on her delivery voyage to Marmagoa in India. (*The Scotsman*)

which were initially fitted to ferries carrying vehicles.

Although converted ships were cheap, great care was needed to balance the books so that conversion costs did not run out of control and overcome the purchaser's budget. Such was the case with the conversion of the sloop HMS *Enchantress* into the luxury Thames pleasure steamer *Lady Enchantress*. She was bought for £22,500 which was almost the same purchase price as *Halladale*. Estimated conversion cost was £72,000, again comparable with that for *Halladale*. Overrunning of the conversion costs, due to supplementary orders for luxury fittings in plush public rooms, increased the final conversion cost to a massive £174,000. No wonder, that after only a short six week season, the owners of *Lady Enchantress* were reluctant to spend even more money to refit her for work the following year.

A number of conversions were carried out to provide stopgap tonnage to fill the role of ships lost at war until more suitable replacement tonnage could be sourced. Others provided short-term tonnage to cope with a sudden and unexpected demand from shippers. Some filled niche roles, that of the Fairmile launch *Wallasey Belle*, for example, as a late-night cross-Mersey ferry.

Some projects went awry due to lack of experience on the part of the purchaser. Numerous former convoy escorts were bought by single-ship owners for conversion into coastal cargo ships and many changed hands before the conversion work was finished. The failure of Forth Ferries Limited in December 1952, with its four former Landing Craft, Tank was due to delays in getting the service going with ships being ready for service but with no slipways modified and ready for their use. John Hall should have foreseen these delays when he planned his new ferry service, and his past shipping experience should have told him to proceed more cautiously with such a venture. In other cases, new purchases of naval shipping were never put to gainful employment as the projects

Charles Mcleod (1945), seen at Malta in 1958, was one of twenty-three Landing Ships, Tank managed by Frank Bustard's Atlantic Steam Navigation company, five of which maintained the commercial services. (Tim Cornwell)

were condemned by their new owners as not worthy of further investment. These cases were few and far between with the vessel usually being sold for scrap.

Surplus naval ships even allowed one British entrepreneur to build up a viable business while holding neither capital nor assets. Frank Bustard was able to charter Landing Ships, Tank at knock-down prices in order to develop a regular freight service between Tilbury and Hamburg. This initially depended on a military contract to carry hardware between Britain and the British Army in Germany, and the service only took off on a commercial basis once the Continental terminal was moved to Antwerp. Bustard next established an Irish Sea link between Preston and Larne. This too was slow to develop and in its first year of trading showed a loss of £52,800, but the service quickly picked up after that.

Both Coast Lines and the General Steam Navigation Company watched this new competitor but paid little serious attention to it. In his history of the Belfast Steamship Company, Robert Sinclair wrote:

Bustard would need capital to develop and expand but such was the potential for his new technology that it should have been clear … that sooner or later someone would supply the capital …

In April 1954, the British Transport Commission, in a move of surprising swiftness, purchased the Atlantic Steam Navigation Company and placed it under the wing of its subsidiary, British Road Services.

It was not long before tenders were invited for a pair of purpose-designed freight and passenger ferries to champion the Tilbury and Preston-based services. The result was *Bardic Ferry* and *Ionic Ferry*, the first of five similar ships commissioned between 1956 and 1964 funded, to all intents and purposes, with government money. Frank Bustard's dream had come about and with it the death knell sounded for both Coast Lines Limited and the General Steam Navigation Company which, in due course, were subsumed within the P&O empire.

Despite his lack of capital, the entrepreneur Frank Bustard achieved far more than building up a vibrant and successful shipping company. He demonstrated to the world that the future for cross-Channel traffic and, indeed, for some deep-sea services, lay in the roll-on roll-off freight mode albeit, at that time, also supported with unit load traffic craned on and off the main deck of the old LSTs. That neither the Board of Coast Lines nor of GSNC recognised the technical progress that Bustard had demonstrated reflected the conservative outlook of these companies; they were too proud of their histories to embrace radical change that would have safeguarded their futures. Frank Bustard is remembered as the champion of the modern-day freight ferry; he could not have aspired to this role without the availability of surplus Landing Ships, Tank which, after the war, the Government needed to keep in reserve or make available for charter.

The dumping of large numbers of cheap shipping at the end of two world wars did have a potential negative impact. The hundreds of small naval motor fishing vessels, built to a fishing-industry design standard and produced from prefabricated parts, was a great source of cheap tonnage, but might it also have impacted on the development of that sort of boat? The answer is no: the fishing vessels were already at the optimum design stage, although largely steam driven after the Great War. That the design did not significantly change and improve thereafter is more likely a reflection on there being little room for improvement of a tried and tested vessel rather than a market saturated with redundant boats. Besides, motor fishing vessels continued to be ordered and built commercially between the wars and after the Second World War, as their increased fuel efficiency extended operational range with lower manning costs.

The same arguments can be applied to other types of ships. The one role that did suffer was that of the deep sea towage and salvage tugs due to the abundance of former military tugs available for purchase or charter after both world wars. The design of these ships did not significantly advance until the late 1950s, despite attempts by one Dutch owner to modernise in the late 1930s. Former military tugs remained in gainful employment alongside the new and more efficient tonnage until rising operating costs forced them out of the towage and salvage businesses.

Former naval tonnage was mainly bought to fill niche roles and the converted ships did this economically and efficiently. Without such conversions some sections of the merchant service would have been hard pressed to recover after each of the two world wars. Conversion of convoy escorts, for example, allowed ferry operators to recover from ship losses incurred during the wars and the whaling industry to recover and provide much-needed food, while numerous specialist ships were reconfigured for a host of other purposes.

The conversions, almost without exception, allowed ships to be successfully altered within the safety margins prescribed by the Classification Societies and State Regulatory Authorities. While some of these converted ships could be uncomfortable in heavy seas, they were essentially safe and few of them foundered. Of those that were lost at sea, the more likely cause, apart from fire or stranding, was inappropriate loading and ballasting, rather than any shortcomings in the final configuration of the vessel.

Many well-known and respected shipping companies embraced the idea of converting former military vessels. The German companies Norddeutsche Lloyd and HAPAG, the Hamburg Amerika Line, did so after the Great War. Others included Christian Salvesen, and the Egyptian Khedivial Mail Line S A E after the Second World War. Some companies were nervous about the prospect, one such being the Isle of Man Steam Packet Company which, after much thought, managed to build to an essentially pre-war design immediately after the Second World War. The decision to build or convert taxed the company as Adrian Sweeney described (personal communication):

> It appeared there was a possibility of purchasing an unneeded frigate and converting her for passenger use. She had reciprocating engines, a speed of 18 knots and water tube boilers and she could be ready for service in the second half of 1945. The Company decided to pursue the matter, especially if a second frigate could be obtained. The Marine Superintendent followed the matter up over the following weeks and visited Swan Hunter and Vickers where the engines were being built. By October 28th the Marine Superintendent was reporting that he

The 21-knot turbine steamer *King Orry* (1946), seen arriving at Llandudno in July 1965, was the preferred option for the Isle of Man Steam Packet Company Limited rather than an 18-knot converted frigate. (Author)

was not too sure how successful a passenger conversion would be and the Company began to go cold on the idea. It was formally rejected in December of 1944.

The outcome of this decision was a series of six new ships of similar design delivered by Cammell Laird & Company at Birkenhead. The first of these was *King Orry*, and she was built for a fixed price of £360,000 although this rose to just over £400,000 due to the post-war pay awards authorised by Government. Although twice the cost of a converted frigate, *King Orry* provided almost 30 years of reliable service to the Isle of Man Steam Packet Company, and maintained the desired service speed of 21 knots rather than just the 18 knots of a frigate.

The degree of conversions ranged from light touch with fishing vessels, fleet tugs and some convoy escorts, to the total reconstruction of the ship from the lower deck upwards. Perhaps the most bizarre conversions were the big-ship rebuilds of German tonnage authorised after the Great War, for example, the conversion of the destroyers *S178* and *S179* into sailing schooners was certainly the most unlikely project. Unlikely it may have been, but it was successful and the former *S178* served commercially for 14 years before being sold for demolition while her sister, the former *S179*, was scuttled in 1944. Their bow sections were replaced during conversion so that they could not easily be converted back into fast warships. Another example after the Second World War was that of turning the Type 1 Landing Ship, Tank HMS *Bruiser* into the luxury cruise ship *Silverstar*; a successful if equally unlikely conversion.

Some of the better-known conversions were from frigate and corvette into cargo ships and passenger ships, some of the latter modified at a later stage as roll-on roll-off vehicle and passenger ferries. Many of these vessels gave long and trouble-free commercial service to their owners. If success can be judged as a ship that returned both her depreciation costs and her operational costs with a margin of profit, then almost all the passenger and cargo conversions were successful.

One former German minesweeper became the Liverpool-based excursion steamer *St Elian* just four years after the Armistice; a case of commerce outbidding politics. The same happened after the Second World War when two German 'R' class minesweepers were bought by Yacht Holidays Limited and converted into British-registered passenger cruise ships for service on the River Rhine. There was even a former German submarine tender that offered passenger excursions in Dublin Bay under the name *Clearwater* during the 1959 summer season.

The roles of the numerous Fairmile launches that were bought for commercial service after the Second World War is a story yet to be told. Not only were they a familiar sight at the end of the pier at British seaside resorts, but they also served in the excursion trade in the Mediterranean, the United States, Canada, in Australian waters and elsewhere. Many of these wooden-hulled ships, with a design life of just five years, provided passenger excursion trips well into the 1960s and some even beyond. A key to their success in the commercial world was the need for only modest conversion to qualify for an inshore passenger certificate.

There were also the immigrant ships working after the Second World War between Europe and Australia or New Zealand. With one exception these were hugely successful, some evolving into cruise ships in later life. The exception was *Hellenic Prince*, a converted seaplane carrier and later a convoy escort that attracted notoriety due to the conduct of her senior officers, although the ship itself was barely suited for its intended purpose.

The numerous other roles fulfilled by former naval vessels provided valuable service in diverse ways. Some were used just as floating platforms for cranes and other equipment, some became workboats and support boats, others salvage ships, dredgers, tank cleaning vessels or were used for diverse other applications. The ships were also valuable as survey vessels, of which the best known was the former British Yard Minesweeper *Calypso* of Jacques Cousteau fame.

There were also conversions to private ownership for use as yachts or houseboats. At the top of the luxury scale were John Wayne's yacht *Wild Goose* and Aristotle Onassis' yacht *Christina*, formerly an American Yard Minesweeper and a Canadian 'River' class frigate respectively. There were many others but none quite reached the glamour or glitz offered by *Wild Goose* and *Christina*.

The conversion of ships from naval to merchant use certainly fulfilled a variety of roles, some niche and some more general. All these ships helped towards the development of commerce and trade and ultimately towards wealth creation. They did this by providing tonnage at times of shortages after the Great War and the Second World War, by providing tonnage at modest cost to sustain uses that could not afford to build new ships, and by providing tonnage quickly after hostilities ended when shipbuilders could not guarantee delivery dates. In addition, conversions filled roles at times of high demand, such as the short-lived mid-Victorian boom in the Continental trades from London, and to provide stopgap tonnage to develop trade, for example, the purchase and conversion of what became *Baltic Ferry* and *Celtic Ferry* in the mid-1960s by the Atlantic Steam Navigation Company.

Many of the ships are fondly remembered, not

Baltic Ferry (1945) was converted for commercial service in 1965 in order to develop trade prior to the introduction of purpose-built vessels. (Author)

least by the holidaymakers who enjoyed trips round the bay aboard the converted Fairmile launches and HDMLs. Some vessels survive to this day either preserved as static museum ships or as operational vessels, while others are currently being renovated and refurbished. Unfortunately, the renovation projects, almost without fail, reconstruct the ship back into its original military guise and the important merchant-service years become overlooked. However, there remain a few that are still in commercial operation and proud of their military provenance; it is these, *Wild Goose*, *Christina O* and *Sunnhordland*, for example, that are the best reminders of this once abundant type of merchant ship.

BIBLIOGRAPHY

Burtt, Frank (1949), *Steamers of the Thames and Medway* (London: Richard Tilling).

Chalk, David (1980), *Anyone for the Skylark? The Story of Bournemouth's Pleasure Boats* (Bournemouth: David Chalk).

Dittmar, F J, and Colledge, J J (1972), *British Warships 1914-1919* (London: Ian Allan Limited).

Dodson, Aiden, and Cant, Serena (2020), *Spoils of War, the Fates of Enemy Fleets After the Two World Wars* (Barnsley: Seaforth Publishing).

Farr, Grahame (1967), *West Country Passenger Steamers* (Prescot: T Stephenson & Sons Ltd).

Ferguson, Sand (2008), *From Burma to Barra, The Life and Times of a Marine Superintendent* (Isle of Gigha: Argyll Ardminish Press).

Forrester, Robert (2006), 'The General Steam Navigation Company c1850-1913: a Business History'. Unpublished PhD thesis, University of Greenwich. https://gala.gre.ac.uk/id/eprint/8535/4/Robert %20Edward%20Forrester%202006&20&20Redacted.pdf

Lambert, John, and Ross, Albert (2018), *Allied Coastal Forces Volume I Fairmile Designs and US Submarine Chasers* (Barnsley: Seaforth Publishing).

Lambert, John, and Ross, Albert (2019), *Allied Coastal Forces Volume II Vosper MTBs and US Elcos* (Barnsley: Seaforth Publishing).

Lenton, H T, and Colledge, J J (1963), *Warships of World War Two Part Seven: Landing Craft* (London: Ian Allan Limited).

Lenton, H T, and Colledge, J J (1963), *Warships of World War Two Part Eight: Coastal Forces* (London: Ian Allan Limited).

McNeill, David (1969), *Irish Passenger Steamship Services, Part 1, North of Ireland* (Newton Abbot: David & Charles).

Mooney, James (ed) (1976), *A Dictionary of American Naval Fighting Ships Volume 4* (Washington: Naval History Division Department of the Navy).

Robins, Nick (2009), *An Illustrated History of Thames Pleasure Steamers* (Kettering: Silver Link Publishing Limited).

Robins, Nick (2017), *Wartime Standard Ships* (Barnsley: Seaforth Publishing).

Sinclair, Robert (1990), *Across the Irish Sea, Belfast Liverpool Shipping since 1819* (London: Conway Maritime Press Limited).

Taylor, James (1976), *Ellermans: a Wealth of Shipping* (London: Wilton House Gentry Limited).

Thornley, Frank (1962), *Past and Present Steamers of North Wales* (Prescot: T Stephenson & Sons, Limited).

INDEX

Merchant ships are listed under the name registered following conversion, subsequent names are not generally shown.

Aagtekerk, ex-*Chaser* 90
Abeille XXII, ex-*St Minver* 46
Aconit (FRA) 'Flower' class corvette, see *Southern Terrier*
Action (US) *Action* class patrol boat and cargo ship 114
Adherent (UK) *Assurance* class fleet tug, see *Hermes*
Adolf Sommerfeld, ex-*Gefion* 11, 57
Aetna (UK) *Hecla* class bomb vessel and Polar exploration ship 24
African (UK) survey ship 26
Aghios Spyridon, ex-*Kilmelford* 77
Ägir (GER) coastal defence ship and commercial cargo ship 56, 57
Air Cormorant, ex-*SC536* 117
Air Mallard, ex-*SC772* 117
Aktion, ex-*M10* 60
Alarm, ex-*St Ewe* 46
Albatross (AUS) seaplane carrier, see *Hellenic Prince*
Albatross (US) auxiliary MMS, see *Dorado*
Alblasserdijk, ex-*Trumpeter* 89–90

Alexandroupolis, ex-*Mignonette* 68
Alisima (UK) 'Flower' class corvette, see *Laconia*
Allegiance (UK) *Assurance* class fleet tug and commercial tug 130, 131
Almdijk, ex-*Hunter* 89
Almkerk, ex-*Patroller* 90
Amber, ex-*Isaac Arthan* 49
Amberley Castle (UK) 'Castle' class corvette, see *Weather Advisor*
Ameer (UK) *Attacker* class escort carrier, see *Robin Kirk*
Amokura, ex-*Sparrow* 29
Anchusa (UK) 'Flower' class corvette, see *Silverlord*
Anglesey (UK) fast minelayer, see *Anglia*
Anglia, ex-*Anglesey* 44
Anzio, ex-*ML 140*
Appledore (UK) 'Hunt' class minesweeper, see *Kamlavati*
Arabis (UK) 'Flower' class corvette, see *Katrina*
Arbiter (UK) *Ruler* class escort carrier, see *Coracero*
Arctic Whale (UK) Admiralty trawler, see *Bermudian*
Argo, ex-*Gillstone* 129
Argon (UK) patrol vessel, see *Peninnis*

Arion, ex-*Kilmarnock* 77
Armant, ex-*LCT(4)675* 95
Army tugs 135
Arnfinn Bergen, ex-*Aubretia* 67
Arrow (UK) harbour defence vessel and civilian crane 28
Arrowhead (UK) 'Flower' class corvette, see *Southern Larkspur*
Arrowhead, ex-*TRV8* 155, 157
Artillero, ex-*Smiter* 87
Arvida (CAN) 'Flower' class corvette and cargo ship 124
Ascot class minesweeper 10, 11, 41–4
Assiduous (UK) *Assurance* class fleet tug, see *Irving Tamarack*
Atheling (UK) *Attacker* class escort carrier, see *Roma*
Atherstone (UK) *Ascot* class minesweeper, see *Queen of Kent*
Athinia, ex-*Kilmington* 77
Atlantic Steam Navigation Co. (UK) 12, 106–11, 167, 168
Attacker (UK) *Attacker* class escort carrier, see *Fairsky*
Attacker (UK) Type 3 LST, see *Empire Cymric*
Aubretia (UK) 'Flower' class corvette, see *Arnfinn Bergen*

Baddeck (CAN) 'Flower' class corvette, see *Rushbrooke*
Baltic Ferry, ex-*Pima County* 118, 119
Bambo, ex-*ML 146*–7
Barnard Castle (UK) 'Castle' class corvette, see *Empire Shelter*
Barnes Park, ex-*LST386* 105
Barnstaple (UK) 'Hunt' class minesweeper, see *Lady Cynthia*
Barrie (CAN) 'Flower' class corvette, see *Gasestado*
Basset (UK) *Basset* class trawler, see *Radford*
Battler (UK) Type 3 LST, see *Empire Puffin*
Beacon, ex-*Meteor* 24
Begum (UK) *Attacker* class escort carrier, see *Raki*
Belgium, ex-*Großherzog von Oldenburg* 25, 26
Bengal, ex-*Kokanee* 123
Bergamot (UK) 'Flower' class corvette, see *Syros*
Bermudian, ex-*Arctic Whale* 35
Bismarck, ex-*FM25* 63
Blyth (UK) *Blyth* class minesweeper, see *Radborne*
Boa Viagem, ex-*Monaghan* 35, 36
Bogue class escort carrier 85–90

INDEX

Bolson & Son Ltd. (UK) 139, 140, 143, 152, 162
Bombay Steam Navigation Co., Ltd. (IND) 35, 36
Bonnie Prince Charlie, ex-*LCT(4)673* 93–5
Bournemouth Skylark No 4, No 5, No 6, ex-*LCG(M)184, LCG(M)185, LCG(M)186* 98, 99
Boxer class LST 102
Bradfield (UK) 'Hunt' class minesweeper, see *Champavati*
Brandram, ex-*X67* 54
Brantford (CAN) 'Flower' class corvette, see *Olympic Arrow*
Bremen (German Confederation) corvette, see *Hanover*
Bridlington (UK) Bangor class minesweeper 15, 151
Bridport (UK) Bangor class minesweeper 15, 151
Brisk (US) Action class patrol boat and cargo ship 115
Bruiser (UK) Type 1 LST, see *Silver Star*
Burhou, ex-*MFV613* 127
Bustard, Frank 15, 106, 167
Bustler class fleet tug 132–4
Bustler (UK) Bustler class fleet tug, see *Mocni*
BYMS2001 (UK) yard minesweeper, see *Radcliffe*
BYMS2026 (UK) yard minesweeper, see *Capypso G*
Byron, ex-*Leith* 80, 81

Calypso G, ex-*BYMS2026* 154–5, 171
Cambrian Prince, ex-*ML253* 144
Canadian National No 2, ex-*St Catherine* 45
Canadian Pacific Railway 46
Cape Pine, ex-*SC715* 117
Captain Theo, ex- *Searcher* 90
Carmelo, ex-*M131* 61
Carnation (UK) 'Flower' class corvette, see *Southern Laurel*
Caroline Moller, ex-*Growler* 134
Caroline Moller, ex-*St Mabyn* 46
Castel Forte, ex-*Attacker* 85, 86
'Castle' class frigate 15, 69, 70, 72, 73
'Castle' class trawler 48
Cautious (UK) Assurance class fleet tug, ex-*Prudent* 131
Cawarstone, ex-*X65* 53
Celtic Ferry 120–2, 171
Champavati, ex-*Bradfield* 35, 36
Channel Belle, ex-*RML* 139, 140
Channel Trader, ex-*TRV* 155, 157
Charger (UK) Albacore class gunboat and salvage vessel 27
Charger (UK) Attacker class escort carrier, see *Fairsea*
Charger (UK) Type 3 LST, see *Empire Nordic*
Charles Mcleod, ex-*LST3021* 103, 108
Charybdis (UK) Astraea class cruiser and passenger liner 33–5
Chaser (UK) Attacker class escort

carrier, see *Aagtekerk*
Chieftain, ex-*Mutine* 28
Christian Ivers, ex-*M607* 163, 164
Christian Salvesen (UK) 66, 67
Christina, ex-*Stormont* 122, 123, 171
Chrysanthemum (UK) Anchusa class sloop and drill ship 15–16
Clover (UK) 'Flower' class corvette, see *Cloverlock*
Cloverlock, ex-*Clover* 68
Clupea, ex-*LST3030* 105
Coaster Construction Co. (UK) 22, 37, 40
Commodore Cruises Ltd 141, 155, 157
Confiance (UK) Cherokee class sloop, survey ship 26
Coppercliff (CAN) Algerine class minesweeper, see *Fairfree*
Coracero, ex-*Arbiter* 87
Coreopsis (UK) 'Flower' class corvette and film set 68, 69
Corrientes, ex-*Tracker* 86, 87
Cresset, ex-*No 298* 163
Crowlin (UK) 'Isles' class trawler and cargo ship 128, 129
Cuckoo (UK) harbour defence vessel and civilian crane 28
Cutty Sark (UK) ex-'V&W' class destroyer 21, 44
Cyclamen (UK) 'Flower' class corvette, see *Southern Briar*

David MacBrayne Ltd. 14, 152–3, 161
Denmark, ex-*Hamburg* 25, 26
Dennistoun, Sir Charles 124
Der Königliche Ernst August (German Confederation) corvette, see *Edinburgh*
Deshulper, ex-*Wem* 36, 37
Despina, ex-*Kilmore* 76
Destiny (UK) Favourite class fleet tug, see *Frosty Miller*
Devon Princess, ex-HDML 160, 161
Dextrous (UK) Assurance class fleet tug and commercial tug 131
Doomba, ex-*Wexford* 36, 37
Dorado, ex-*Albatross* 115
Dorbie, ex-*Poleaxe* 50
Dove (UK) Albacore class gunboat and tug/tender 27
Dragonet (UK) boom defence vessel, see *Foundation Venture*
Drente, ex-*Rajah* 91
Droogdok 18, ex-*Elfin* 158, 159
Duchess of Holland, ex-*LSM558* 11, 99–101
Dunkirk, ex-*ML* 140

Eastern Princess, ex-*MGB347* 147, 148
Echo (UK) survey ship 26
Edinburgh, ex-*Der Königliche Ernst August* 25, 26
Elfin (UK) torpedo recovery vessel, see *Droogdok* 18
Elk (UK) composite screw sloop and dredger 28
Ellerman's Wilson Line (UK) 8–9
Elsa, ex-*Quadrille* 129

Emerson K, ex-*Marauder* 130
Eminent (UK) Favourite class fleet tug, see *Ming* 105
Empire Baltic, ex-*LST3519* 106–10, 171
Empire Cedric, ex-*LST3524* 106, 108–10
Empire Celtic, ex-*LST3512* 106, 108–10
Empire Comfort, ex-*York Castle* 70
Empire Curlew, ex-*Hunter* 108–9
Empire Cymric, ex-*Attacker* 108–9
Empire Doric, ex-*LST3041* 108–10
Empire Fulmar, ex-*Trumpeter* 108–9
Empire Gaelic, ex-*LST3507* 107–10
Empire Gannet, ex-*Tromsø* 108–9
Empire Grebe, ex-*Fighter* 108–9
Empire Guillemot, ex-*Walcheren* 108–9
Empire Gull, ex-*Trouncer* 108–11
Empire Kittiwake, ex-*Slinger* 108–9
Empire Lifeguard, ex-*Maiden Castle* 70
Empire Nordic, ex-*Charger* 108–11
Empire Peacemaker, ex-*Scarborough Castle* 70
Empire Petrel, ex-*Thruster* 108, 109
Empire Puffin, ex-*Battler* 108–10
Empire Rest, ex-*Rayleigh Castle* 70
Empire Shearwater, ex- *LST3033* 108–10
Empire Shelter, ex-*Barnard Castle* 69, 70
Empire Skua, ex-*St Nazaire* 108–9
Empire Tern, ex-*Pursuer* 108, 109
Emulous (UK) Director class fleet tug, see *St Christopher*
Enchanter (UK) Envoy class fleet tug, see *Englishman*
Enchantress (UK) Bittern class sloop, see *Lady Enchantress*
Encore (UK) Envoy class fleet tug, see *Salvaliant*
Englishman, ex-*Enchanter* 134
Englishman, ex-*Reward* 132, 133
Erebus (UK) Hecla class bomb vessel and Polar exploration ship 24
Eriskay, ex-*LCT(4)668* 93–5
Erna David, ex-*M147* 62
Esso 5, ex-*LCT1052* 95
Euginie M Moran, ex-*Masterful* 132
Evan Gibb, ex-*LST3037* 103, 108
Evening Star, ex-*Strenuous* 115, 151–2
Excellent, ex-*Handy* 29, 31
Explorer, ex-*John Felton* 49

Fairfield (UK) 'Hunt' class minesweeper, see *Flechas*
Fairfree, ex-*Coppercliff* 124
Fairsea, ex-*Charger* 85, 86
Fairsky, ex-*Attacker*, ex-*Castel Forte* 85, 86
Favourite (UK) Favourite class fleet tug, see *Susan Moran*
Fencer (UK) Attacker class escort carrier, see *Sydney*
Fighter (UK) Type 3 LST, see *Empire Grebe*
Fiumana I, ex-*FM37*; *Fiumana II*, ex-*FM38*; *Fiuama III*, ex-*FM49* 64
Flechas, ex-*Fairfield* 41
Fleet Commodore, ex-*RML534* 141,

143
Flora Macdonald, ex-*LCT895* 93–5
Flora Sommerfeld, ex-*Victoria Louise* 11, 57
'Flower' class corvettes 15, 19, 65–9, 73
FM Type minesweeper (GER) 63–4
FM1 (GER) FM Type minesweeper, see *Siegfried*
FM3 (GER) FM Type minesweeper and commercial tug 63
FM5 (GER) FM Type minesweeper, see *Georgios Galaos*
FM25 (GER) FM Type minesweeper, see *Bismarck*
FM29 (GER) FM Type minesweeper, see *Westfalen*
FM36 (GER) FM Type minesweeper, see *Socrates*
FM37 (GER) FM Type minesweeper, see *Fiumana I*
FM38 (GER) FM Type minesweeper, see *Fiumana II*
FM49 (GER) FM Type minesweeper, see *Fiumana III*
Ford (UK) 'Hunt' class minesweeper, see *Forde*
Forde, ex-*Ford* 12, 37–40, 70
Foreign Liquidation Commission (US) 10
Forth Ferries Ltd (UK) 93–5, 166, 167
Foundation Francis, ex-*Freedom* 135
Foundation Josephine, ex-*Samsonia* 133
Foundation Venture, ex-*Dragonet* 135
Fowey (UK) Shoreham class sloop, see *Rowlock*
Frankfurt (German Confederation) corvette, see *Holland*
Frankin, ex-*St Finbarr* 46
Franzeska Kimme, ex-*S178* 59, 170
Frederick Clover, ex-*LST3001* 103, 108
Freedom (UK) Director class fleet tug, see *Foundation Francis*
Friesland, ex-*Rance* 90
Frisky (UK) Assurance class fleet tug, see *Hasan*
Frisky (UK) Frisky class fleet tug, see *Gustavo Ipland*
Frisky class fleet tugs 45, 47
Frithjof (GER) coastal defence ship and commercial cargo ship 57–9
Frosty Miller, ex-*Destiny* 124
Fury (UK) Hecla class bomb vessel and Polar exploration ship 24

Gannet (UK) Osprey/Doterel class sloop, see *President*
Garm, ex-*St Enoder* 45
Gasestado, ex-*Barrie* 124
Gay Commodore, ex-*ML* 141
Gay Corsair, ex-*MGB507* 9
Gay Viking, ex-*MGB506* 8, 9
Gefion (GER) cruiser, see *Adolf Sommerfeld*
General Steam Navigation Co. (UK) 25, 26, 167, 168
Genista (UK) 'Flower' class corvette,

see *Weather Recorder*
Georg Kimme, ex-*S179* 59, 170
Georgeos F, ex-*Kilhampton* 77
Georgios Galaos, ex-*FM5* 63
German Confederation, Deutscher Bund 11, 24, 25
Gillstone (UK) 'Isles' class trawler, see *Argo*
Glenfinnan, ex-*LCT1048* 93–5, 166
Glenrodian, ex-*ML* 144
Golden Galleon, ex-*RML162* 13, 14, 147
Granny Kempock, ex-*MFV137* 126
Greyhound class sloop 28
Greystoke Castle, ex-*Trouncer* 88, 89
Grille, ex-*M158* 63
Grimsby class sloops 80, 81
Griper (UK) *Assurance* class fleet tug and commercial tug 131
Griper (UK) Polar exploration ship 23
Großherzog von Oldenburg (German Confederation) corvette, see *Belgium*
Growler (UK) *Bustler* class fleet tug, see *Caroline Moller*
Gustavo Ipland, ex-*Frisky* 47

H187 (GER) destroyer, see *Hoisdorf*
Halladale (UK) 'River' class frigate and car ferry 12, 40, 70, 71, 165–7
Hamburg (German Confederation) corvette, see *Denmark*
Hamburg America Line (GER) 61, 169
Handy (UK) gun trials ship, see *Excellent*
Hanover, ex-*Bremen* 25, 26
Hansdorf, ex-*Hawaldstwerke* 60
Harbour Defence Motor Launchs (HDMLs) 150, 159, 160
Harold Ivers, ex-*M608* 163, 164
Hasan, ex-*Frisky* 131
Haste (US) *Action* class patrol boat, see *Porto Azzuro*
Haugesund, ex-*Kilbirnie* 75
Hawaldtswerke (GER) destroyer, see *Hansdorf*
HDML1396 (UK) HDML, see *Pride of the Dart*
HDML1400 (UK) HDML, see *Sepia*
Hecla (UK) bomb vessel and Polar exploration ship 23
Helgoland, ex-*M139* 61
Hellenic Prince, ex-*Albatross* 15, 81–3, 170
Henry Burton, ex-*St Bees* 45
Hermes, ex-*Adherent* 131
Heros, ex-*St Erth* 45
Hibernia, ex-*Sheppey* 44
Hoisdorf, ex-*H187* 60
Holland Amerika Liijn (NED) 89, 90
Holland, ex-*Frankfurt* 25, 26
Hooghly, ex-*Waskesiu* 123
Hopewell, ex-*MGB504* 8
Humfrey Gale, ex-*LST3509* 103, 108
'Hunt' class minesweepers 12, 20, 35–8
Hunter (UK) *Attacker* class escort carrier, see *Almdijk*
Hunter (UK) Type 3 LST, see *Empire Curlew*

Hyaena (UK) *Albacore* class gunboat and salvage vessel 27
Hörnum, ex-*M140* 61, 62

Indian Co-operative Navigation and Trading Co. (IND) 35, 36
Instow (UK) 'Hunt' class minesweeper, see *Tilak*
Intensity (US) 'Flower' class corvette, see *Olympic Promoter*
Ironaxe (UK) trawler and salvage vessel 50
Irving Tamarack, ex-*Assiduous* 131
Isaac Arthan (UK) 'Castle' class trawler, see *Amber*
Island Commodore, ex-*TRV2* 156, 157, 159

J & A Brown (AUS) 45, 46
Jaunty (UK) *Frisky* class fleet tug, see *Rio Tejo*
John Burlingham, 'Castle' class trawler, see *Rehearo*
John Felton (UK) 'Mersey' class trawler, see *Explorer*
John MacLeod, ex-*RML* 148
Jose Mart, ex-*LSD11* 119–22
Jylland, ex-*Kilbride* 76, 77

Kallsevni, ex-*Loosestrife* 68
Kamlavati, ex-*Appledore* 35, 36
Katrina, ex-*Arabis* 68
Khalifa, ex-*St Giles* 46
Khedive (UK) *Attacker* class escort carrier, see *Rempang*
Khedivial Line (EGY) 95, 169
'Kil' class patrol boats 51
Kilbirnie (UK) PCE, see *Haugesund*
Kilbride (UK) PCE, see *Jylland*
Kilchattan (UK) PCE, see *Stavanger*
Kilchrenan (UK) PCE, see *Sunnhordland*
Kildary (UK) PCE, see *Rio Vouga*
Kildwick (UK) PCE, see *Sunnfjord*
Kilham (UK) PCE, see *Sognefjord*
Kilhampton (UK) PCE, see *Georgios F*
Kilkenzie (UK) PCE, see *Naddodd*
Kilmalcolm (UK) PCE, see *Rio Agueda*
Kilmarnock (UK) PCE, see *Arion*
Kilmarten (UK) 'Kil' class patrol boat, see *Mandrake*
Kilmartin (UK) PCE, see *Marigoula*
Kilmelford (UK) PCE, see *Aghios Spyridon*
Kilmington (UK) PCE, see *Athinia*
Kilmore (UK) PCE, see *Despina*
Kokanee (CAN) 'River' class frigate, see *Bengal*
Kosmos I, ex-*M151* 62
Kyuqot, ex-*St Florence* 46

Laconia, ex-*Alisima* 68
Lady Adriana, ex-German R class minesweeper 14
Lady Cecilia, ex-*Swindon* 40
Lady Constance, ex-German R class minesweeper 14
Lady Cynthia, ex-*Barnstaple* 40
Lady Enchantress, ex-*Enchantress* 78–80, 134, 167
Lady Nugent, ex-*LCM* 99
Lancero, ex-*Speaker* 87
Landfall, ex-*LCT7074* 101
Lariat (UK) *Favourite* class fleet tug, see *Ming* 108
Laugen (NOR) *Laugen* class minesweeper, see *Rosenburg VI*
Lauro Line (Achille Lauro) (ITA) 86
LCG(M)127 (UK) LCG, see *Sauda*
LCG(M)184, LCG(M)185, LCG(M)186 (UK) LCG, see *Bournemouth Skylark No 4, No 5, No 6*
LCG(M)194 (UK) LCG, see *Sanda*
LCG(M)196 (UK) LCG, see *Sark Coast*
LCG181 (UK) LCG, see *Rochester Queen*
LCT399 (UK) LCT, see *Topmast 20*
LCT474 (UK) LCT, see *Topmast 16*
LCT(4)668 (UK) LCT, see *Eriskay*
LCT(4)673 (UK) LCT, see *Bonnie Prince Charlie*
LCT(4)675 (UK) LCT, see *Armant*
LCT828 (UK) LCT, see *Norris Castle*
LCT895 (UK) LCT, see *Flora Macdonald*
LCT1048 (UK) LCT, see *Glenfinnan*
LCT1052 (UK) LCT, see *Esso 5*
LCT7074 (UK) LCT, see *Landfall*
Leith (UK) *Grimsby* class sloop, see *Byron*
Lend-Lease Agreement 12, 19, 74, 85
Lenrodian, ex-*RML525* 144
Lindfield, ex-*St Claude* 45
Lingay (UK) 'Isles' class trawler, see *Tulipglen*
Linnet (UK) gun vessel second class and salvage ship 29
Liverpool and Glasgow Salvage Association (UK) 29
Liverpool & North Wales Steam Packet Co. (UK) 61, 62
Llandudno (UK) *Ardrossan* class minesweeper, see *Rorvick*
Loch Arkaig, ex-*MMS233* 152, 153
Loch Toscaig, ex-*MFV* 14, 126
Locust (UK) *Lizard* class gunboat and survey ship 26
London and North Western Railway 44
Loosestrife (UK) 'Flower' class corvette, see *Kallsevni*
Lord Byng, ex-*William Jackson* 48, 49
Lord Talbot, ex-*William Westernbugh* 49
Lowland Lancer, ex-*Sir Lancelot* 111–13
LSD11 (US) Landing Ship Dock, see *Jose Marti*
LSM558 (US) Landing Ship Small, see *Duchess of Holland*
LST365 (UK) Type 2 LST, see *Mowbray Road*
LST386 (UK) Type 2 LST, see *Barnes Park*
LST3001 (UK) Type 3 LST, see *Frederick Clover*
LST3003 (UK) Type 3 LST, see *Rio Tejo*

LST3009 (UK) Type 3 LST, see *Reginald Kerr*
LST3018 (UK) Type 3 LST, see *Rio Minho*
LST3021 (UK) Type 3 LST, see *Charles Mcleod*
LST3023 (UK) Type 3 LST, see *Rio Guardiana*
LST3024 (UK) Type 3 LST, see *Maxwell Brander*
LST3028 (UK) Type 3 LST, see *Snowden Smith*
LST3030 (UK) Type 3 LST, see *Clupea*
LST3032 (UK) Type 3 LST, see *Rio Mondego*
LST3033 (UK) Type 3 LST, see *Empire Shearwater*
LST3037 (UK) Type 3 LST, see *Evan Gibb*
LST3039 (UK) Type 3 LST, see *Rio Duoro*
LST3041 (UK) Type 3 LST, see *Empire Doric*
LST3507 (UK) Type 3 LST, see *Empire Gaelic*
LST3509 (UK) Type 3 LST, see *Humfrey Gale*
LST3512 (UK) Type 3 LST, see *Empire Celtic*
LST3519 (UK) Type 3 LST, see *Empire Baltic*
LST3534 (UK) Type 3 LST, see *Empire Cedric*
Lubec (German Confederation) corvette, see *Newcastle*
Luwen 3, ex-*M72* 61

M Type minesweeper (GER) 60–3
M10 (GER) M Type minesweeper, see *Aktion*
M42 (GER) M Type minesweeper, see *Nymph*
M72 (GER) M Type minesweeper, see *Luwen 3*
M131 (GER) M Type minesweeper, see *Carmelo*
M139 (GER) M Type minesweeper, see *Helgoland*
M140 (GER) M Type minesweeper, see *Hörnum*
M147 (GER) M Type minesweeper, see *Erna David*
M151 (GER) M Type minesweeper, see *Kosmos I*
M158 (GER) M Type minesweeper, see *Grille*
M607 (GER) M Type minesweeper, see *Christian Ivers*
M608 (GER) M Type minesweeper, see *Harold Ivers*
Macklin, Noel 136, 138
Mae MacLeod, ex-*RML* 148, 149
Maiden Castle (UK) 'Castle' class corvette, see *Empire Lifeguard*
Maj Vinke, ex-*Rhododendron* 67
Manchester Ship Canal Co. (UK) 28, 29, 135
Mandrake, see *Kilmarten* 51
Marauder (UK) *Brigand* class fleet

INDEX

tug, see *Emerson K*
Marguerite (UK) 'Flower' class corvette, see *Weather Observer*
Marigoula, ex-*Kilmartin* 77
Mariner (UK) *Mariner* class composite sloop and salvage ship 29
Maritime and Coastguard Agency (UK) 17
Martha Vinke, ex-*Stonecrop* 67
Master Standfast, ex-*MGB508* 9, 14
Masterful (UK) *Favourite* class fleet tug, see *Euginie M Moran*
Matapan, ex-*ML180* 140
Maxwell Brander, ex-*LST3024* 103, 108
Melita (UK) *Mariner* class composite sloop, see *Ringdove's Aid*
Melton (UK) *Ascot* class minesweeper, see *Queen of Thanet*
Merrie Golden Hind, ex-*MGB346* 147
'Mersey' class trawlers 48
Meteor (UK) *Hecla* class bomb vessel and Polar exploration ship, see *Beacon*
MFV137 (UK) *MFV1* class, see *Granny Kempock*
MFV613 (UK) *MFV601* class, see *Burhou*
MGB504 (UK) Camper & Nicholson type gunboat, see *Hopewell*
MGB505 (UK) Camper & Nicholson type gunboat, see *Nonsuch*
MGB506 (UK) Camper & Nicholson type gunboat, see *Gay Viking*
MGB507 (UK) Camper & Nicholson type gunboat, see *Gay Corsair*
MGB508 (UK) Camper & Nicholson type gunboat, see *Master Standfast*
MFV1003 (UK) *MFV1001* class, see *Pre-eminent*
Might (US) 'Flower' class corvette, see *Olympic Explorer*
Mignonette (UK) 'Flower' class corvette, see *Alexandroupolis*
Ming 105, ex-*Eminent* 132
Ming 108, ex-*Lariat* 132
Ministry of Transport and Ministry of War Transport (UK) 10, 11
ML1 et seq Fairmile launch 138–49
MMS233 (UK) MMS, see *Loch Arkaig*
MMS372 (UK) MMS, see *Southern Paul*
MMS378 (UK) MMS, see *Southern Peter*
Mocni, ex-*Bustler* 133
Monaghan (UK) 'Hunt' class minesweeper, see *Boa Viagem*
Monkswood (UK) 'Flower' class corvette, see *W R Strang*
Motor fishing vessels (UK) 125–7
Motor Minesweepers (MMS) 150, 152–5
Mount Independence, ex-*SC1013* 117
Mountain Ash, ex-*X219* 53
Mowbray Road, ex-*LST365* 105
Muncaster Castle, ex-*Puncher* 88, 89
Mutine (UK) *Greyhound* class sloop, see *Chieftain*

Naddodd, ex-*Kilkenzie* 76

Nairana (UK) escort aircraft carrier, see *Port Victor*
Naval Inter-Allied Commission of Control 56
Neave (UK) 'Isles' class trawler, see *Tulipbank*
Neidermair, John 102
New Medway Steam Packet Co. (UK) 11, 42, 43
Newcastle, ex-*Lubec* 25
Newport (UK) *Philomel* class gunboat and Polar exploration ship, see *Pandoro II*
Nisos Kerkyra, ex-*Turmoil* 80, 133–4
No 298 (UK) steam harbour launch, see *Cresset*
Nonsuch, ex-*MGB505* 9
Nordeutsche Lloyd 63, 169
Norfolk Line (NL) 11
Norking, ex-*SC1039* 117
Norris Castle, ex-*LCT828* 12, 92, 93
Nymph, ex-*M42* 60, 61

Oakham Castle (UK) 'Castle' class corvette, see *Weather Reporter*
Oberschlesien, ex-U boat hulls 60
Ocean Eagle, ex-*St Arvans* 45
Ocean Mist, ex-*Samuel Green* 48
Ocean Pride, ex-*Oriana* 132
Odin (GER) coastal defence ship and commercial cargo ship 57
Olympic Arrow, ex-*Brantford* 124
Olympic Champion, ex-*Parry Sound* 124
Olympic Chaser, ex-*Pictou* 124
Olympic Explorer, ex-*Might* 124
Olympic Lightning, ex-*Smiths Falls* 124
Olympic Promoter, ex-*Intensity* 124
Olympic Runner, ex-*Trillium* 124
Onetwenty, ex-*ML120* 149
Oriana (UK) *Favourite* class fleet tug, see *Ocean Pride*
Ostpreussen, ex-U-boat hulls 60
'Overlord', Operation 91, 92, 137

Pacific Laurel, ex-*SC504* 117
Pandoro (UK) *Philomel* class gunboat and Polar exploration ship 26
Pandoro II, ex-*Newport* 26, 27
Papua (UK) 'Colony' class frigate and passenger and cargo ship 80
Parana, ex-*St Teath* 46
Parry Sound (CAN) 'Flower' class corvette, see *Olympic Champion*
Parry, William Edward 23
Patroller (UK) *Attacker* class escort carrier, see *Almkerk*
PC842 Patrol Escort class (US) 115
Pendennis, ex-*ML113* 140, 141
Peninnis, ex-*Argon* 50, 51
Peninsular & Oriental Steam Navigation Co. 27
Peter P, ex-*X57* 53
Pevensey Castle (UK) 'Castle' class corvette, see *Weather Monitor*
Philomel class gunboat 26
Phlox (UK) 'Flower' class corvette, see *Southern Lotus*
Pictou (CAN) 'Flower' class corvette,
see *Olympic Chaser*
Pima County (US) LST, see *Baltic Ferry*
Poleaxe (UK) trawler, see *Dorbie*
Pollock, Walter 52
Port Victor, ex-*Nairana* 84
Port Vindex, ex-*Vindex* 83, 84
Porto Azzuro, ex-*Haste* 115
Pre-eminent, ex-*MFV1003* 126, 127
Premier (UK) escort aircraft carrier, see *Rhodesia Star*
President, ex-*Gannet* 31, 32
President, ex-*Saxifrage* 15, 16
Pride of Paignton, ex-*RML492* 146
Pride of the Dart, ex-*HDML1396* 160
Procher (UK) 'Isles' class trawler, see *Tulipdale*
Prudent (UK) *Assurance* class fleet tug, see *Cautious*
Pullman Standard Car Company (US) 74
Puncher (UK) escort aircraft carrier, see *Muncaster Castle*
Pursuer (UK) Type 3 LST, see *Empire Tern*

Quadrille (UK) 'Dance' class trawler, see *Elsa*
Queen (UK) *Attacker* class escort carrier, see *Roebiah*
Queen of Kent, ex-*Atherstone* 10, 41–3
Queen of Thanet, ex-*Melton* 11, 41–3

Radborne, ex-*Blyth* 151
Radcliffe, ex-*BYMS2001* 154
Radford, ex-*Basset* 127, 128
Rajah (UK) *Attacker* class escort carrier, see *Drente*
Raki, ex-*Begum* 90
Rance (UK) *Attacker* class escort carrier, see *Friesland*
Ranger (UK) *Algerine* class gunboat and salvage ship 29, 30
Ranonculus (UK) 'Flower' class corvette, see *Southern Lily*
Ravager (UK) *Attacker* class escort carrier, see *Robin Trent*
Rayleigh Castle (UK) 'Castle' class corvette, see *Empire Rest*
Reaper (UK) escort aircraft carrier, see *South Africa Star*
Recruit (UK) ex-*Salamander* (Prussia) gun vessel and cargo ship 27
Red Commodore, ex-*RML537* 141–3
Reginald Kerr, ex-*LST3009* 103, 108
Rehearo, ex-*John Burlingham* 49
Reindeer (UK) *Mariner* class composite sloop and salvage ship 29
Rempang, ex-*Khedive* 90
Repton (UK) 'Hunt' class minesweeper, see *Rupavati*
Resolve class fleet tugs 45–7
Reward (UK) *Bustler* class fleet tug, see *Englishman*
Rhodesia Star, ex-*Premier* 88, 89
Rhododendron (UK) 'Flower' class corvette, see *Maj Vinke*
Ringdove's Aid, ex-*Melita* 29
Rio Agueda, ex-*Kilmalcolm* 76

Rio Duoro, ex-*LST3039* 105
Rio Guardiana, ex-*LST3023* 105
Rio Minho, ex-*LST3018* 105
Rio Mondego, ex-*LST3032* 105
Rio Tejo, ex-*Jaunty* 47
Rio Tejo, ex-*LST3003* 105
Rio Vouga, ex-*Kildary* 76
Riouw, ex-*Stalker* 90
'River' class frigates 65, 70, 71
River Lady, ex-*ML309* 148
RML1 et seq Fairmile rescue launch 138–49
Robin Kirk, ex-*Ameer* 90
Robin Mowbray, ex-*Slinger* 90
Robin Trent, ex-*Ravager* 90
Rochester Queen, ex-*LCG181* 12, 96–7
Rocky River, ex-*Satinleaf* 117–18
Roebiah, ex-*Queen* 90
Rollcall (UK) *Resolve* class fleet tug, see *Romsey*
Rollicker (UK) *Resolve* class fleet tug and commercial tug 47
Roma, ex-*Atheling* 86
Romsey, ex-*Rollcall* 46, 47
Rorvick, ex-*Llandudno* 151
Rosenburg VI, ex-*Laugen* 164
Ross, James Clark 24
Rowlock, ex-*Fowey* 68
Royal Army Service Corps 12, 103, 108–10
Royal Forth Lady, ex-*RML* 143–4
Royal Sovereign (UK) Third Rate, see *Worcester*
Royal Tay Lady, ex-*RML* 143–4
Rupavati, ex-*Repton* 35–6
Rushbrooke, ex-*Baddeck* 124
Rushen Castle (UK) 'Castle' class corvette, see *Weather Surveyor*
Rutland, ex-*X178* 53

S178 (GER) destroyer, see *Franziska Kimme*
S179 (GER) destroyer, see *Georg Kimme*
Safeguard (UK) patrol vessel, see *Safeguarder*
Safeguarder, ex-*Safeguard* 51
'Saint' class fleet tugs 45, 46
Salford (UK) 'Hunt' class minesweeper, see *Vegavati*
Salta, ex-*Shah* 86, 87
Salvaliant, ex-*Encore* 134, 135
Samsonia (UK) *Bustler* class fleet tug, see *Foundation Josephine*
Samuel Green (UK) 'Strath' class trawler, see *Ocean Mist*
Sanda, ex-*LCG(M)194* 96
Sark Coast, ex-*LCG(M)196* 97, 98
Satinleaf (US) net layer, see *Rocky River*
Saucy (UK) *Frisky* class fleet tug and commercial tug 47
Sauda, ex-*LCG(M)127* 96
Saxifrage (UK) 'Flower' class Q ship, see *President*
SC504 (US) submarine chaser, see *Pacific Laurel*
SC536 (US) submarine chaser, see *Air Cormorant*

SC715 (US) submarine chaser, see *Cape Pine*
SC772 (US) submarine chaser, see *Air Mallard*
SC1013 (US) submarine chaser, see *Mount Independence*
SC1039 (US) submarine chaser, see *Norking*
Scarborough Castle (UK) 'Castle' class corvette, see *Empire Peacemaker*
Searcher (UK) *Attacker* class escort carrier, see *Captain Theo*
Secretary of State for Scotland (fisheries protection) 129, 130
Sepia, ex-*HDML1400* 160
Shah (UK) *Attacker* class escort carrier, see *Salta*
Sharpshooter (UK) gun vessel and cargo ship 27
Sheppey (UK) fast minelayer, see *Hibernia*
Shiga (JPN) Type B escort, see *Shiga Maru*
Shiga Maru, ex-*Shiga* 74
Siegfreid, ex-*FM1* 63
Silver Commodore, ex-*RML449* 141
Silver Star, ex-*Bruiser* 12, 103-4, 170
Silverlord, ex-*Anchusa* 68
Sir Lancelot (UK) Landing Ship Logistics, see *Lowland Lancer*
Sitmar Line (GRC) 85, 86
Skylark I, ex-harbour launch 162
Slinger (UK) *Attacker* class escort carrier, see *Robin Mowbray*
Slinger (UK) Type 3 LST, see *Empire Kittiwake*
Smiter (UK) *Ruler* class escort carrier, see *Artillero*
Smiths Falls (CAN) 'Flower' class corvette, see *Olympic Lightning*
Snowden Smith, ex-*LST3028* 103, 108
Snowflake (UK) 'Flower' class corvette, see *Weather Watcher*
Socrates, ex-*FM36* 63, 64
Sognefjord, ex-*Kilham* 75
South Africa Star, ex-*Reaper* 88, 89
South American Tours Ltd. (ARG) 41
South Western Steam Navigation Co., Ltd. (UK) 15, 151
Southern Briar, ex-*Cyclamen* 66, 67
Southern Broom, ex-*Starwart* 66
Southern Larkspur, ex-*Arrowhead* 66
Southern Laurel, ex-*Carnation* 66
Southern Lily, ex-*Ranonculus* 66
Southern Lotus, ex-*Phlox* 66
Southern Lupin, ex-*Woodruff* 66
Southern Paul, ex-*MMS372* 153
Southern Peter, ex-*MMS378* 153
Southern Princess, ex-*ML293* 147, 148
Southern Terrier, ex-*Aconit* 66
Sparrow (UK) gun vessel second class, see *Amokura*
Speaker (UK) *Ruler* class escort carrier, see *Lancero*
Spitfire (UK) survey ship 26
Spithead, ex-*X44* 54
St Anne (UK) 'Saint' class fleet tug and commercial tug 45
St Aristell (UK) 'Saint' class fleet tug and commercial tug 45
St Arvans (UK) 'Saint' class fleet tug, see *Ocean Eagle*
St Athan (UK) 'Saint' class fleet tug and commercial tug 45
St Aubin (UK) 'Saint' class fleet tug and commercial tug 45
St Bees (UK) 'Saint' class fleet tug, see *Henry Burton*
St Boniface (UK) 'Saint' class fleet tug, see *Toia*
St Catherine (CAN) 'River' class frigate and weather ship 123
St Catherine (UK) 'Saint' class fleet tug, see *Canadian National No 2*
St Christopher, ex-*Emulous* 135
St Claude (UK) 'Saint' class fleet tug, see *Lindfield*
St Clears (UK) 'Saint' class fleet tug and commercial tug 45
St Day (UK) 'Saint' class fleet tug, see *Ursus*
St Dominic (UK) 'Saint' class fleet tug and commercial tug 45
St Eileen, ex-*St Tudy* 46
St Elian, ex-*Hörnum* 61, 62, 170
St Enoder (UK) 'Saint' class fleet tug, see *Garm*
St Erth (UK) 'Saint' class fleet tug, see *Heros*
St Ewe (UK) 'Saint' class fleet tug, see *Alarm*
St Finbarr (UK) 'Saint' class fleet tug, see *Franklin*
St Florence (UK) 'Saint' class fleet tug, see *Kyuqot*
St Giles (UK) 'Saint' class fleet tug, see *Khalifa*
St Helier (UK) 'Saint' class fleet tug and commercial tug 46
St Hilary (UK) 'Saint' class fleet tug and commercial tug 46
St Keyne (UK) 'Saint' class fleet tug, see *Times*
St Kitts (UK) 'Saint' class fleet tug, see *Uco*
St Mabyn (UK) 'Saint' class fleet tug, see *Caroline Moller*
St Minver (UK) 'Saint' class fleet tug, see *Abeille XXII*
St Nazaire (UK) Type 3 LST, see *Empire Skua*
St Olaves (UK) 'Saint' class fleet tug and commercial tug 46
St Seiriol 7
St Stephen (CAN) 'River' class frigate and weather ship 123
St Teath (UK) 'Saint' class fleet tug, see *Parana*
St Tudy (UK) 'Saint' class fleet tug, see *St Eileen*
Stalker (UK) *Attacker* class escort carrier, see *Riouw*
Starwart (UK) 'Flower' class corvette, see *Southern Broom*
Stavanger, ex-*Kilchattan* 75
Stone Town (CAN) 'River' class frigate and weather ship 123
Stonecrop (UK) 'Flower' class corvette, see *Martha Vinke*
Stormking (UK) *Assurance* class fleet tug, see *Tryphon*
Stormont (CAN) 'River' class frigate, see *Christina*
'Strath' class trawlers 48
Strenuous (UK) *Auk* class minesweeper, see *Evening Star*
Submarine Chasers (US) 51, 52
submarine engines (GER) 64
Sulphur (UK) *Hecla* class bomb vessel and Polar exploration ship 24
Sunnfjord, ex-*Kildwick* 75
Sunnhordland, ex-*Kilchenan* 76, 171
Susan A Moran, ex-*Favourite* 131
Swindon (UK) 'Hunt' class minesweeper, see *Lady Cecilia*
Sydney, ex-*Fencer* 86
Syros, ex-*Bergamot* 68
Szamos (Austro-Prussian) river monitor, see *Tivador*

Tankard, ex-*X8* 54
Terror (UK) *Vesuvius* class bomb ship and Polar exploration ship 24
Thais store ship and tug 27
Thruster (UK) Type 3 LST, see *Empire Petrel*
Thunder (UK) *Hecla* class bomb vessel and Polar exploration ship 24
Thyme (UK) 'Flower' class corvette, see *Weather Explorer*
Tilak, ex-*Instow* 35, 36
Times, ex-*St Keyne* 46
Tivador, ex-*Szamos* 60
Tobago (UK) 'Colony' class frigate and passenger and cargo ship 80
Toia, ex-*St Boniface* 45
Topmast 16, ex-*LCT474* 96
Topmast 20, ex-*LCT399* 95, 96
Townsend, Captain Stuart 37
Tracker (UK) *Attacker* class escort carrier, see *Corrientes*
Treaty of Versailles, the 55
Trillium (CAN) 'Flower' class corvette, see *Olympic Runner*
Triton (UK) survey ship and training ship 32
Tromsø (UK) Type 3 LST, see *Empire Gannet*
Trouncer (UK) escort aircraft carrier, see *Greystoke Castle*
Trouncer (UK) Type 3 LST, see *Empire Gull*
Trumpeter (UK) *Attacker* class escort carrier, see *Alblasserdijk*
Trumpeter (UK) Type 3 LST, see *Empire Fulmar*
TRV2 (UK) torpedo recovery vessel, see *Island Commodore*
TRV8 (UK) torpedo recovery vessel, see *Arrowhead*
Tryphon, ex-*Stormking* 131
Tucalif, ex-*Kilbirnie* 22
Tulipbank, ex-*Neave* 128
Tulipdale, ex-*Procher* 128
Tulipglen, ex-*Lingay* 128
Turmoil (UK) *Bustler* class fleet tug, see *Nisos Kerkyra*

Uco, ex-*St Kitts* 46
Ukuru (JPN) Type B escort, see *Ukuru Maru*
Ukuru Maru, ex-*Ukuru* 74
Ulster Queen 7, 29
United States Maritime Commission (US) 10, 11
Ursus, ex-*St Day* 45

Vegavati, ex-*Salford* 35, 36
Vesuvius class bomb vessels 23
Victoria Louise (GER) cruiser, see *Flora Sommerfeld*
Vindex (UK) escort aircraft carrier, see *Port Vindex*

W R Strang, ex-*Monkswood* 67
Walcheren (UK) Type 3 LST, see *Empire Guillemot*
War Assets Corporation (CAN) 10
Waskesiu (CAN) 'River' class frigate, see *Hooghly*
Weather Advisor, ex-*Amberley Castle* 73, 74
Weather Explorer, ex-*Thyme* 72, 73
Weather Monitor, ex-*Pevensey Castle* 73, 74
Weather Observer, ex-*Marguerite* 72–3
Weather Recorder, ex-*Genista* 72, 73
Weather Reporter, ex-*Oakham Castle* 73, 74
Weather Surveyor, ex-*Rushen Castle* 73, 74
Weather Watcher, ex-*Snowflake* 72, 73
Weems, ex-*YMS268* 115
Wellington (UK) *Grimsby* class sloop and club house 81
Wem (UK) 'Hunt' class minesweeper, see *Deshulper*
Western Lady et seq, Western Lady Ferry Service 13, 144–6
Western Princess, ex-*RML 148*
Westfalen, ex-*FM29* 63
Wexford (UK) 'Hunt' class minesweeper, see *Doomba*
White Commodore, ex-*ML445* 141
Wild Goose, ex-*La Beverie*, ex-*YMS328* 116, 171
William Jackson (UK) 'Mersey' class trawler, see *Lord Byng*
William Westernburgh, 'Mersey' class trawler, see *Lord Talbot*
Woodruff (UK) 'Flower' class corvette, see *Southern Lupin*
Worcester, ex-*Royal Sovereign* 31

X Lighter 52–4

Yacht Holidays Ltd. (UK) 14, 170
Yard minesweepers (US) 115, 153–5
YMS268 (US) auxiliary MMS, see *Weems*
YMS328 (US) auxiliary MMS, see *La Beverie*
YMS470 (US) auxiliary MMS and research boat 115, 116
York Castle (UK) 'Castle' class corvette, see *Empire Comfort*